The Case for Animal Experimentation

The Case for Animal Experimentation

An Evolutionary and Ethical Perspective

Michael Allen Fox

UNIVERSITY OF CALIFORNIA PRESS

Berkeley • Los Angeles • London

University of California Press
Berkeley and Los Angeles, California

University of California Press, Ltd.
London, England

Copyright © 1986 by The Regents of the University of California

Library of Congress Cataloging in Publication Data

Fox, Michael Allen.
    The Case for animal experimentation.

    Bibliography: p.
    Includes index.
    1. Vivisection. 2. Animal experimentation.
3. Vivisection—Moral and ethical aspects. 4. Animal
experimentation—Moral and ethical aspects. I. Title.
HV4915.F67   1985   179′.4   85-1036
ISBN 0-520-05501-2

PRINTED IN THE UNITED STATES OF AMERICA

2 3 4 5 6 7 8 9

To Kevin, Jason, Tim, Randy, and Jasper

CONTENTS

Acknowledgments

This book was begun during a 1979–80 sabbatical leave from Queen's University at Kingston, and much of the basic research was done at the University of Waterloo. I am grateful to Queen's University for providing the leave, and especially to the Advisory Research Committee for a grant in aid of research. I wish to express my appreciation as well to the University of Waterloo for furnishing office space and for extending other scholarly privileges.

The Canadian Council on Animal Care deserves special thanks for sharing its library resources and generally keeping me up to date on literature and events in several areas of interest, for enabling me to participate in some of its on-site inspections of research facilities, and for allowing me to reprint its "Ethics of Animal Experimentation" guidelines. I am deeply indebted, in particular, to Dr. Harry C. Rowsell, scientist and humanitarian, for his helpful advice, encouragement, tireless support and advocacy, and friendship.

An instrumental part of this book is the brief outlines, in chapter 4, of ongoing research conducted at the Hospital for Sick Children in Toronto and at the Department of Psychology, Queen's University. I owe much to the staff of the Research Institute at Sick Children's and especially to Dr. Carl Grant who handled the necessary arrangements. I am grateful to those who consented to be interviewed and to let me observe their work and to the hospital administration for permission to publish the results of my investigations. To my colleagues in the Queen's Psychology Department, particularly Dr. Barrie Frost, who smoothed the way, and Dr. Richard J. Beninger, who wholeheartedly supported this project, many thanks.

Professor Warner Wick first suggested the conception of the moral community which I develop in chapter 3, and conversations with Duncan MacIntosh inspired the discussion of value and the value of nature in chapter 1. These individuals contributed more to the formation of my position than they are aware of. Nancy Zettler, a brilliant and promising doctoral candidate in chemical engineering at Queen's University, also offered some helpful ideas about the preceding topics in chapter 1. I regret that her untimely passing prevented her from seeing this book appear in print. Professor John Whyte assisted me in formulating my thoughts on legal rights for animals in chapter 7. Professors Jan Narveson, Kristin Shrader-Frechette, Christine Overall, and anonyous referees contributed valuable input during the final stages of revising the manuscript.

Appreciation is also due to the students who have taken my courses in environmental ethics and from whose suggestions and critical discussion of my views both in class and out I have benefited.

Dr. Sandra Olney's comments, criticisms, and ideas were of great help in general and in relation to some of the topics in chapter 5 in particular. The general encouragement and advice Professor Kerry McSweeney and Dr. Franklin M. Loew gave were invaluable.

All of these people have helped show me the way; the arguments and statements of fact herein, however, are my responsibility alone.

Finally, my appreciation to those who have labored long and hard to type and/or word process the manuscript and who nonetheless kept smiling: Karen Hermer, who patiently and good naturedly carried the major responsibility; Joy Howe; Jackie Doherty; and Linda Hall.

Kingston, Ontario   M. A. F.
November 1984

It is sometimes held by some people that ethical decisions are easy to make, that they come down almost as telegrams from heaven. I am not one of those people myself. If I do receive that kind of telegram, I am always suspicious about where it comes from and sometimes I fear I may have unwittingly sent it to myself. No, in complex issues there is no substitute for the discipline of the facts, understanding what is at issue.

—Hugh Montefiore

Introduction

WHY DEFEND ANIMAL EXPERIMENTATION?

This book is an essay in support of the use of animals for human ends. Not just any animals and not just any ends, and most important of all, not without important qualifications. This is a view with which the majority of readers would probably agree. Why, then, is it necessary to write a book defending it? There are two main reasons. One is that a new generation of dedicated antivivisectionists are presenting a very one-sided, often distorted picture of animal welfare issues, focusing on animal suffering in scientific research and devoting little or no attention to current intensive efforts to maintain and improve the standards of animal care or to the benefits gained from such research. Media attention everywhere is, as always, easily and frequently captured by emotional appeals on behalf of animals and by sensationalistic tactics like "guerrilla" raids on scientific laboratories aimed at "liberating" experimental animals and exposing them to the press and TV.[1] Most of us are scarcely or only intermittently aware of these episodes. Here are three examples:

> On January 18, 1982, a member of the Animal Liberation Front entered the Royal Society Headquarters in London where the Wellcome Art Gallery is housed. Upon reaching the gallery, he proceeded to slash a portrait which was hanging there several times with a knife. The man escaped without being caught. The portrait was a representation of René Descartes, a 17th century philosopher who, as the ALF points out, was also one of the founders of modern vivisection.[2]

August 31, [1982] a "screaming mob" of 700 antivivisectionists, some armed with flares, sticks and stones, fought a two-hour running battle with 100 police while forcibly trying to enter Europe's largest toxicity testing laboratory, the U.S.-owned Huntingdon Research Centre in Cambs., U.K. A policeman was thrown in a ditch and punched; 21 arrests were made.

The mob reportedly dispersed when an Animal Liberation Front member said they would return to destroy the centre. The raid has been called the biggest in the ALF's six year anti-research campaign.[3]

... animal activists ... recently broke into a lab at [the University of Toronto's] Scarborough College, stole some rats, crushed others under overturned cages and took cards off the cages, destroying a long-standing experiment to treat epilepsy. "Those animals now have to be destroyed, and the whole thing has to be started again". . . . As a result of these attacks, $62,000 is being spent on new security measures at the medical faculty.[4]

It is interesting to note how the media play the game of sensationalizing such events, featuring them under misleading headings on page one. For example, when twenty-one cats were stolen from the research unit at the Hospital for Sick Children in Toronto in 1981, a newspaper that carried the story on its front page announced: "Group saves animals from hospital laboratory" (note: saves, rather than "saves"). However, when the Canadian Council on Animal Care, the agency responsible for inspecting the hospital's facilities and passing judgment on its ethical standards, spoke in defense of the research project in question, this story appeared on page 56 of the same newspaper.[5] (The evident discrepancy between sensationalizing animal rights groups' mayhem and running regular features on medical progress through animal experimentation—itself often prematurely and sensationalistically described—apparently passes unnoticed by members of the press.)

This sort of behavior is unfortunately characteristic of our age, and is clearly calculated to have shock value and to polarize public opinion. There is, of course, always great danger in a populace that reacts without thinking, but the aim of many zealots promoting one cause or another is to create a widespread, intense emotional response backed by a spurious sense of moral superiority. Responsible members of the "animals rights" movement, however, have condemned these acts of violence and vandalism and have presented their ideas in a more dispassionate manner, appealing instead to argument and moral and political suasion. But in general, the public, which eventually has to make the decisions affecting, for example, the future of scientific research and to accept the consequences of such decisions (such as better or inferior standards of health care), has heard in recent times only that side of the argument that advocates the moral equality of all species and focuses on human guilt for causing animal suffering.

In the face of these influences, it is important to develop a reasonable position in support of what most human beings have believed and practiced for thousands of years—that animals are *not* our moral equals and that therefore there is no compelling ground for treating them as such. We do not have to possess the sensitivity of a St. Francis of Assisi or an Albert Schweitzer to be aware that animals are capable of suffering greatly, that some are remarkably like us in important respects, and that countless abuses of animals occur daily in every part of the world. These facts obviously have to be taken into account in arriving at a satisfactory position on our use and treatment of animals; but it does not follow, as I try to show, that a traditional, anthropocentric interpretation of morality and of humans' relationship to other species cannot be maintained. No doubt many animal welfarists and antivivisectionists will react to this position with extreme disfavor, dismissing it as essentially conservative or even reactionary. I would prefer to think of it as an antidote to extremism of all sorts—a sensible, middle-of-the-road point of view for which adequate support can be given.

Perhaps we should pause to ask what is to count as an "animal"—lions, whales, armadillos, zebras, and mice, surely; even oysters, ants, butterflies, and mosquitoes if we are willing to stretch our concept a bit. But what about viruses, bacteria, and other primitive or single-cell organisms? Where do we draw the line? It will do no good to protest that *everyone knows* what animals are and that therefore some of these examples are farfetched. In common usage anything living that is not a plant is an animal; and the universally accepted system of biological classification used by scientists includes among the animal phyla, or major divisions, everything from protozoans, sponges, and annelids (insects, scorpions, earthworms, leeches, and the like) to chordates (all organisms with vertebrae). The animal kingdom thus runs the gamut from species that respond to stimuli but are very rudimentary in function and structure, lacking a nervous system altogether (amoebas, sea cucumbers, certain molluscs) through those that are sentient and possess some limited mode of consciousness (fish, insects, reptiles, birds) to those with large and highly complex brains, highly evolved nervous systems, a wide range of social and communicative behaviors, sophisticated problem-solving capacities, and so on (chimpanzees, dolphins, humans). Exactly which of these characteristics make a species an object of our moral concern is a moot point; but even if all living things are in a sense such objects, the degree of concern that is appropriate to each species is surely a function of how we regard the characteristics it possesses. A major burden of the argument of this book is to establish and elaborate this point.

A great deal of what has been said and written about the moral status of animals over the past two decades is characterized by sentimentalism and exemplifies the "pathetic fallacy," or the illegitimate attribution of human qualities to nature. Sentimentalism appears in two guises: the plain, old-fashioned, tug-at-the-heartstrings type and the modern, intellectualized variety. The latter is frequently present in the work of speculative ecologists, theologians, and academics who have joined the animal rights movement but appear to possess scanty firsthand knowledge of animals or the uses to which they are put by humans. These tendencies are so commonplace now that they form part of a shared ambience, which helps foster animal liberation crusades, intolerance toward opposing views, and an adversarial approach to discussion of issues like experimentation on animals.

The second reason for writing this book is that I believe much of the attention and energy committed to improving the lot of animals would be put to better use ameliorating human need and suffering and in fact constitutes a diversion from this more important and indeed critical task.[6] Now it may be replied that, of course, everyone *could* devote more time and energy to helping those who are less privileged. If we add that everyone *should* do so, then the logical extreme of this position is that anyone who fails to give up everything else he or she might otherwise be doing, including getting eight hours of sleep at night, is guilty of not putting forth enough effort to improve the lot of humankind! This is an absurd view which no one would want to endorse. My point is not that everyone should work twenty-four hours a day to improve human welfare or that everyone should work full time for a charitable or human rights organization such as Oxfam, the Foster Parents Plan, or Amnesty

International, which would plainly lead to equally absurd consequences. Rather, it is that human welfare is a more vital concern than
animal welfare and deserves more of our dedication because humans
are more important than animals. Relieving human need and suffering
is an extremely urgent priority without which our species—and
indeed the natural world as such—may not survive the century.
Relative to this cause, that of animal welfare, though not unimportant,
appears of considerably lower priority. Lamentably, it often seems
that among the most vociferous proponents of animal welfare there is
an abundance of concern for the plight of other species and very little
for that of our own.

WHAT IS AT ISSUE IN ANIMAL EXPERIMENTATION?

In the modern era (and particularly in the nineteenth and twentieth centuries), those who object on moral grounds to the traditional
ways in which nonhuman creatures have been made to serve humans
have tended to adopt one of two viewpoints. The first of these is that
any use of animals as means to human ends must be defended or
argued for, its moral acceptability demonstrated. This position is
based on the standing presumption that it is prima facie wrong to put
animals to human use at all, which itself derives from fundamental
convictions of the following sort: "Animals have a right to live and to
be free from interference"; "Animals are sacred"; "Animals' lives are
of intrinsic value, just like all of nature"; "Animals have interests that
deserve equal consideration." Proponents of this view argue that any
use of animals must be morally justified and often express their
orientation in the idiom of rights; for example, "What *right* do we
have to use animals for experimentation (even if no pain is
involved)?" "What *entitles* us to interfere with the natural course of
animals' lives so that we may obtain knowledge (or whatever)?"
This kind of thinking lies behind the following remark by Brigid
Brophy: "That I like the flavour of mutton no more entitles me to kill
a sheep than a taste for roast leg of human would entitle me to kill
you."[7]

To answer the foregoing questions in their own terms would, in a
way, be to share in a misconception, both of our relation to animals
and of what is fundamentally at issue ethically concerning the uses to
which animals are put. As I argue, the fundamental reason why we
are "entitled" to use animals for experimentation—if we are forced to

speak this way—is that they are in no sense the moral equals of humans, and therefore we are under no moral obligation to refrain from so using them. Since anything that is not prohibited by a moral imperative of some kind (that is, not morally wrong) is morally permissible, and since the use of animals for experimentation is not morally prohibited, then this use falls within that class of actions that are morally permissible. We do not need a correlative right to give the seal of approval to everything we do, to "justify" it. Animal liberationists frequently talk as if we do to show, allegedly, how shameful our normal practices are. But if we have no obligation toward animals to refrain from using them, as in experimentation, then we may so use them and need invoke no special entitlement, moral or otherwise, to defend this practice. The argument in favor of continuing to use animals in certain ways, then, is that the uses in question are, in and of themselves, morally neutral or morally permissible. We might indeed go beyond this and assert that animal experimentation is morally imperative or obligatory if there is no other way to obtain certain kinds of knowledge needed for the alleviation of much greater suffering in both humans and animals. (More on this later.)

This difference of opinion between those who think that using animals for human ends always needs to be justified and those who do not may also stem from conflicting beliefs about whether making animals the instruments for carrying out our aims ipso facto constitutes the causing of a harm, that is, adversely affects the animals' interests (health, well-being, quality of life, and so on). It will be clear from what follows (especially in chapter 3) that I do not think this is the case and that putting the matter in this way anthropomorphizes the lives of animals to an unwarranted extent. But plainly, experimenting on animals does sometimes harm them. Is this wrong? We can, if we so choose, define *harm* in such a way that injuring any sentient being—or any living thing, for that matter—is always wrong; but this would be to beg the question just posed. Some people would insist that it is always wrong (or at any rate always prima facie wrong) nonetheless. This shows, I believe, that something more basic still is at issue; namely, whether harming another creature (or life form) is a type of act that always takes place in a context of moral appraisal and which, because of this, we should uniformly judge to be wrong. Those who adhere to such a position extend what certain ethicists call the principle of nonmaleficence to animals. According to this view, it is first and foremost our duty not to harm other beings (including, of course, other humans) and only secondarily to help or benefit them (that is, to observe the principle of beneficence or benevolence). At bottom, however, this stand cannot be argued for or derived from beliefs or assumptions of a more rudimentary kind; rather, I think, it springs from a fundamental moral intuition. So the debate over the justification of animal experimentation, then, is in the final analysis over conflicting moral intuitions, neither of which is demonstrably preferable to the other. I must confess that I do not share the intuition that it is always wrong to do anything that might cause harm to an animal or that we must always have very strong and overriding reasons for doing so—especially if "harming" is taken to include (as it often is) curtailing an animal's freedom, affecting its welfare, or interfering in the normal pattern of its life in any way.[8] For my part, it is just not self-evident that we should transfer the principle of nonmaleficence to animals. (I am assuming, for the sake of argument, that it does self-evidently apply to other persons.) Nor is it even apparent that what we know of animal behavior and mental life from empirical studies should compel us to apply the principle to other species. However, this is not to say or imply that we may feel free to harm or abuse animals whenever we wish or that we lack sufficient grounds to support moral concern over animal suffering, particularly when caused by humans. Animals may not be moral agents or persons, but they may still be moral patients, that is, beings that may be affected for better or worse by our acts and which we should therefore treat with care. This point is stressed in chapters 3 and 7.

The second prevalent moral viewpoint on our use of animals avoids the inflexibility of the position just discussed. Conceding that perhaps the human use of animals does not by itself pose a moral problem, many would still maintain that because pain is a bad thing, no matter who or what experiences it, any practice that involves inflicting suffering on sentient beings is prima facie wrong and therefore requires arguments to show why it ought not to be morally condemned. (Some would extend this claim to the taking of animal life as well, contending that a rationale must always be given to warrant such an action. Those who adhere to a Schweitzerian reverence-for-life principle, for example, would hold such a position.

Others concern themselves with suffering only, allowing that killing does not pose a serious moral issue, as long as it is done painlessly or without causing undue suffering.)

This, I believe, is a much more plausible perspective and expresses a more common challenge to our present animal-use practices. For we simply do find repellent the idea of deriving benefits from suffering. In the following chapters I address the problems it raises in some detail. I argue that there are a number of confusions in the usual formulation of this position and indicate the conditions under which experimentation on animals can be justified even when it results in their suffering or death.

ORIGINS OF THE PRESENT CONTROVERSY OVER ANIMALS

It is important initially to understand the context in which the current debate over animal welfare has evolved. During the seventies and the present decade, interest in understanding humans' relationship to the rest of nature and in moral issues concerned with our use and treatment of animals has increased dramatically. The number of publications devoted to these topics has grown exponentially—so much that it is virtually impossible for anyone to survey the recent literature and be confident that he or she has not omitted anything of importance.

What has caused this boom, which shows no sign of abating? Why has animal welfare emerged as the burning moral issue of our time, alongside (or for some even overshadowing) nuclear war? Three factors are worth noting. Foremost among these is the tremendous increase in knowledge about the natural world due to rapid developments in all areas of science. Because of the speed with which information now is accumulated and can be processed and transmitted, new discoveries are often topics of household conversation within days or weeks of their initial presentation at professional conferences or in specialized journals. An instance of this general trend is the constantly enlarging fund of information about animal capacities and behavior. As a result of studies conducted within both artificial environments and the natural world, much more is now becoming known about the nature of diverse animal species. This research is slowly shrinking the perceived gulf between humans and the rest of the animate world in certain important respects, as anyone who has tried to keep pace with these new discoveries will attest. As we shall see, however, it is vital to be aware of the differences that actually remain between *Homo sapiens* and other species because they are what establish humans as moral beings.

A second factor is the rise of ecology as a major scientific field over the past two decades and the consequent change that has begun to occur in people's thinking about nature. We have witnessed during this period the dawning consciousness that humans cannot set themselves above the ecosystem of which they are a part, continuing to overexploit and despoil it thoughtlessly.

A third and different source of stimulus can also be discerned. This is the general broadening of the horizon of moral concern that is the legacy of the counterculture and the civil rights and antiwar movements in the United States and elsewhere during the sixties. In addition to generating debate over such issues as the safety of nuclear energy, genetic manipulation, abortion, euthanasia, civil disobedience, sexism, and racism, this expansion of moral concern has also stimulated discussion of the use and abuse of animals by humans. It has been argued that moral concern over the plight of animals can be straightforwardly derived from that over the status of blacks or women in today's society and that by simple parity of reasoning we ought to extend basic ethical precepts and considerations from disadvantaged humans to animals. One of my purposes in writing this book is to show why this view is mistaken. The civil rights and feminist movements may have played an instrumental role in bringing the animal rights debate before the public, but it would be a serious error to infer that therefore animals have rights or that "animal liberation" is a cause which all right-thinking people should support as merely a logical extension of considerations of equality and justice.

STATEMENT OF PURPOSE

I have chosen, in the chapters that follow, to concentrate on just one issue concerning the ethics of humans' use of animals: laboratory experimentation on other species in biomedical and behavioral research, which accounts for 40 percent of all animals used for scientific purposes (the other major uses being drug development, 26 percent and toxicity testing, 20 percent).[10] The reason for this is, first, that to treat the problem in as complete a manner as it deserves and requires, no less than a book will suffice. Though there have been many other full-length discussions of animal experimentation, this is the first that considers the subject against the background of (a) a careful review of evolutionary findings; (b) a critical consideration of our ethical views as they pertain to animals; (c) an examination of past and current research; and (d) the possible alternatives to animal experimentation.

Second, because I have endeavored to apply the ethical conclusions I have arrived at to the issues raised by scientific research, and have done this within the larger context of ongoing research projects, it is hoped that the reader will be assisted by this specific example in the task of reasoning through the issues surrounding other uses of animals. (See final section of chapter 7.)

SCIENCE AND ANTIVIVISECTIONISM

By long tradition, the dispute over the ethics of animal research has been one between researchers and antivivisectionists. *Vivisection* means, literally, the cutting of a living organism and by common usage refers to the performance of surgical procedures upon animals. Since only some of the many experiments on animals today involve invasive (or surgical) procedures, *antivivisectionism* is something of a misnomer. Though I generally avoid using this term to label the opponents or critics of animal research, it may be useful for a moment to look at the origins of antivivisectionism.

Antivivisectionism, in one form or another, has been around almost as long as research using live animals, because in former times abuse of animals in laboratories (as in society at large) was relatively widespread and because anesthetics were not yet discovered, making for untold suffering in both humans and animals. Though certain animals had been cultivated as companions and domesticated as livestock for thousands of years, throughout much of the Christian era animals were regarded as "soulless brutes," which had little, if any, conscious life of their own, no capacity for language, and even lacked the ability to feel pain. The rise of modern science in the seventeenth century brought with it the view known as mechanism—that living systems could be understood on purely mechanical principles—and this, combined with the belief that animals had no souls, yielded the position that animals are mere machines (whereas humans might be machines somehow inhabited and animated by souls). René Descartes (1596–1650), the so-called father of modern philosophy and by training both cleric and mathematician-scientist, held such a position and is generally cited as the most important source of the image of animals as insensate machines. Whatever the source of this view may be and however incredible it may sound today, it is clear that it, or something like it, was the received opinion for decades and even centuries, and many scholars locate the origin of antivivisectionism in the protest against this mechanistic outlook.

One other point to note about antivivisectionism is that when it began as a major movement, in Victorian England, it served not only as a focus for concern over animal suffering, but also as an outlet for anxieties stemming from changes in society, values, and the image of what it is to be human. Thus antivivisectionism was part of a mental set, a constellation of (mostly reactionary) ideas and outlooks composing opposition to aseptic medical practice, compulsory vaccination programs, the rise of the medical establishment, and the scientific worldview, as well as xenophobia (the notion of experimental medicine as an imported aberration), the perception of experimental medicine as a threat to the moral and religious foundations of society (the notion of disease as a product of sin and folly), and manifestations of psychological conflict over the biological and behavioral implications of evolution.[11] Although it would be historically inaccurate to assert that all of these ideas have continued to fuel antivivisectionism (some have, some have not), or that antivivisectionists did not come to see and value the alleviation of suffering by medical research (many did), it remains true now, as a century ago, that beyond its more obvious preoccupation with animal suffering, antivivisectionist activity is often motivated by concerns that have little or nothing to do with animals.

It is not my purpose, however, to give a detailed history of antivivisectionist thought, but rather to indicate that it encompasses a variety of views. This applies even to views about animal experimentation itself. Certain antivivisectionists oppose animal experimentation as such because they are sure that it is by its nature cruel. Others oppose all but the most "crucial" experimentation, where it is supposed that the criteria for selecting such essential procedures already exist or can be formulated readily. (This is not the case, as we shall see later.) Still others argue that if not all, then at any rate most, experiments could be eliminated in the interests of humaneness and reducing unnecessary suffering. Finally, a small number oppose animal experimentation (in whole or in part) largely on philosophical or ethical grounds. As might be expected in a group as diverse as this, the quality of argument varies greatly, and emotionalism, the nemesis of reason, often predominates. Although I concentrate on examining the views of the last-mentioned group, a reasoned case for experimentation on animals should serve as a response to all these expressions of opinion and belief.

A MIDDLE GROUND

We are all being buffeted by the winds of change, and many of our most basic ideas and values are subject to scrutiny and challenge. No one can be very happy in this atmosphere advocating either humans' unrestricted dominion over all living things or the complete abolition of all activities that cause animals suffering or loss of life or normal freedom. It is my hope that the reader will discern in what follows a reasonable position on the use and treatment of animals, which avoids these extremes, helps promote understanding of the moral issues arising from present practices involving animals, and incorporates adequate humane principles.

1

Fallacies in Our Thinking About Humans and Animals

SOME PERPLEXITIES

Moral issues relating to our use and treatment of animals are very difficult to sort through. This is due in part to the emotionalism that seems inevitably to accompany even the most elementary stages of discussion. But the problem is also a function of the complexity of the moral issues themselves and the ambiguity that surrounds our notions of what it is to be a human and what it is to be an animal. Many people simply lack the ability to think clearly, objectively, and consistently about animals. Emotional responses play an important role in placing moral issues close to the heart of everyday experience; but they seldom contribute to the solution of moral dilemmas, more often clouding the matter and blocking the progress of rationality. This is as true in issues of animal welfare as it is in religious disputes, politics, and debate over sensitive social issues like abortion and euthanasia.

Taking a moral perspective on animals is challenging because it forces us to reexamine and question the assumptions of our system of moral beliefs, a process that is always hard and for some painful as well. Answers to questions like What is the basis of our moral community? What are rights? What sorts of beings have rights? Can we have obligations toward nonhumans? and Is it always wrong to cause suffering? lie at the center of any system of moral beliefs, and the average individual is generally ill equipped to answer them readily or cogently or to modify answers to encompass animals. Indeed, such questions pose quandaries even for professional philosophers, and there is no unanimity among them concerning the correct answers.

In dealing with such questions, we must bear in mind that the issue of humans' place in nature is far from being resolved and may never be. Is *Homo sapiens* an animal or more than an animal? If more, then how much weight should be assigned to this "more" in thinking through the moral issues before us? What is an animal anyway? We know and yet we do not know; we are accustomed to saying that we are animals or at least have an animal side to our nature, yet there is a world of difference between almost any animal we care to name and a human being. As for animals themselves, it seems altogether too misleading to classify all nonhuman organisms under such a broad heading. Controversies about animals and morals have been most unsatisfactory in this respect, featuring blanket statements about animals' capacities and moral status that utterly fail to differentiate between forms of life as widely separated on the evolutionary scale as oysters and chimpanzees.

My purpose in this chapter is to address some of these preliminary issues and thereby clear ground for the construction of a moral theory that can be applied to our dealings with animals and later to the specific area of animal use in experimentation.

IRRATIONAL ATTITUDES TOWARD ANIMALS

Many dedicated individuals have labored long and hard in the cause of humane animal care, the preservation and protection of wildlife, and the strengthening of laws regulating our use and treatment of animals. These efforts deserve to be commended. A civilized society ought to be able to make some provision for the needs and well-being of other species, which cannot speak for themselves, particularly those which humans have chosen to domesticate. However, it is undeniable that emotionalism colors and frequently overwhelms the good judgment of animal lovers and advocates, as a few examples will show. On October 10, 1979, the Toronto *Globe and Mail* reported that a two-week-old baby girl was severely mauled by the family pet, a six-week-old mongrel puppy. The infant lost both ears and a finger and suffered multiple lacerations to the face, arms, and scalp, as well as eye damage.[1] The *Toronto Star* of the same date quoted the head of the Ontario Humane Society as asserting that "this is one dog I am not going to see killed. I can't believe that a six-week-old puppy has any concept of what it is doing. It can't be vicious in any concept of the term."[2] Despite the family's threat that it would go to court to have the dog destroyed, it was taken into custody at the order of this official and placed with another family. More than one hundred persons reportedly offered to adopt this "nonvicious" pet. Another case in point is that of a leading antivivisectionist, Hans Ruesch, who voices approval in his book *Slaughter of the Innocent* of violent assaults on scientific researchers using animals in their work. This same author apparently condones the intentions of two Italian medical students who, upset by physiological experiments they were required to perform on animals, vowed to kidnap and dissect alive one of their professors![3]

This sort of irrationality evidently knows no bounds and is capable of reaching frightening extremes more often than we may care to admit. Iris Nowell, in *The Dog Crisis*, relates two such episodes from the mid-seventies:

> In 1975 the Mayor of Pisa, Italy, banned dogs from the center of town because of fouling, and he received a murder threat.
>
> A New Jersey yachtsman was charged with manslaughter in the drowning deaths of two crew members when he refused to throw his Labrador overboard to make room for the men in the lifeboat. He was acquitted.[4]

It is a well-known phenomenon that people's hearts go out quickly and spontaneously to pet animals and to infants of all species, perceived as utterly defenseless and innocently lovable. Sadly, they do not warm as readily to young children or adolescents in need, as we saw in the recent "International Year of the Child," a travesty of high-sounding speeches, vacuous ceremonies, and little substantive action. Still less do we respond to the plight of the suffering millions of adult fellow human beings around the globe.

Perhaps the main problem here is the widespread tendency to anthropomorphize and idealize pets and other animals. Most of us grow up nourished by a diet of animal fairy tales, cartoons, "cute" stuffed animals, Disney nature "documentaries," performing animals, zoo visits, and TV pet food commercials. As adults we cannot entirely escape being bombarded by the pseudoprofundities of best-sellers like *Jonathan Livingston Seagull*, *Watership Down*, and *The*

Plague Dogs or the heartwarming, edifying animal tales of Gerald Durrell, James Herriot, and the *Reader's Digest*. The tendency of which I am speaking is not confined to the products of popular entertainment, however. A leading animal behaviorist, for instance, has written, "An animal like a dog clearly must have a sense of self and therefore an ego, together with the capacity for superego development since it is social. As in man, it also possesses an id."[5] Immersed in an environment of fantasy, sentiment, and overgeneralization of this sort, it is very difficult for the average person to construct and retain a realistic perspective on animals' capacities and on the important differences between animals and humans. The extent to which this is the case is illustrated by studies of people's attitudes toward pets conducted in the United States, Canada, and England.[6] These reveal that in a world of increasing social and family instability and alienated urban life, pets are relied on to a greater and greater degree as surrogate humans whose primary role is to fill an emotional vacuum in their owners' lives. As Nowell puts it,

> Pet adoration will continue unabated as long as human relationships have deficiencies and offer no guarantees. . . . One life in touch with another can be hurtful, and when the bruises of interaction turn into permanent scars a person retreats, unwilling to take any more chances with unreliable humans. All too frequently these people settle for a safer outlet for their emotions—a dog, a cat, or a bird in a cage.[7]

This "pets are people" mindset makes it possible for American taxpayers to foot without complaint an estimated annual bill of $500 million to clean up after dogs and cope with the damage, injuries, and diseases they cause.[8] It also leads to bizarre relationships between people and their pets and hysterical responses to any perceived threat to the sanctity of pets and pet ownership, such as suggestions that urban dwellers give up pet keeping or that they be compelled by municipal bylaws to clean up after their dogs (as is the case now, for example, in New York City). The fallout from North America's pet fetishism has reached such alarming proportions that a leading Toronto veterinary clinic reports receiving as many as twenty calls a week to arrange counseling sessions for pet "behavioural upsets." One vet, reflecting on this trend, remarked, "As people get crazier, so do the animals. People just pass their neuroses on."[9] Meanwhile, dog bites and attacks, attributed largely to poor breeding, the preponderance of guard dogs, and the stresses of urban life, range from one to four million annually in the United States alone.[10]

People are inconsistent, not only in valuing pets above people, but also in the way they discriminate among animal species. Experiments performed on cats or dogs provoke outrage, whereas the same procedures may be carried out on harmless mice, frogs, or pigs without a murmur of protest. A now classic case is a 1973 U.S. Defense Department plan to test poison gas on beagles, which had to be canceled owing to the massive public outcry it caused. However, criticism was stilled when it was announced that the possibility of using other animals would be investigated.[11] Hunters kill and maim deer, moose, geese, ducks, rabbits, and other gentle animals by the tens of millions every year and little concern is voiced. But the annual slaughter of approximately 200,000 baby harp seals on Arctic ice floes was a *cause célèbre* in our time, triggering heated confrontations between hunters and environmentalists, plus an avalanche of letters to politicians and newspapers, antifur consumer campaigns, boat rammings, and the like. Seal pups, however, are cute and cuddly, whereas beavers, muskrats, wolves, foxes, and other animals lack these qualities or are considered nasty predators and pests and therefore are permitted to languish in cruel leghold traps. Sentimentalism over animals reveals its unpleasant side once more here. Finally, nearly everyone hates spiders and snakes (the latter invariably and incorrectly called "slimy"), even when they are known to be harmless, though no one can say why.[12]

It seems, then, that there is a large element of irrationality in our attitudes toward different animals and in our sense of the sort of treatment of them that is appropriate and morally acceptable. There is nothing wrong with preferring one species to another provided we have good reasons for doing so; nor is there anything amiss in thinking that we must relate differently to dissimilar animals on the basis of the characteristics they possess, to which we may or may not be able to respond. I have only tried to indicate some of the ways in which our behavior and attitudes fall considerably short of reasonableness and therefore complicate the task of thinking clearly about our relationship to and treatment of other species.

THE PROBLEM OF HUMANS' PLACE IN NATURE

There is also much confusion about humans' proper place in nature, which aggravates the preceding situation. The Judeo-Christian tradition teaches that humankind shall "have dominion over the fish of the sea, and over the fowl of the air, and over the cattle, and over all the earth, and over every creeping thing that creepeth upon the earth." God's words in Genesis have customarily been interpreted as giving our species divine authorization to exploit the natural world and its resources as it chooses, without considering anything other than our own needs and desires. In the present century some commentators have argued that this passage calls for us to be, first and foremost, responsible "shepherds" or "stewards" of nature. However, it is difficult to see how any useful inferences could be drawn from God's pronouncement here (or his subsequent indication that humans are by nature vegetarians) to guide present-day conduct, since his words pertain to a hypothetical state of paradise before the Fall. Those who consider themselves obliged to follow the spirit or the letter of the Bible will work out this problem as they see fit; I have only cited it to indicate that for those who do give allegiance to the Bible, and for all of us so far as we participate in a Judeo-Christian culture, values and attitudes about nature are born in ambiguity.[13]

Another notion that has been particularly vexing through history to anyone seeking a clearly stated moral imperative is that humans should somehow live in accordance (or in harmony) with nature. Rousseau inspired many of his contemporaries and followers with the image of the "noble savage," guided by instincts and flourishing in the allegedly innocent and simple state of nature. Kant, Hegel, and William James held, however, that humans achieve true human-ity and the highest attainments only when they emerge fully as unique beings by subduing nature and putting it to work for them; and John Stuart Mill, in his essay "On Nature," wrote that "confor-mity to nature has no connection whatever with right and wrong,"[14] that is, cannot be looked to for a principle capable of guiding conduct.

There are two senses in which living in accordance with nature *is* a meaningful concept. One is the ecological sense in which natural balances have to be maintained or there will be severe repercussions in the future for all species (including our own), dependent as they are upon environmental integrity and balance. The other is the esthetic sense in which the things that we value (wilderness, clean air and water, fertile soil) can be preserved only if we avoid over-exploiting nature. Though perhaps somewhat helpful in setting limits to conduct or providing disaster warnings, these ideas can scarcely be said to provide adequate guidelines for human conduct or to define our species' place in nature.[15]

Why is it so difficult for us to know where we fit in the natural order? The answer may be found in the fact that we are part of nature and also stand outside it. *Homo sapiens* is an animal, a natural biological system that has evolved from other, simpler forms of life over millions of years, but is also self-conscious and capable of abstract symbolization, judgment, and self-criticism. Thus we can see our own as one among many species on earth and at the same time reflect, ponder courses of action, choose, and alter ourselves and our behavior, possibly even our very nature. We can shape ourselves in whatever way we decide is best. We need not act instinctively or according to genetically stereotyped patterns of behavior; nor need we wait for hundreds of generations to pass in order to adjust our fitness for survival in certain desired ways. Our species is therefore a paradox, being both firmly planted within nature and apart from and projecting out of nature; both a natural system obeying the same physical laws as all other inanimate and animate systems and yet capable of judging, valuing, and self-making. We could summarize this by saying that unlike any other creature we know of, humans can, within certain obvious constraints, choose and fashion their environmental niche as they wish.

To make any progress at all toward understanding our place in nature, this paradox must first be accepted as a given. *Homo sapiens* is accordingly neither purely animal, as some zealous ethologists and behavioral psychologists seem to suggest, nor uniquely other as pre-Darwinian religionists believed and present-day fundamentalists still hold. Another fact from which we must begin is that humans are part of the total ecosystem for better or worse and will continue to have a significant shaping influence on the environment as long as they survive. It follows that much of what *Homo sapiens* has done to alter the environment should be seen as living in accordance with nature, that is, our own nature and its demands. Human nature is ineradicably inquisitive and innovative. As Karl Marx was one of the first to point out, in his *Economic and Philosophical Manuscripts* of 1844, new desires and needs develop as soon as basic ones are fulfilled, and a great many characteristic human activities are designed to achieve second- and higher-order goals.

It is, of course, not easy to state which activities should be included within the category of living in accordance with nature, and I do not wish to digress into a discussion of this theme. My intention is only to indicate that because of our dual nature or paradoxical position vis-à-vis the rest of the biosphere, much of our impact on the environment can be viewed as either natural or unnatural relative to our evolutionary and ecological niche, depending on our standpoint or perspective. I do not deny for a moment that our species has severely damaged the ecosystem in numerous respects or that some of the harm we have caused may be irreparable. These shameful facts cannot be whitewashed over. But at the same time, discussion of environmental issues, including our use and treatment of animals, cannot prove fruitful if we fail to acknowledge certain elementary truths about our species' place in nature.

A number of authors have done just this, having contributed to an image of humans as the great despoilers, the beings who are always out of place and can do nothing right in the natural world.[16] Some paint an idyllic and completely unrealistic picture of pristine, peaceful nature, beyond our blundering, rapacious hands. Others exclaim despairingly that the world would be a better place without humans—a meaningless assertion as I show presently. What these ideas have in common is a nostalgia for simpler times and a veiled lament for a lost Edenic paradise. In fact, guilt and the need for repentance through self-punishment pervade much contemporary writing on the environment and our relationship to animals. The fable of the Fall of Man has now acquired a secular guise, and a group of righteous pop environmental philosophers and animal liberationists are the new self-appointed apostles of redemption. Unfortunately, however, collective feelings of guilt and a refusal to acknowledge humans' inclusion and formative role in the ecosystem will not help solve any of the world's problems.

Another unconstructive idea that has attained currency in recent discussions on our use of other species is that *Homo sapiens* is a herbivore by nature. It is argued that if we returned to our "natural" vegetarian diet, we would not have to kill other creatures for food, which would somehow be a better state of affairs. Evidence has been marshaled to support the first of these contentions—for example, that modern humans have the short canine teeth and incisors of grain-eating mammals, rather than the longer, sharper ones of carnivores like lions, hyenas, and some of the great apes. Although one theory suggests that *Homo sapiens* descended from prehistoric hominids (humanlike creatures) who were tree dwellers, lacked tools, and ate grains,[17] the best anthropological evidence thus far indicates that of our distant ancestors only bush-dwelling *Australopithecus robustus*—thought to have been an evolutionary dead end—was a natural vegetarian. The other important precursors of *Homo sapiens*, *Australopithecus africanus*, *Homo habilis*, and *Homo erectus*, are all believed to have been omnivorous.[18] (One author even claims provocatively that the carnivorous predilections of our early ancestors and their pursuit of game led them to develop a "dynamic view of the world," which was an important stimulus to tool use and further evolutionary advances.[19] The role of hunting in the formation and consolidation of social groups throughout nature is too well known to require documentation here; whatever we might think of hunting today, the contribution of this process to human evolution was obviously vital.)

Some "moral vegetarians" also cite the length of human intestines to establish our herbivorous nature. According to this view, our species "has the long bowels of herbivores," and meat should be shunned because it cannot pass through quickly enough for the toxic (carcinogenic) by-products of its digestion to be expelled before they do any damage.[20] However, such reasoning is purely speculative and thus irrelevant to the animal welfare debate, particularly in view of these well-established facts: that *Homo sapiens* appears always to have been omnivorous; that the practice of livestock husbandry is at least eleven thousand years old; and that agriculture postdates hunting and fishing by tens of thousands of years.[21]

Even if we did choose to convert (or "return") to a vegetarian diet, we would not thereby avoid killing for food. *Homo sapiens* is in the business of killing, whether we like it or not. If we do not kill animals, we must kill plants, for there is no alternative to consuming living things to fulfill our nutritional needs. This is again a consequence of being part of the ecosystem. Of course, I do not mean to imply that there is no choice open to us in what we kill to survive. I only wish to underscore here the fallacy of supposing that a herbivorous existence precludes killing or that ecological wisdom and living in harmony with nature are incompatible with large-scale human destruction of living things.

SOME REFLECTIONS ON VALUE

Let us turn now to the question of nature's value apart from humans. I have called the assertion that the world would be a better place without humans meaningless. The reason is that nothing in the world (let alone the world as a whole) can be of value in a purely self-contained or nonrelational sense, that is, apart from the awareness of conscious beings of the sort that are capable of valuing things. Philosophers commonly distinguish between (a) things having intrinsic or inherent value, which are ends in themselves or may be enjoyed for their own sakes (such as a sunset or a painting) and (b) things possessing extrinsic or instrumental value, which are useful or serve as means to something else (such as raw materials and tools). Neither category of things, however, is conceived of as possessing value totally independent of the awareness of conscious beings endowed with the capacity to make the discriminations and judgments necessary to evaluate the properties these things have. Apart from the context just specified (that is, if there were no sophisticated minds like our own in the world or in the universe), then, nothing would be of value, either actually or potentially, intrinsically or extrinsically, since apart from the realm of conscious awareness, "value" has no vantage point and hence no reference. The world is, literally, value-*less* in the absence of beings capable of forming and articulating value preferences. Therefore, to speak of the world as being potentially a better place without humans is non-sensical (unless, of course, this were judged by some other valuing species or a transcendent being like God). It also follows that when people think they are valuing a feature of the world for its own sake, they must be doing something else instead, such as valuing it for the fact that it produces in them certain desired experiences.

To see more clearly why this is so, consider the following counterargument.

> Let us imagine one world exceedingly beautiful. Imagine it as beautiful as you can; put into it whatever on this earth you most admire—mountains, rivers, the sea; trees, and sunsets, stars and moon. Imagine these all combined in the most exquisite proportions, so that no one thing jars against another, but each contributes to increase the beauty of the whole. And then imagine it simply one heap of filth, containing everything that is most disgusting to us, for whatever reason, and the whole, as far as may be, without one redeeming feature. Such a pair of worlds we are entitled to compare. . . . The only thing we are not

entitled to imagine is that any human being ever has or ever, by any possibility, can, live in either, can ever see and enjoy the beauty of the one or hate the foulness of the other. Well, even so, supposing them quite apart from any possible contemplation by human beings; still, is it irrational to hold that it is better that the beautiful world should exist, than the one which is ugly? Would it not be well, in any case, to do what we could to produce it rather than the other? Certainly I cannot help thinking that it would.[22]

The author of this example is G. E. Moore, a celebrated Cambridge University philosopher of the early twentieth century. Here Moore offers a classic defense of the view that value is to be found in the things of the world as they exist in and of themselves. For if we accept that his hypothetical "beautiful world" is better than its "ugly" counterpart, we also accept that the former has value completely independent of a valuing consciousness. But if it does, then so does our real natural world and at least some of the things in it.

I believe Moore's argument to be faulty on two counts. First of all, the judgment that the beautiful world is better is a value judgment formulated by outside observers, namely, ourselves. The problem arises when we consider what it is that we value in Moore's imaginary world, for what we value are certain things which we already believe to be of value in our real world. In other words, Moore has us introduce into his fictitious world precisely those things we do value and no others. Clearly, then, when we are asked to contemplate the two worlds and compare them, we apprehend the beautiful world as better because it is entirely our own creation in accordance with what we value and the ugly world as worse because it is filled with things we already disvalue and cannot think of otherwise. Moore has simply given us loaded dice with which he asks us to play a fair game, and the outcome can hardly surprise us.

Second, Moore asks us to assume the existence of these worlds "quite apart from any possible contemplation by human beings." He thus "begin[s] by requesting that the reader become non-existent, or make himself scarce, and then call[s] upon him from this state of nothingness to make value judgments regarding the contrived world."[23] But there is no such thing as an outside observer in a thought experiment of this kind; we can no more imagine an imaginary world that is incapable in principle of being perceived or thought of than we can eat without putting food into our mouths. Moore's imaginary game must be conducted wholly within the limits of thought and cannot be used to draw inferences extending beyond it.[24] The experiment and thus the counterargument are failures because the "better" world is better by definition, not by being discovered to be so; and we cannot be asked to contemplate two uncontemplatable worlds to judge them better and worse respectively. Last, if no one is around to care whether a world is beautiful (as in Moore's example), then it matters to no one and no valuing or judgment could conceivably take place.

May it not still be the case that the objects of our real world possess some kind of self-contained value even if those in Moore's imaginary world cannot? The question of the origin of value judgments is far too complex to be dealt with here, but we may proceed a little farther. If we reject the notion of values inhering in the world taken by itself but still wish to avoid the conclusion that all value judgments represent merely subjective or purely personal preferences (the opposite extreme), then we must locate an objective foundation for such judgments; that is, there must be something about things which we judge, for instance, to be beautiful that gives rise to this judgment in each of us. Only in this manner can we avoid the pernicious doctrine that beauty (or goodness, rightness, or the like) is in the eye (or mind) of the beholder. Now it has proven very difficult to specify what this objective ingredient in things might be, but I think it is possible to find a middle ground between a Moorean theory of intrinsic values inhering in the world and pure subjectivism. Such a view would identify certain features of the world that tend to elicit fairly uniform aesthetic, moral, and other responses from beings capable of valuing, like ourselves. Yet it would not be necessary to attribute the values solely to the things themselves or to their qualities. The things of the world would be the occasions for value judgments, and values could be thought of as existing, but only in the interaction that takes place between things and valuing beings.

A relational theory of value of the foregoing type enjoys a clear advantage over a Moorean objectivism, as it avoids the incoherence of supposing that values would remain in nature if we subtracted valuing beings from the picture. It is also superior to any form of subjectivism that takes value judgments to express purely private or personal preferences. If subjectivism were true, our aesthetic, moral, and other preferences could not be regarded as educable (though, of course, they could still be conditioned). But the fact is that these sensibilities can be cultivated and altered by rational arguments, appeals to universal standards, examples, disciplined discipleship, and so forth. Subjectivism founders on its inability to take all of this into account, whereas a relational view (and, of course, an objectivist view) has no trouble doing so.

It would take us too far afield to explore the precise nature of the relational aspect of value, though a number of authors have recently attempted to come to grips with it in various ways.[25] It may be pointed out, however, that it is difficult to see how any relational view can avoid a commitment to an anthropocentric locus of valuation. But I do not necessarily see this as a serious limitation on our capacity to deal wisely and humanely with the world around us.

The view I have been defending—that nature has no value in and of itself—may strike many nature lovers as preposterous. I can almost hear some exclaim, "The starry heavens, beautiful scenery, lush gardens, magnificent wild animals, natural wonders, and the products of millions of years of evolution—are these things which we venerate and enjoy absolutely without value?!" But notice that I have not said that they are without value, only that they lack independent value, value apart from conscious, sentient beings who can make value discriminations and corresponding judgments. Natural objects and animals cannot have value in themselves, though they can and do have value if conscious beings capable of valuing can perceive and interact with them or if such beings' lives can be rejuvenated or enriched by them in some way. Whenever we suppose that nature has value apart from humans, it is solely because we are articulating this judgment or performing the requisite thought experiment and thereby introducing our value preferences into the picture.

THE VALUE OF NATURE

It is easy to miss recognizing that values and value judgments arise and that talk of them makes sense only in relation to a being such as *Homo sapiens*. In their haste to appear humble and to avoid any taint of anthropocentrism, many writers on nature and on animals have overlooked this, treating values as if they could be straight-forwardly contained in or possessed by the biosphere or some of its parts. Thus, for example, Aldo Leopold wrote in his memorable naturalist's credo, *A Sand County Almanac*, "A thing is right when it tends to preserve the integrity, stability and beauty of the biotic community. It is wrong when it tends otherwise."[26] Here it is assumed that in addition to self-regulating systems in nature, "beauty" also is an inherent, naturally occurring feature. We must begin to ask ourselves what we are saying when we make such statements. If we think carefully about the matter, we shall see that apart from the awareness of beings that have a highly sophisticated mental life, the world is not beautiful, nor is anything in it marvellous or valuable; it just *is*, as it just *was* for millions of years before our species appeared.

This issue might be made clearer if we consider for a moment the reasons why we value the animal life around us. The explanation is not too difficult to come by. We value the freedom of wild horses running at full tilt on a deserted beach; the spontaneity and playfulness of river otters; the grace of deer in an unspoiled misty meadow at dawn. We marvel at the soaring eagle, the migrating butterfly, the age-old tortoise, the intricate pattern of blood vessels in the tiniest creature. What actually inspires our awe, our exhilaration?—simply the fact that we human beings highly value freedom, experiences of things we call beautiful, and the thousand and one ways in which animals enrich our lives. Some of us are even capable of valuing obscure forms of life, like the snail darter, a minute fish whose fate was thought to have been sealed by a major American power dam project, or other endangered species that are of no obvious use to us and may never be seen by more than a handful of naturalists. Ecological findings suggest that the stability of ecosystems is related to their fundamental complexity and to other factors that are as yet not fully understood.[27] It behooves us therefore to preserve every species we can, for it may make some unknown contribution to the health and survival of the whole of which it is a part. Evolutionary biology would also point out that once a species dies out, a potentially useful gene pool that might have been tapped to create new animals with greater disease resistance or some other desirable trait is lost forever.[28] But beyond these prudential motives for being conservationists, is there not a purely altruistic one—to assure that species that have been around for thousands, perhaps millions, of years do not become extinct, because they are "valuable in themselves" or "have an inherent right to survive"? I deal with the topic of rights in the next chapter, but so far as value is concerned, I submit that conservationist goals appeal to us because we feel good (that is, have experiences that we value or prefer) and have a sense of accomplishment when we do something to preserve creatures possessing characteristics we value most in ourselves or species that enrich our lives in certain valued ways. In this manner even the desire to preserve animals that one will never come into contact with can be explained, for just knowing that they are there, that the natural world is richer for them than it would otherwise be, can be a source of satisfaction.

One explanation of what we may call the indirect, but nonetheless anthropocentric, value of the world of fauna to humans may make my position more plausible. Animals often function as important cultural symbols and as such can and do serve humans by helping to provide a deep sense of satisfaction, contentment, and significance in their lives. Thus animals, whether we directly experience them or not, may produce states of awareness in us that relate to the core of our human identity and to our collective heritage and positively reinforce these self-images.[29]

Let us return for a moment to Moore's example. In my earlier discussion I deliberately left out of consideration the experiences of animals themselves. Few would deny that certain species of animals are conscious and sentient, that like ourselves they experience pleasure and pain in response to various stimuli, and that they prefer pleasure to pain. Does it follow that animals' pleasurable experiences are valuable (to them) and that their presence in the world gives the world value apart from humans after all? Does it follow, contrary to my previous assertions, that because animals have experiences to which we would ascribe value if we had them, this bestows value on their lives irrespective of whether their lives are valued by humans? Neither of these consequences follows. Animals' pleasurable experiences are not valuable to them because animals are incapable of judging and articulating that they are.[30] It would be meaningful, however, to say that it is in their interest (accords with their observed preferences) to have pleasurable experiences repeat themselves or occur more frequently and be more enduring, though this is not an interest that they can be aware of having. Furthermore, that animals have valuable experiences (experiences that we would value if we had them) does not furnish grounds for our ascribing value to their lives. It is we who judge their experiences to be valuable by empathetic comparison of what we believe animals experience with our own range of conscious states and psychological preferences. Hence the world is still dependent on humans for its value, and accordingly attempts to ascribe independent worth to animals' lives and experiences must fail.

Anthropocentrism in morals has become a dirty word. Yet if the arguments presented here are sound, it is unavoidable, and those who think otherwise have not generally considered carefully enough the tenability of their own alternative perspectives. I show later on, however, that anthropocentrism need not be arrogant and narrow or foster inhumaneness and ecological insensitivity, as has often been thought.

There may be exceptions to the generalizations laid down in this chapter. Some mammals, particularly primates, may have a degree of intelligence and sufficient abstract reflective capabilities to formulate and even articulate value discriminations and judgments throughout at least some part of the range of their experience, as opposed to just demonstrating preferences behaviorally. It seems very doubtful that this will ever prove to be so, but it is a possibility that must be taken into account. More likely, perhaps, is the prospect of coming into contact with extraterrestrial species that are at least as intelligent and sophisticated as we. This is why I have intermittently suggested that "beings like ourselves" rather than "men," "members of our species," or "humans" are the originators of valuing and value talk.

A final note: In view of what has been said so far, we can only be puzzled when encountering the claim that "each [animal's] life is the life of a distinct individual."[31] Of course, in an obvious sense each animal *is* a unique individual; each is numerically distinct from every other. But so are pebbles, cigarette butts, ticks of a clock, and whatever else you care to name. In another sense, animals are also unique individuals; each is a subject of its own sensations, experience, or awareness. In a third sense, we may say that animals are unique individuals, by which we mean that they have "personalities"— distinctive dispositional traits, looks, behaviors, dietary preferences, ways of being playful, and so on. But in a further sense (most relevant to our discussion), animals do not show any signs whatever of being individuals—the sense in which we could legitimately speak of their lives as more or less "full," "satisfying," and so forth or in which we could meaningfully state that animals "have their own lives to lead" or have a "capacity to enjoy the good life."[32] These expressions are simply appropriated without caution or qualification from the human sphere, where we have a fairly clear idea of their meaning, and introduced into another, quite different context, where their application is completely spurious. Animal advocates who speak this way presuppose, contrary to fact, that animals can reflectively evaluate the quality of their lives and find them a cause for either satisfaction or regret.[33]

It appears that writers who have employed such expressions and see nothing conceptually odd in doing so endorse anthropomorphism (the attribution of human qualities to animals) at the same time as they denounce anthropocentrism (the adoption of a human-centered worldview or value system). This position should strike us as at least questionable, if not straightforwardly inconsistent.

A more sophisticated approach is developed by Tom Regan in his recent book *The Case for Animal Rights*.[34] Regan claims that although animals may be moral patients rather than moral agents, "normal mammalian animals aged one or more" and others are nonetheless conscious, goal-oriented beings and hence may be said to be "subjects-of-a-life" that is in itself either better or worse in quality. He then argues that "the subject-of-a-life criterion can be defended as citing a relevant similarity between moral agents and patients, one that makes the attribution of equal inherent value to them both intelligible and nonarbitrary," adding that this criterion is a sufficient, not a necessary, condition for ascribing inherent value to animals' lives. Finally, according to Regan, "since inherent value is conceived to be a categorical value, admitting of no degrees, any supposed relevant similarity must itself be categorical. The subject-of-a-life criterion satisfies this requirement."

It is ironic that although Regan rejects the categorical criterion embodied in speciesism, he endorses such an uncompromising principle of his own, indeed one that assigns equal intrinsic value to only some of the many species that exist. As I show in chapter 3, however, our moral concern for animals has to be conceptualized as admitting of varying degrees, depending on the capacities possessed by the species or individual in question. It is apparent from the arguments in this chapter that for a being's life to have independent or inherent value, it must be a valuing being in its own right. It will also become clear in chapter 3 that being a subject-of-a-life is not a condition we can attribute to animals to support the claim that their lives are of equal value to those of autonomous moral agents (such as humans), as autonomy entails possessing the ability (species-typically, at maturity, given normal development) to generate a life plan in relation to which such agents guide their lives as a whole and monitor and evaluate the varying conditions of their lives. It would therefore be more appropriate to think of certain higher animals not as subjects-of-lives but rather as subjects-of-consciousness (or as subjects-of-consciousness-with-rudimentary-thought) and of some primates as subjects-of-consciousness-with-rudimentary-thought-and-self-awareness.

2

An Evolutionary Perspective on Humans and Animals

THE UNIQUENESS OF *HOMO SAPIENS*

A wealth of information about nonhuman species accumulated in the last two decades has tended to narrow in certain respects the evolutionary gap once thought to establish beyond doubt the uniqueness of *Homo sapiens*. To mention only the best-known examples, chimpanzees' ability to learn and manipulate symbols has been well documented, and the intelligence and social life of cetaceans (particularly dophins and whales) as well as complex whale communications (or "songs") have begun to receive careful study.[1] The discoveries that have been made so far are impressive and as yet the picture is very incomplete.

An attitude of humility and awe before the intricate ways of nature unfolding to our understanding is always appropriate and even healthy for the mind. Having said this, however, it is surely fitting to add that there are many misconceptions in relation to this new knowledge. Although it is true that certain findings in the biological and behavioral sciences force us to reconsider firmly entrenched preconceptions, evolutionary hypotheses, explanatory models, boundary lines, and methods of comparative behavioral research, it is equally true that important differences between humans and other animals remain and will survive these controversies. Contemporary discussions of the capacities of animals and humans often seem to lose sight of this fact and to accept more or less uncritically the prevalent view that all significant differences between our own and other species have been relativized away. This situation is due in large measure to the inaccuracies disseminated by popularizers and journalists presenting new findings to the lay reader. Thus, for example, an article entitled "Field Report: The State of the Apes" begins: "Man is not unique. . . . [M]an is forced to concede the last significant attribute that was his and his alone—language."[2] Serious scientists, however, have also been purveyors of this view. For instance, Gordon G. Gallup, Jr. (who first demonstrated rudimentary self-awareness in chimpanzees) and his associates write that "psychologically and biologically, most of the differences between humans and chimpanzees are a matter of degree, not a matter of kind."[3]

There is another viewpoint. W. H. Thorpe contends in *Animal Nature and Human Nature*, an extensive review of biological and behavioral continuities between animals and humans: "We are left with a tremendous chasm—intellectual, artistic, technical, linguistic, moral, ethical, scientific, and spiritual—between ape and man. And we have no clear idea as to how this gap was bridged. Man is unique in all these aspects, and we may never know how this happened."[4] Similarly, Stephen Walker, in a recent, wide-ranging, and detailed study of all the relevant scientific evidence to date, concludes, "The contrast between human history and civilisation and the relatively fixed and constant adjustment of other species to natural environments is a complete and unassailable discontinuity."[5] I wish to elaborate this position here, because recognition of the significant differences between humans and animals is paramount in any discussion of humans' proper sphere of moral concern for their fellow creatures.

To understand correctly what is meant by humans' uniqueness, we must be careful to distinguish three views: (1) that humans are totally unique; (2) that humans possess characteristics that are unique, but only in superficial and insignificant ways (unique in degree perhaps, but not in kind); and (3) that although not totally unique, humans are still different from all other animals in significant respects (they possess characteristics that are different in kind, not just in degree).[6] The first of these positions, associated by tradition with certain doctrines of special divine creation ("creationism"), is now thoroughly outmoded and deservingly discredited. The second position is put forward by those who believe that new discoveries about animals' capacities eliminate any substantive difference between our own and other species or that *Homo sapiens*[7] is an ordinary product of nature and therefore does not present the paradox discussed in chapter 1. This position has a distinguished lineage, dating from at least the mid-eighteenth century.[8] It was forcefully advanced by no less a thinker than Charles Darwin, who wrote that "the difference in mind between man and the higher animals, great as it is, certainly is one of degree and not of kind."[9] Nevertheless, I believe this view is wrong and that if the ways in which humans are truly unique are properly appreciated, it will become clear that the third position is the correct one.

SIMILARITIES BETWEEN ANIMALS AND *HOMO SAPIENS*

From the time of Darwin to the present day, critics of the theory of evolution by natural selection of adaptively advantageous traits have repeatedly charged that it cannot be proven and is "just a theory." But the converging circumstantial evidence in favor of the evolution of species, to anyone who studies it carefully, is simply overwhelming. One interesting and relevant aspect of this evidence is the biochemical continuity between *Homo sapiens* and other species. Consider, for example, serum albumin, "the principle protein in the blood plasma of vertebrates."[10] Not only is some form of this substance, which contains roughly 570 units of twenty different amino acids, found in the blood of all vertebrates but also chimpanzee and gorilla albumin "show only a 1 percent immunological difference from our own." Identical immune reactions have been observed in human, gorilla, and chimpanzee T cells ("white blood cells found in the thymus gland that attack invading organisms directly") in response to the introduction of foreign (different animal species') antibodies.[11] Hemoglobins are present in humans as well as in other vertebrates, some invertebrates, and even plants. Human hemoglobin comprises "574 amino acid units arranged in four interconnected chains."[12] Though there are many different hemoglobins in nature, the chimpanzee's is identical to our own. In addition, biologists Allan Wilson and Marie-Claire King have demonstrated that in humans and chimpanzees "99 percent of the protein structure is the same."[13] Studies of DNA recombination or "hybridization" between humans and chimpanzees show a degree of combination of 97.5 percent, revealing a very close "genetic relatedness . . . at the molecular level." [14] By the same measure, our genetic complementarity with other primates has also been found to be quite high. [15]

Beyond these startling biochemical relationships, numerous behavioral similarities between chimpanzees and humans have been observed. Through the patient fieldwork of Jane Goodall and others, much has been learned about the complex patterns of social interaction within communities of chimpanzees and gorillas as well as about tool use among chimpanzees. [16] According to anthropologist Richard E. Leakey and coauthor Roger Lewin, "A troop of chimpanzees . . . has access to a pool of knowledge greater than any one individual would possess." Individual experiences are somehow passed on to other members of the troop, and this "group wisdom" they regard as "the rudiments of culture." [17] Other authors are more explicit in extending the concept of culture to nonhuman species. Bernard G. Campbell, for instance, defines culture as "the totality of behavior patterns of a social group of men or animals that are passed from generation to generation by learning." [18]

Psychological experiments have also disclosed that chimpanzees have much more sophisticated problem-solving or analytic abilities than anyone suspected. It appears that some of the intellectual tasks which they have mastered give evidence of a capacity to form and manipulate to some degree both mental images and concepts—to exercise visualization, some level of reasoning, and inventive ingenuity to achieve a desired goal. Nor is the capacity for self-awareness, once thought by some to be the hallmark of human uniqueness, any longer possible to deny chimpanzees. [19]

Finally, an abundant literature on chimpanzee language learning accomplishments has changed many long-standing ideas about the communicative abilities of our closest biological relative. Chimpanzees cannot talk (vocalize), but have been taught to use American Sign Language and other symbolic systems (up to 130 signs or combinations of signs) to formulate meaningful, if primitive, sentences and to name novel objects and experiences. [20]

The chimpanzee is, of course, not the only animal with which our species shares many attributes. Indeed, if this were not so, evolutionary continuity would be an empty concept and biomedical and psychological research would be impossible to imagine. Investigators in these fields have at their disposal in fact a vast amount of information on the resemblances between corresponding systems in

Homo sapiens and other species accumulated from paleontological and comparative studies and past experiments. Some animals as far removed from humans as mice, hamsters, and guinea pigs exhibit very similar physiological reactions; dogs share many of the same diseases; and pigs have been noted to be strikingly like humans physiologically and anatomically.[21] Continuities between our own and other species have also been amply demonstrated by neurobiology, the science of the brain. In a special issue of *Scientific American* devoted to the brain, one author remarks,

> The principles of neuronal function are remarkably similar in animals as far apart as the snail and man; most of what is known about the nerve impulse was learned in the squid. Even the major structures of the brain are so similar in, say, the cat and man that for most problems it seems to make little difference which brain one studies.[22]

As far as behavior is concerned, displays of surprisingly human-like qualities have been well known for centuries in animals other than our closest evolutionary relatives, particularly among cats, dogs, horses, and other domesticated species. Dolphins mimic almost any human or animal behavior that is anatomically possible for them and therefore learn a variety of tricks with great ease and less frequent reinforcement (or reward) than other species.[23] Birds exhibit "a capacity for organizing their auditory perception and their vocalizations with [a] precision exceeded only by man, and possibly by bats, but seldom even approached by other mammals."[24] Altruistic behavior has been observed among several species, notably dolphins, elephants, baboons, and African wild dogs, the last of which, along with chimpanzees, are the only social carnivores other than *Homo sapiens* that actively share their spoils. These dogs will even regurgitate food to nourish sick animals left behind at the pack's den.[25] Gorillas are monogamous and wolves frequently so. Murder, infanticide, and cannibalism are found among chimpanzees in the wild.[26] Anecdotal reports abound, containing even more surprising testimony about remarkable animal behaviors. One I encountered not long ago tells of a domesticated chimpanzee that can plow with a tractor, mow lawns manually or with a riding mower, build fences, bay cattle, bait its own hook and fish, eat with a fork and knife at the family table, and use the toilet when it is in the house![27]

What are the implications of such close similarities? Do they seriously weaken or perhaps destroy the concept of humans' uniqueness? No—and it is important to understand why not, for anyone who thinks they do is either oversimplifying or laboring under a misconception. We remain in many respects importantly different from all other animals, but the difference has to be examined with more care than is usual in the literature devoted to this subject. We must proceed with caution when advancing any claim on behalf of human uniqueness. Books written only a decade or two ago and expressing then-current notions about our singular endowments now sometimes seem almost as antiquated and quaint as those published a century ago. The fact is that there appear to be few biological or psychological processes in humans of which some degree or aspect has not also been discovered elsewhere in the animal kingdom. This is especially true in areas like the neuroanatomy of the brain, perception, immunological reactions, information processing, and communications, which have been studied thoroughly enough to yield interesting and valuable results.

DIFFERENCES BETWEEN *HOMO SAPIENS* AND ANIMALS

What are the differences, then? First of all, there are many ways in which *Homo sapiens* is biologically singular. For instance, as Richard M. Tullar reflects in *The Human Species*,

> We are bigger and stronger than most mammals. We can climb, swim, jump, kick, and throw. We can run faster than most mammals and can outwalk any of them, including the horse. In all-around physical prowess, we rank high among the animals. . . . We are fully erect, wholly terrestrial, and zealously protective of our territorial hunting ground and its home base. We are the most intelligent, hairless, sweaty, not to mention sexy, primate on earth.[28]

George Gaylord Simpson adds, from an ecological perspective,

> [Man] is, on the whole, the most adaptable of animals. He is about as independent of environment as any animal, or, as it may more accurately be put, is able to get along in about as wide an environmental range as any. He is almost the only animal that really exerts any significant degree of control over the environment. His reproductive efficiency is the highest in the animal kingdom, with a prenatal protection at least as high as in any other animal and postnatal care decidedly higher.[29]

It is useful to remember these things to call ourselves back from idle reveries in which we depict ourselves as merely "featherless bipeds," *lupus homini*, "naked apes," "fetalized (neotenic) apes," or what have you.

Discussions of humans' uniqueness have often emphasized such features as the extraordinary size and complex structure of our brain, the possession of an opposable thumb, and the capacity for language. However, these characteristics, although not altogether unrevealing, cannot be put forward as unequivocal marks of humans' essential difference. It is instructive to take a closer look at these salient features of our nature.

THE BRAIN

In terms of absolute size, the human brain is obviously surpassed by those of elephants, whales, and even some extinct mammalian species. In addition, the normal range of human brain sizes is from 1,000 cc to 2,000 cc, and there have been extremely bright and gifted people with brains that would fall at the lower end of this scale.[30] Furthermore, there seems to be no direct and uniform correlation between body size and brain size. In a survey of the literature on this subject, Carl Sagan suggests that "even the simplest 'housekeeping' functions of the brain must require some minimum brain mass,"[31] and Stephen Jay Gould remarks that "a large brain may reflect nothing more than the needs of the large body that house[s] it."[32] Because of this, numerous attempts have been made to find some formula for comparing different species' brain sizes and hence to determine their relative levels of intelligence. The most widely cited index of interspecific intelligence devised thus far is the ratio of brain mass to body mass. Though precise measurements are not always easily obtained and a range of variation is also a complicating factor, much intriguing work has been done in this area. However, reports of the accumulated data conflict, some suggesting that our species rates highest whereas others note exceptions and anomalies. Additional characteristics that have commonly been made the focus of attention are the degree of convolution and thickness of the cortical surface (neocortex) and the overall density of cerebral neurons. Since the human brain is outstandingly well developed in all these respects, and since the cerebral cortex is the locus of thinking, it has been widely held that humans have a clearly superior capacity for reflection and intelligent behavior. In contrast, however, Peter Morgane, a senior scientist at the Worcester (Massachusetts) Foundation for Experimental Biology and coauthor of *A Dolphin Brain Atlas*, notes,

The whales [including dolphins and porpoises] . . . appear to fill such criteria as we presently have to assume advanced brain development. . . . The cortex of whales is relatively thinner than comparable regions in other large brains, including human brains, but the total surface area is far greater due to the tremendous infolding. Hence, as a whole we may be dealing with the same essential numbers of cells, but the cells that are present are more spread out.[33]

The evolution of the brain and relative brain sizes of both extinct and living mammals has been most exhaustively studied by Harry J. Jerison, a scientist who has developed a method of making endocasts, or latex molds, of intracranial spaces. Jerison has also worked out a mathematical analysis that compares the brain weight of a species with the brain weight of an average animal of the same approximate body weight. From this computation he derives a value for the "expected brain size" (weight) of a given species, then compares its actual (measured) size by taking the ratio of the actual to the expected brain size. According to this formula, or "encephalization quotient," the actual brain size of humans comes out to six times what should be expected of a typical comparable mammal.[34] We must note, however, that Jerison also places dolphins in this range and that there simply is not a comparable set of mammals to use in order to obtain a meaningful statistic for whales.

TOOL USE

Much has been made of *Homo sapiens'* hand structure and its role in shaping human evolution and culture.[35] To begin with, we must recognize that our species is not the only one equipped with a prehensile (grasping) hand instead of a paw, claws, a hoof, or with an opposable thumb or a "precision grip, in which the thumb and index finger meet at their tips to form a circle."[36] These attributes are present elsewhere among the primates, being possessed by the gelada baboon and the chimpanzee. But as Leakey and Lewin point out, ours is the only species in which the precision grip is fully developed, meaning that humans alone are capable of very fine manipulative maneuvers, such as those employed in carving, sewing, carpentry, painting, and electronics assembly. Because of this endowment, humans can make use of any tools their intelligence can devise, either manually or as indirect or remote extensions of manual techniques. The importance of this capacity cannot be overstated, for because of it sophisticated exploratory behavior, creative artistry/design, and technology become possible—in short, our species' adaptation to and high degree of formative influence upon its environment.

An ape, in contrast, is very limited in its tool-inventing and -using activities. Though its tool use represents intelligent behavior, an ape is "able only to use a natural object as a tool with, perhaps, slight modification. An ape cannot conceive the tool without seeing it."[37] Nor has one ever been observed to fabricate a tool to use in making other tools.[38]

Still, we should not overemphasize the role of tool use in establishing human uniqueness nor consider it in isolation from other characteristics. As one science writer has remarked, reporting on new discoveries that date the first use of fire at 1.4 million years ago, "The use of fire is the quintessence of the human condition, even more so than the use of tools since some animals at least use sticks as primitive tools but none, other than man, uses fire at all."[39]

LANGUAGE

The capacity for language used to be thought of as *Homo sapiens'* most distinctive behavioral trait. We now realize that this belief was naive. Animals of a wide variety communicate among themselves in their own often complex and indecipherable ways, and captive chimpanzees can be taught to manipulate humanly meaningful symbols, teach their young to do likewise, and communicate with one another using these same signs.[40] Unfortunately, much of what has been reported about chimpanzees' language skills is inaccurate, leading to exaggerated claims by popularizers of this research. E. Sue Savage-Rumbaugh, director of the language project at the Yerkes Regional Primate Center in Atlanta, and her husband/research associate, Duane M. Rumbaugh of Emory University, have conducted some of the most advanced research in this area, with the objective of applying what is learned to training mentally retarded children in language skills.[41] In a 1978 survey of all ape language training efforts to date, they conclude that previous work (including much of their own) was methodologically defective and proceeded from "an inherent bias toward a set of presumptions about the significance of symbol manipulation formerly reserved for children." They add that "a dramatic and significant difference between symbol use in children and in chimpanzees . . . is obvious even at the earliest

stages of language acquisition" (about one year, eight months) and
that "apes may not understand the symbolic communicative significance of the symbols they have learned to use."[42] The following
conclusion is then drawn by this research team after seven years of
the Yerkes project:

> Thus, it appears that chimpanzees, even with intensive linguistic
> training, have remained at the level of communication they are endowed
> with naturally—the ability to indicate, in a general fashion, that they
> desire another to perform an action upon or for them when there exists a
> single unambiguous referent.[43]

In contrast to this form of communication, they remark, "We see true
symbolization as the use of arbitrary symbols to refer to objects and
events that are removed in time and space." Surprisingly, though,
these investigators also state that "our own recent work indicates that
the ability to use symbols representationally can be acquired by the
chimpanzee."[44]

Another group of specialists in ape language training offers a
much less promising prognosis. Four collaborators, headed by H. S.
Terrace, studied "more than 20,000 combinations of two or more
signs . . . for evidence of syntactic and semantic structure" and
summarize their results in this manner:

> For the moment, our detailed investigation suggests that an ape's
> language learning is severely restricted. Apes can learn many isolated
> symbols (as can dogs, horses, and other nonhuman species), but they
> show no unequivocal evidence of mastering the conversational, seman-
> tic, or syntactic organization of language.[45]

Thomas A. Sebeok and Donna Jean Umiker-Sebeok, who claim to
have detected an "experimenter effect" (body language cues given
unconsciously by scientists to their subjects) in many now-classic ape
language experiments, contend that "there is no solid evidence that an
ape has ever invented a composite sign by understanding its parts."[46]
There is also evidence—as yet incomplete—that animals lack the
specialized brain regions known to be responsible for linguistic skills
in humans.[47]

These critical reservations notwithstanding, chimpanzees' language abilities are remarkable. But far more exceptional are the innate
linguistic skills of human beings, the only beings that invent their
own languages:[48]

Under anything like normal circumstances it is virtually impossible to prevent a child's learning to speak. What is more, children master what appears to be one of the most complex intellectual skills with virtually no formal tuition. From the cacophony of sounds that the infant hears it is able to construct the elements of its native language, so that by the age of five it uses perhaps two thousand words of spoken vocabulary and comprehends at least another four thousand; that these words, furthermore, are strung around at least a thousand rules of grammar adds up to a very impressive achievement.[49]

Because the underlying structure of the thousands of different languages in the world is thought to be the same, and because the number of basic sound units (phonemes) humans are capable of forming is limited to about forty, any infant can become equally fluent in whatever linguistic environment he or she happens to be reared in. Whereas the chimpanzee's symbolic vocabulary and capacity to make sentences equals that of a two-year-old, the average human adult has a working vocabulary of approximately 100,000 words from which he or she can construct limitless original sentences, giving expression to countless variations on old ideas and to entirely new ones. Although definitions of language vary, the following three characteristics are generally agreed to be essential features: *productiveness* (completely novel utterances can be generated by any speaker and can be understood by any other speaker whether or not he or she has ever heard them); *displacement* (language is used to refer to objects, events, people, and places removed in time and space; it is abstract); and *duality of patterning* (phonemes, which themselves have no meaning, can be used in combination to construct meaningful utterances).[50] Apes' capacities in the first two appear to be so primitive that they scarcely fit the descriptions given, and, of course, since they do not speak, in the usual sense, their linguistic skills omit the third entirely. Furthermore, it is not clear what significance should be attached to such linguistic performances in apes, since they do not represent species-typical behavior but only emerge in an enriched artificial environment such as a laboratory.

Whether language precedes thought or thought language in human development is a conundrum that philosophers, psychologists, and experts in linguistics have debated for ages. No one will contest the immense importance of language in the refinement of human cognitive skills. This relationship has been well expressed by evolutionist Bernhard Rensch as follows:

Homo sapiens is the first species to be capable of envisioning his own ego as a significant concept and of seeing himself objectively against an extramental background. This has enabled him to measure matter, space and time, . . . to recognize causal, logical and psychological laws . . . , [and to come] to an understanding not only of his own phylogenetic evolution but also of the structure of the universe from the most distant galaxy to the interior of the atom. And he has done this through language, writing and printing, which have enabled him to hand on tradition and to develop a supra-individual memory and a global range of knowledge.[51]

The equally vital role in shaping language of the innate conceptual apparatus that is characteristic of *Homo sapiens* is succinctly summarized by Mortimer J. Adler:

Man's ability to name or designate objects and to make significant declarative sentences about them cannot be explained except in terms of man's having the ability to understand what different kinds of objects are like and his having the ability to make judgments about them in the light of such understanding. These two abilities, together with the additional ability to draw inferences from the judgments made or to construct arguments out of them, constitute the power of conceptual thought, the root of which is the ability to form and employ concepts.[52]

The remarkable achievements of our species as social and civilized beings, looked at in the optimistic and affirmative spirit of a Sir Kenneth Clark or a Jacob Bronowski, stand as evidence of the fruitful interaction between language and thought and demonstrate too the radical disparity between humans' and animals' capacities. As Stephen Walker states,

Of all the discontinuities between man and animals that could be quoted, including the exclusively human faculties for abstraction, reason, morality, culture and technology, and the division of labour . . . the evergreen candidate for the fundamental discontinuity . . . is language.[53]

Against the background of an exhaustive discussion of all the ways in which consciousness and thought may be attributed to animals, Walker concludes, "It is still reasonable to say that animals do not think as we do, when we think in words, and that in so far as we are only conscious when we think in words, they lack conscious awareness."[54]

FURTHER CAPACITIES

There are other important characteristics that set humans off from animals. The learned component of human behavior is vast and far surpasses that of any known nonhuman species.[55] Human nature is capable of endless expression through flexible responses to environmental challenges. Humans can modify their behavior and way of life, learning whatever is required to survive in a given habitat or to alter the habitat itself to enhance their survival. They can make and follow rules to govern social interactions and to ensure group security. These can be modified or changed by conscious and rational choice.

Leakey and Lewin, René Dubos, Alexander Alland, Jr., Ashley Montagu, and others have argued that aggression is not innate in humans as has been popularly claimed;[56] on the contrary, the evolutionary progression from hominids to modern humans can best be understood in terms of a basic cooperative drive, which is the moving force behind the astonishing miscellany of cultural patterns observed throughout the world. Human beings' high degree of sociability and capacity to learn, according to this view, have accounted for their ability to diversify and survive. Ritualized behavior is, of course, quite common among our own species as it is among other animals, but human cultural variability shows that in ours alone such behavior is not genetically stereotyped or preprogrammed.[57] As C. F. Hockett notes, "The ratio of goal-directed acts to automatic or random responses is much greater for us than for other animals, so that, as seen from the outside, human behavior is much less predictable. No other species manifests nearly so wide a variety of conduct and goals from one community to another as we do."[58] This high component of goal-directedness is responsible for the unparalleled adaptability of the human species. Tullar attributes the malleability of human nature to an inborn exploratory drive:

> We also are born with a drive to explore that is unmatched by any other creature. We carry this exploratory urge throughout our lives so that we retain the option for change despite the traditional (imitative) nature of much of our learning. This has made possible one of man's main strengths, the great flexibility of his behavior.[59]

The combination of high intelligence, a capacity for invention, infinitely rich linguistic communication, enormous capacity to learn, and strong genetic predisposition to sociability, then, accounts in large measure for *Homo sapiens'* singular adaptability as a species. As Leakey and Lewin remark, a human is "an animal capable of tackling whatever challenge the environment might offer," "an animal with the potential to achieve virtually anything."[60]

SUMMARY

Homo sapiens possesses a number of significant traits that differentiate it from all other species, past and present, and that should contribute to our understanding of what human nature means. It should be evident from the preceding discussion that the contrast between humans and the other animals is not just a difference of degree but also of kind. We possess important capacities that are not present elsewhere in nature and additional capacities (such as language and conceptualization) that, although present to some degree in other species, are in humans so highly developed as to be qualitatively distinct from those of animals. This is often erroneously denied by those who fashionably overdramatize animals' capacities while underrating those of humans or who consider parsimony in scientific explanation to be the highest virtue. Similarities and analogies between animal and human behavior may be drawn and often direct our attention toward fruitful avenues of research and suggestive interpretations of human experience. However, attempts to explain our behavior reductively (in terms of principles applicable to simpler organisms or inanimate objects) have always failed to make sense of those features that are most characteristically and uniquely human, and have thereby obscured the data from which they began. This is no less true of sociobiology and other forms of determinism today than it was of post-Cartesian mechanism in the seventeenth century or social Darwinism and naive behaviorism in the early twentieth century.

AUTONOMY AND THE FULL MEANING
OF HUMANS' UNIQUENESS

The foregoing discussion tells only part of the story of humans' distinctiveness and says little that pertains directly to capacities that signify we are moral beings. Crucial to the concerns of this book are attributes that mark out the autonomy of humans and the foundation for their mutual moral concern, as these are the characteristics that most clearly manifest our species' uniqueness. They provide as well the necessary groundwork for a realistic perspective on the moral issues concerning our use and treatment of other species.

When I speak of an *autonomous being* I mean one that is critically self-aware and has the capacity to manipulate concepts in complex ways, use a sophisticated language, reflect, plan, deliberate, choose, and accept responsibility for acting. In other words, an autonomous being can act freely, choose and decide rationally in the fullest sense, and engage in self-making or self-realizing activities. Such a being possesses a range of specialized cognitive abilities, which are the essential tools or vehicles by means of which its autonomy evolves, is made known to that being reflexively, and is manifested or expressed to others. We call this kind of being an *agent* because it has the capacity for fully self-conscious, voluntary, and deliberate action—action that can be evaluated, appraised, judged, or otherwise normatively assessed.

I have referred to critical self-awareness, complex concept manipulation, and sophisticated language, but we now need to look at these more closely. Saying that human beings are critically self-aware does not just mean that, apelike, they can recognize and respond to a mirror image of themselves; it implies a whole gamut of qualities. We are aware of ourselves perceptually to be sure, but also of ourselves as objects among objects, as persons, as independent individuals with our own integrity, sense of purpose, and worth. We have a concept of our own lives—their origin, duration, self-guided direction, and terminus in death—of world history, and of the limitless reaches of time and space beyond the self. We can foresee the possible consequences of our acts and estimate the relative probabilities of each. We can appreciate the necessity for both self-expression and self-regulation. Humans are the beings who because of their acute sense of self experience anxiety, guilt, despair, shame, remorse, internal conflict, pride, hope, triumph, and so many other emotion-laden states. Initiative, the choice of values, judgment, and role playing are also expressions of self-awareness in humans. This sort of reflexive act of consciousness I call *critical self-awareness* because humans intermittently monitor their own activities, interactions with others, inner states, and levels of self-development. We are complicated feedback systems psychologically as well as neurologically. The flow of our conscious life is constantly altered by self-examination, revision, addition and deletion, and thought experiments aimed at improving either mental or physical performance are regularly conducted. As a consequence, our behavior is and expresses itself as subject to our own scrutiny, self-direction, and subtle alteration. Each of us has a self-image, which is itself a product of self-activity and open to modification through self-criticism as we express ourselves through various ongoing engagements with the world. It is in this sense that existentialists speak of creative self-making or self-realization.

Now only a being with highly evolved cognitive capacities, such as the ability to symbolize, think abstractly, reflect, imagine, calculate, invent and solve complex problems, recollect, and project, could have this kind of awareness and the degree of freedom from and control over the world that it affords. The evolution of languages that can serve as vehicles for self-expression and convey the subtleties of human cognitive processes extends the domain of freedom and control manyfold by opening up the possibility of pooled mind power and cooperative effort. Along with the high degree of freedom from natural necessity possible for *Homo sapiens* comes deliberation, choice, and responsibility—the essential ingredients of moral decision making. Our critical self-awareness enables us to envision alternatives, reflect on possible scenarios and outcomes, and optimize benefits through the careful selection and organization of appropriate behavior. The self, then, is essentially expressed in many of our voluntary acts, namely, those governed by deliberation and choice. The context of such acts is agency and autonomy, and it is here we find the assigning of responsibility and the willingness to accept it.

We can readily see that far from being of merely passing interest, even those characteristics with which we began to explore humans' uniqueness—a highly developed brain, the precision grip, and sophisticated languge skills—are quite important in the evolution of our species' autonomy, for they make it possible for us to range fairly freely through the environment, overcoming obstacles, not only to our survival, but also to our will. Indeed, there probably has been a reciprocal interaction of humans' capacities and their autonomy, such that the latter has also exercised an influence on the speed if not the direction of human evolution.[61] This is nowhere more evident than in the sphere of culture, where morality first makes its appearance.

3

Animals and the Moral Community

TWO CURRENT VIEWS OF THE MORAL STATUS OF ANIMALS

We have seen in chapter 2 that there are important evolutionary continuities between *Homo sapiens* and other species as well as significant quantitative and qualitative differences. The questions that must now be raised are whether any of the differences are morally relevant, that is, have a bearing on the issue of our use and treatment of animals, and if so which, and what weight should be assigned to them in our deliberations. According to a view classically stated by Jeremy Bentham in the eighteenth century and often reiterated today, the paramount question to be asked when deciding how we ought to treat animals "is not, Can they *reason*? nor Can they *talk*? but, *Can they suffer*?" [1] This position derives from Bentham's utilitarianism, a moral theory about which more is said presently. To the utilitarian, only animals' capacity to experience pain (or to suffer) [2] and to experience pleasure (or to enjoy) are morally relevant. Since they also hold that this is true for humans, the characteristics that make our species unique are considered to be irrelevant, in general, to the moral issue of the treatment of animals and may be appealed to, if at all, only on a case-by-case basis to determine whether the interests of humans outweigh those of animals with which they conflict or vice-versa. In brief, humans are obligated to take animals' interests into account whenever these may be adversely affected by our actions, and therefore the boundary of our sphere of moral concern does not coincide with that which biologically separates our own from other species. (There are, of course, other varieties of utilitarianism that do not focus so narrowly on pleasure and pain; but hedonistic utilitarianism predominates in discussions of the ethics of our treatment of animals.)

Another view that is currently popular among spokespersons for animal welfare is that which endorses the notion of animal rights. To different individuals, the ascription of rights to animals means different things. To some, it is a way of expressing their conviction that animals' lives have intrinsic value or value to themselves. I have already shown in chapter 1 that no meaning can be attached to the notion of anything's having totally self-contained value; and as animals cannot reflectively examine their lives to arrive at qualitative assessments about them, their lives also cannot have intrinsic value or value to themselves. Others seem to think that granting rights to animals is like waving a magic wand or uttering incantations, as if by doing so they could change overnight the attitudes and behavior of their fellow human beings.

The origin of the idea of animal rights is not easy to trace. One view is that this notion is a natural spin-off or even a logical extension of the civil rights and women's rights movements; another is that it represents nothing more than another symptom of the tendency, particularly prevalent in the United States, to couch all demands for change in the language of rights. Arthur L. Caplan has referred to this contemporary phenomenon as the "hortatory or political usage of rights," remarking on "rights language". . as a politically expedient device to focus social concern on any ethical or political question."[3] Thus we hear daily of employees' rights, students' rights, the right to die with dignity, a bill of rights for nonsmokers, the right to work, the right to strike, tenants' rights, landlords' rights, the right to a safe environment, prisoners' rights, gay rights, the rights of future generations, the rights of the handicapped, and so on. Lately, even the rights of left-handers and the right of parents to spank their children have been defended in the media! Some of these rights claims are surely legitimate. But there is little doubt that the concept of rights has been much abused, having been stretched almost beyond recognition and frequently invoked when other terminology would do just as well or when basic constitutional or civil rights could be cited instead. In any event, a sizable and growing number of people think that animals have (or should have) rights, such as the right to life, the right not to suffer, and the right to a certain minimum quality of life, and that it makes perfectly good sense to talk this way.

I think it can be shown that both the utilitarian position on animals and the advocacy of animal rights are fundamentally mistaken. To see why and to develop a sensible alternative position on the moral status of animals, it is necessary to examine the foundations of our system of moral beliefs. This in turn requires that we consider the nature of a moral community, for only within such a social organization can the basic concepts and principles of morality arise.

FOUNDATIONS OF THE MORAL COMMUNITY: PRELIMINARIES

Few people will dispute the statement that we all belong to a moral community, though we may have different ideas about the nature of such a community (for example, whether it is rooted in religion or in purely secular precepts) and its scope (such as whether morality is relative to a given culture or is universal; whether it includes only human beings or other species as well). What, then, is a moral community? Most generally, it is a group of beings that shares certain characteristics and whose members are or consider themselves to be bound to observe certain rules of conduct in relation to one another because of their mutual likeness. These rules create what we call obligations and derive in some intimate way from the characteristics which the beings composing the moral community have in common. Thus a moral community is a society in the broadest sense of the word, and the beings belonging to it are related by natural bonds, whereas their conduct is regulated by bonds of obligation— that is, the beings in question possess certain salient characteristics, are capable of recognizing these in other, similar beings, and acknowledge possession by other beings of the characteristics in question as grounds for following certain rules of conduct toward them.

Note, however, that not all people who are members of a moral community necessarily accept that they are bound to follow specifiable standard rules of conduct even by virtue of recognizing and acknowledging that others share important characteristics with them. Sociopaths and terrorists, for instance, do not. Most moral theorists, however (as well as most laypersons), would argue that such exceptions do not seriously undermine our moral community or threaten to destroy the bond of association that holds it together, any more than the occasional act of anarchism or civil disobedience harmfully erodes the basic principles of political obligation and community.

MEMBERSHIP IN THE MORAL COMMUNITY

Now what sorts of beings do actually belong to a moral community such as I have just described? Clearly, they must be beings that, by their nature, are capable of functioning within one. This means, in effect, that they must possess the sorts of characteristics that we have already discussed: critical self-awareness; the ability to manipulate complex concepts and to use a sophisticated language (especially for the purpose of communicating wishes, desires, needs, decisions, choices, and so on);[4] and the capacity to reflect, plan, deliberate, choose, and accept responsibility for acting. The importance of these attributes in humans' evolutionary adaptation and in establishing their uniqueness has already been stressed. What we need to emphasize here is that these characteristics make humans autonomous or self-directing and capable of functioning as rational moral agents. It is because they are capable of long-range planning, anticipating consequences, choosing among alternative courses of action, taking responsibility, making and following rules, and the like that humans can engage in moral behavior, or behavior that affects others as well as themselves and that is subject to moral appraisal. Furthermore, the possession of these characteristics, plus the capacity to recognize them in others and to care about others, goes a long way toward explaining what we mean by speaking of ourselves as *persons*. Thus it appears that a moral community is a social group composed of interacting autonomous beings where moral concepts and precepts can evolve and be understood. It is also a social group in which the mutual recognition of autonomy and personhood exist. The latter feature is equally important and indeed inseparable from the former, since the development of moral institutions (such as promise keeping, truth telling, making contractual agreements, and giving mutual aid in emergencies) is contingent on recognition of and respect for persons.

A number of animal protectionist authors have attempted to refute the approach I have followed here, claiming that when we examine critically each of the characteristics differentiating humans from animals, which I have identified as morally relevant differences, we find that none of them succeeds in establishing the moral superiority of humans.[5] But I am not arguing that any one of these characteristics taken in isolation establishes the moral superiority of humans (or better, of autonomous agents or persons), rather that all of them do, when taken together. This is a crucial point: It is the whole cluster of interrelated capacities, and this alone, that constitutes the nature of an autonomous being. The piecemeal approach taken by animal welfarists to undermine, as they suppose, the position advocated here simply succeeds in trivializing the claim being advanced on behalf of autonomy as the focus of full moral status and discourse. Their argument amounts in fact to an illicit *reductio*, much like one that might be offered, say, to "prove" that there is no politically relevant difference between democracy and other forms of government and hence no superiority of the former over the latter. We could imagine such an argument, cast in Socratic form, to run as follows: "'Does freedom of speech, which you claim to be a politically relevant difference between democracy and other forms of government, establish the superiority of democracy over these other forms?' 'No, not taken by itself.' 'Well, then, what about freedom of assembly?' 'Also inadequate taken by itself.' 'Freedom from arbitrary arrest?' 'Not by itself.' 'The right to vote?' 'No.' 'It appears, then, that democracy is not superior to other forms of government because under examination each of its essential characteristics shows itself to be a politically irrelevant difference.'" But, of course, no one would think to defend democracy by placing the entire weight of the argument on one isolated feature. In like manner, no one would seek to support the claim that autonomous beings are morally superior by building the case on a single characteristic of such beings.

ON RIGHTS

I wish to argue now that only within the context of a moral community do rights and obligations (duties) arise at all. This is so first of all because rights are possessed solely by persons. As a preliminary, I want to stress that I am speaking here of basic moral rights as distinct from legal rights. Defenders of animal rights are often unclear in their own minds, as well as in the presentation of their case to the public, whether they are endorsing moral or legal rights for animals or indeed both. This is an important distinction to which I return in the final chapter. For the moment, however, let us concentrate on moral rights. Why are moral rights possessed only by persons? The short answer is that rights are accorded to persons (that is, reflectively self-valuing beings) by other persons in recognition of their inherent independence, dignity, and worth *as persons* (rather than as individuals who have attained or failed to attain some level of moral development in their lives).

Much has been written over the past few centuries on the subject of rights, and a good deal of this literature has mystified rather than clarified the concept. Probably the principal factor in this mystification lies in the traditional doctrine of natural rights. Natural rights are "rights we are alleged to have in a state of nature, independently of human institutions and conventions, simply by virtue of our humanity (or some other set of attributes). Such rights are typically indefeasible, that is, they cannot be overridden (except maybe in great catastrophes . . .)."[6] Now the idea of a "state of nature" is notoriously vague, and for all we know one may never have existed, at least in the way envisioned by natural rights theorists, since *Homo sapiens* and their ancestral hominids have always been highly social creatures. In addition, it has never been made plain what it means to say that we possess rights "by virtue of our humanity." Some have claimed that rights are God-given, others that no grounds can be given for the possession of rights; it is simply self-evident that all humans have them. Still others have asserted both, as in the famous passage from the Declaration of Independence of the United States of America, which reads, "We hold these truths to be self-evident, that all men are created equal, that they are endowed by their Creator with certain unalienable Rights, that among these are Life, Liberty and the pursuit of Happiness."

Because of these and other difficulties with the notion of rights, many philosophers have become convinced that talk of rights, although useful in a civil libertarian (that is, legal) context, has no value in moral theory and in fact should be avoided altogether in our discussion of moral issues. Some have also said that the British libertarian/egalitarian tradition in morality and the law does not depend on a strong conception of rights and that the American system is the exception, rights having been initially enshrined in the Declaration and then later in the Bill of Rights. However, in my view the idea of basic moral rights lies at the core of our system of moral beliefs and is an essential feature of the moral community. In an article on "Rights, Human Rights, and Racial Discrimination," Richard Wasserstrom observes that if the question be raised why ought anyone have a right to anything? or why not have a system in which there are not rights at all? the answer is that such a system would be a morally impoverished one. . . . [for] one ought to be able to claim as entitlements those minimal things without which it is impossible to develop one's capabilities and to live a life as a human being.[7]

Wasserstrom helps to bring out here the crucial role that rights have to play by indicating that they serve to express the moral equality of autonomous beings, each of which has an equal claim to be provided the conditions necessary for self-development as a being of that kind. Rights also serve in this context to protect the interests of each in having certain goods and services on which self-development depends, and this sets the stage for the many compromises and trade-offs that society must assure are justly arrived at and implemented. Some additional points may also be worth noting here.

First, the fact that scores of nations are signatories to the Universal Declaration of the Rights of Man, on which the United Nations was founded, indicates, prima facie at least, that the concept of rights is understandable and significant to people of diverse experience and cultural backgrounds. This remains true in spite of the egregious and often shocking violations of human rights in all parts of the globe that are characteristic of our era. Whether people in general live up to their moral precepts or only pay lip service to them is surely independent of considerations of their validity and significance, for moral beliefs as such are not invalidated by immoral behavior, however widespread.

Second, it seems highly unlikely that an account of fundamental legal or otherwise institutionalized rights (such as the rights of habeas corpus, trial by jury, suffrage, freedom of speech and assembly, and property) could even be formulated if there were no moral rights on which they could rest. One kind of legal right in fact serves the sole function of guaranteeing the exercise of basic moral rights in society and establishes grounds for protecting individuals against violations of their moral rights (in essence, their persons) in practical situations. In other words, this subclass of legal rights gives concrete definition to moral rights within a political framework. (Bills of rights and guarantees of civil liberties are of this type.)

Third, it is questionable whether morality can dispense with a strong assertion of rights. Persistent violation of persons' autonomy in some countries could be said to underscore the necessity of ascribing rights to individuals to serve as a declaration of the dignity and inviolability of the person, as well as some kind of protection against the arbitrary use of power over the person and as a foundation for international laws to protect individuals everywhere against such abuses.

With these points in mind, then, I wish to consider what it means to ascribe moral rights to human beings.

The idea of basic moral rights (the rights to life, liberty, happiness or well-being, freedom from suffering, and the like) need not remain a mystery, because it is possible to retain the attractive features of the traditional natural rights theory while avoiding its pitfalls. To begin with, the possession of those characteristics that make humans members of a moral community also makes them the possessors of rights. It would be a mistake, however, to construe this as simply another way of expressing the natural rights theorist's claim that rights are possessed by virtue of our being humans. Whereas I have endorsed the view that the possession of certain *attributes* is crucial to both autonomy and having rights, there are two important differences between the position I am defending and the traditional natural rights theory. One is that having rights and ascribing them to others are functions of the mutual recognition that occurs within a social group of autonomous beings, that is, of the recognition that they manifest the sorts of characteristics that identify them as autonomous agents. In other words, members of the social group recognize and acknowledge, either explicitly or tacitly, that others in the group, like themselves, possess the prerequisites for autonomous, rational behavior and hence for moral personhood. The ascription of rights, then, is an act signifying the recognition that others are beings of this sort and expresses in symbolic form the resolve that they shall be treated in a manner appropriate to the autonomy and personhood thus perceived. Among other things, this resolve means that each undertakes to guarantee everyone else adequate scope for independent self-expression, responsibility, self-determination, and an equal opportunity to develop to his or her fullest potential. From the standpoint of the individual, rights may be seen, inversely, as claims on others to be recognized and respected in accordance with one's natural capacities, autonomy, and personhood.[8]

Thus rights belong to beings because they are moral agents functioning within a community of which responsibility and accountability are central features and where they are acknowledged to be such. Rights therefore do not need to be thought of as arising in some nebulous "state of nature, independently of human institutions and conventions, simply by virtue of our humanity," even though they do require that we conceive of them by reference to the possession of a certain set of attributes. Nor do rights need to be described or defended as God-given or as self-evidently attached to being a member of the genus *Homo sapiens* or even as self-evidently attached to manifestations of autonomy, personhood, and agency (although they are so attached). As we have seen, criteria for the assignment and possession of rights can be specified, so that religious and intuitionist considerations are unnecessary to give substance to the notion of universal moral rights, as belonging properly to a certain class of beings.

The second principal difference between the position put forward here and traditional natural rights theory is that I have generally avoided speaking of humans or referring to "our humanness" in considering the notions of moral community and rights, opting instead for speaking in more species-neutral terms—of "beings" of a certain type (autonomous beings). In discussing such questions as the comparative moral status of humans and animals, we should try to avoid the sort of species chauvinism or narrow anthropocentrism argued against in chapter 1. Many scientists now believe it is very probable that intelligent life exists elsewhere in the universe. If so, we may well come into contact some day with extraterrestrial forms of intelligent life with which we can communicate and interact at a high level of complexity. We have no reason to suppose that such extraterrestrials would belong to our own or a similar species or even resemble anything with which we are familiar.[9] But by the same token, there appears to be no good reason to assume that they would not share the same sorts of aspirations and have many of the same fundamental needs and interests as we or that they would be instinctively hostile to us. We should therefore recast our moral precepts in a form that could be extended to such creatures, which might very well be like us in all morally relevant respects.

Another reason for framing our moral precepts more cautiously has to do with other species that inhabit the earth. Though I do not think anyone can honestly assert, on the basis of the evidence available, that it is at all likely we shall learn to communicate at a high level with any terrestrial animals (such as chimpanzees, whales, or dolphins), it is at least possible. It is possible too that they are so very similar to us in all important respects that we should be prepared to extend our moral community to include them as equals if this turned out to be the case. However remote these prospects may be, it would be foolishly shortsighted to exclude animals from the moral community merely as a matter of principle or definition. Speaking of "beings" rather than "humans" avoids just these problems.[10]

The argument thus far has been that human beings have basic moral rights because they are beings of the requisite kind, that is, autonomous beings, persons, or moral agents. Even though other species have not been systematically excluded from possible membership in the moral community, I have not hesitated to characterize the central concepts that define the moral community in human or humanly understandable terms. For this I offer no apology. Since the only species we know of that has developed the notions of rights and obligations (and the institutions associated with them) is *Homo sapiens*, there must be something about this peculiar sort of social being that accounts for the phenomenon in question. My claim is that the attributes of humans that explain why they have developed such concepts and institutions are humans' possession of a particular kind of reflexive consciousness, unique cognitive and linguistic abilities, and the capacity to comprehend, undertake, and carry out obligations and to expect the same of similarly constituted beings. Furthermore, it is important to note that autonomous beings have certain types of interests which these institutions exist to ensure are recognized and respected. Only in this manner can such agents' well-being be protected and facilitated.

AUTONOMY AND RIGHTS

Why do only autonomous beings have rights? The answer can now be given quite briefly: (1) Autonomous beings are capable of free (self-determining, voluntary), deliberative, responsible action and have the sort of awareness necessary to see this kind of action as essential to their nature, well-being, and development as individuals. (2) Autonomous beings are capable of recognizing autonomy in others and of full participation in the moral community, as already described.[11] It is not arbitrary to hold that all and only such beings qualify for the possession of rights. Once we demystify the notion of natural rights, we can see that the ascription of rights to other beings and to ourselves is the keystone of the mutual recognition process on which the moral community is founded. Assigning rights to others and claiming them for oneself is tantamount to issuing a declaration

of nonintervention in the self-governing lives of others, by acknowledging the sort of being they are, and acquiring mutual guarantees of
this type by tacit agreement (that is, "All things being equal, I agree
to recognize your autonomy and not interfere with its free expression
and development if you agree to do the same for me").

This is why philosophers have generally regarded rights and
obligations as logically connected or correlative. If I have a right,
then others are deemed to have a duty to respect that right, which
means either to refrain from interfering with my free exercise of it or
to assist me in attaining what I have a right to, as the case may be and
as the circumstances require and permit. It does not follow, of course,
that all such rights are absolute, inalienable, or indefeasible, and here
the present account departs once more from traditional natural rights
theory. Normally, basic moral rights cannot be forfeited, compromised, suspended, or overridden by the acts of others or even of
oneself. Under exceptional conditions, such as self-defense, imprison-
ment for crimes, or declarations of legal incompetence, certain rights
justifiably may be abrogated. In addition, conflicts between individuals are commonplace in society and moral principles and institutions have to be evolved to deal with them in ways that are fair to
those concerned. (A good deal of our political machinery serves just
this function.)

THE POSITION OF ANIMALS VIS-À-VIS
THE MORAL COMMUNITY

The conclusion to be drawn from the foregoing discussion, so far
as it pertains to animals, is that lacking in various degrees the
possession of capacities on which moral autonomy or agency depends,
animals fail to meet the conditions specified for full membership in
the moral community and likewise fail to qualify for having rights.
Joel Feinberg has, I believe, stated fairly clearly why this is so with
particular reference to dogs, but his point is generalizable to all
animals.

> Well-trained dogs sometimes let their masters down; they anticipate
> punishment or other manifestations of displeasure; they grovel and
> whimper, and they even make crude efforts at redress and reconciliation.
> But do they feel remorse and bad conscience? They have been con-
> ditioned to associate manifestations of displeasure with departures from
> a norm, and this is a useful way of keeping them in line, but they haven't

the slightest inkling of the *reasons* for the norm. They don't *understand* why departures from the norm are wrong, or why their masters become angry or disappointed. They have a concept perhaps of the *mala prohibita*—the act that is wrong because it is prohibited, but they have no notion of the *mala in se*—the act that is prohibited because it is wrong. Even in respect to the *mala prohibita* their understanding is grossly deficient, for they have no conception of rightful authority. For dogs, the only basis of their master's "right" to be obeyed is his *de facto* power over them. Even when one master steals a beast from another, or when an original owner deprives it of its natural freedom in the wild, the animal will feel no moralized emotion, such as outraged propriety or indignation. These complex feelings involve cognitive elements beyond an animal's ken. Similarly, to suffer a guilty conscience is to be more than merely unhappy or anxious; it is to be in such a state because one has violated an "internalized standard," a principle of one's own, the rationale of which one can fully appreciate and the correctness of which one can, but in fact does not, doubt.[12]

Since animals could not begin to function as equals in a society of autonomous beings, they cannot be counted within the bond of association that makes morality and its institutions viable and gives them vitality. It should be apparent by now that the intent of this sort of judgment is not to portray the moral community as an exclusive club for membership within which "no animals need apply." Rather, it is to take a realistic look at the considerations that are relevant to regarding a being as having (or lacking) full moral status.

It should also be evident that any attempt to equate the "animal liberation" movement, which claims that animals and humans have equal moral status, with the civil rights and feminist movements is preposterous and indeed insulting to those who have worked long and hard to advance the cause of blacks and women (and children and other underprivileged groups). Blacks and women have been systematically denied full and equal moral status with whites and men. In effect, they have been prevented from enjoying the full membership in the moral community that is their due, on the basis of morally irrelevant differences—skin color and sex. It is precisely this sort of discrimination that we describe as unjust treatment. Animals, however, are denied full and equal moral status (and hence full membership in the moral community) for reasons that *are* morally relevant, namely, their lack of autonomy and moral agency. When women and blacks are granted their rights, these are not invented or "given" to them; rather, granting their rights is simply belatedly acknowledging that women and blacks are the sorts of beings that should have been perceived as autonomous all along and that therefore can claim to have been oppressed.

The characteristics on which this judgment or admission is made do not reduce merely to the capacity to experience pleasure and to suffer but are much more complex, as we have seen. If these characteristics are lacking in animals, then it makes no sense to speak of animals as "oppressed" and as deserving of equal moral concern. Failure to apprehend this crucial difference between animals and humans not only displays moral insensitivity but also denigrates and, by introducing conceptual confusion, weakens the legitimate case of those who genuinely are oppressed by trivializing it and making it appear ridiculous.[13]

I have tried to show why it is inappropriate to think of animals in terms that have meaningful application only to persons and to argue for this position rather than make a stand on faith or dogma. We may now turn to other issues to arrive at a resolution of the question of animals' proper moral status.

THE POSITION OF DEFICIENT HUMANS VIS-À-VIS THE MORAL COMMUNITY

Before we can make any progress on defining animals' moral status, however, we must face an extremely difficult question that is raised by the foregoing analysis and immediately presses itself on our attention. This is the problem of how to classify in relation to the moral community those beings that fall short of autonomy but which we should still consider candidates for rights and therefore to which we have obligations. Examples here would include infants, the severely mentally retarded, and those who are senile, autistic, mentally ill, badly brain damaged, comatose, and so on. Any theory linking full moral status to the possession of rights and the possession of rights in turn to autonomy is bound to encounter this issue and to stand or fall by how well it comes to terms with it.[14] This problem is also relevant because some might contend that certain animals are among those beings that fall short of autonomy but possess in varying degrees at least some of the capacities believed essential to autonomy. If deficient humans qualify for rights in spite of what they lack, it may then be asked, why not also higher animals? The difficulty is aggravated by the previous admission that it is not necessary to membership in the moral community that one be a member of the genus *Homo sapiens*; and if the stress falls on the possession of certain crucial traits, then it would seem that it is also not sufficient for membership that one be human.

Do human beings deficient in autonomy fail to qualify for rights, and do we as a result cease to have moral obligations toward them? Some antivivisectionists maintain that underdeveloped or deficient humans are no more and often less similar to normal humans in morally relevant respects than healthy and mature members of certain other species. Thus, it is claimed, a fully developed horse may be more reflective than a brain-damaged child; a chimpanzee more skilled in language than a newborn infant; a cat better able to reason than a comatose accident victim. It has even been suggested that to be consistent we should consider ourselves morally bound not to use such animals for any purpose for which we would not feel equally justified in using an underdeveloped or deficient human being.[15] However, this line of reasoning seems to me to betray a degree of moral insensitivity which we should all wish to reject.

If, as most would agree, natural emotional responses to and feelings of kinship with other species are allowed to count as factors in shaping our assessment of their moral status, then such responses and feelings should count equally in our dealings with members of our own species. We must also acknowledge differences among the sorts of cases under consideration. Infants are appropriately related to as potential fully autonomous beings, possessing in latency those attributes that will later (typically at maturity, given normal development) find expression, whereas those who are senile, comatose, mentally ill, or incapacitated by disease or accident are generally individuals who have achieved autonomy but whose full functioning is now blocked by conditions or circumstances beyond their control. In the case of children who are severely retarded, autistic, and so on, however, we are dealing with people who may never achieve a semblance of autonomy. In deciding how we ought to look on all these classes of individuals, a reasonable position to take would seem to be that here membership in our own species ought to count for something, in the sense in which a charitable attitude toward those less developed or less fortunate than ourselves, for whom we feel some especially close kinship, is particularly compelling to a morally mature person. Just as our untutored moral sense tells us that we have very strong obligations to members of our immediate families, so it seems that preferential treatment should, under certain circumstances, accordingly be granted to members of the human family.[16]

John Passmore, writing on the subject of our obligations to future generations, has argued that "a chain of love and concern" extends from our children and grandchildren to our grandchildren's grandchildren, and that it also embraces the "places, institutions and forms of activity" that shape our daily life. As Passmore notes, "Such links are sufficiently common and persistent to lend continuity to a civilization" and to explain sacrificing for future human beings.[17] Such a "chain" surely accounts for our concern for those among us who are severely handicapped or grievously disadvantaged. This is not to deny, of course, that a similar chain connects us to the animals, but the latter is not, I think, naturally so strong, direct, or morally compelling. (I have more to say on this important topic later in this chapter.)

Admittedly, for many it is not an easy matter to feel a close kinship to those less fortunate or often even to see them as human. Many cannot even establish an empathetic relationship with a normal, healthy human infant. Probably almost all of us would prefer and choose to spend time with responsive, sociable animals than with humans whose faculties are severely compromised. But none of these facts obviates the responsibility of each of us (whether religious or not) to develop and incorporate into our moral outlook the spirit behind the old saying, "There, but for the grace of God, go I." Let us say, then, that although underdeveloped or deficient humans are also, like animals, not full members of the moral community because they lack autonomy, they must nevertheless fall within the most immediate extension of the moral community and as such are subject to its protection. This sensibility is indeed a cornerstone of civilized society, for failure to cultivate and preserve this frail thread leaves the way open to systematic abuses of the dignity and rights of those designated as second-class citizens. Under certain all-too-common circumstances, it may also lead to Nazilike genocidal campaigns to eliminate "undesirables," "defectives," or "unworthy lives."

We might add that it is also a matter of prudence that we cultivate such a sentiment; for each of us knows that under certain unforeseeable circumstances he or she might suffer an injury or illness that could severely limit or even terminate his or her autonomy.

Membership in the moral community is not a cut-and-dried matter. How many and what kinds of affinities with ourselves a creature must exhibit before being counted as autonomous is not something that can be decided in the abstract but rather has to be examined on a case-by-case basis. Just as animals cannot be looked on as an undifferentiated or virtually identical collection of beings, so too there is no uniform class of underdeveloped or deficient human beings. Because of this, a comparison of such individuals would array them variably according to the presence or absence in them of capacities that are essential for autonomy. At one end of the scale would be those whom we sometimes (less than charitably) identify as hopeless "human vegetables" or "basket cases," whereas at the other end could be found normal infants, less severe retardates, and others who manifest to a greater or lesser degree psychological attributes that are typical of personhood.

To add further complexity to this already very difficult issue, we must bear in mind that conditions considered irremediable at present may yield to scientific inroads with astonishing suddenness. Autism is a case in point. Once considered completely impervious to all therapies and treatments, techniques have been devised in the past few years that promise to give autistic children a semblance of a normal life.[18] This sort of breakthrough, of course, does not happen as often as some try to make out. A cure is not just around the corner for every severe handicap. But the examples that can be cited should give us pause when we feel inclined to lump together as without hope a whole range of diverse conditions affecting normal human functioning and autonomy.

In view of this, it appears that drawing a line to separate human beings who are full members of the moral community from those who are not is probably not only an impossible task but also, even if feasible, extremely dangerous and unwise. If we must nevertheless give a rule that will rationalize including such borderline cases within the framework of the moral community, it might reasonably take the following form:

> All underdeveloped, deficient, or seriously impaired human beings are to be considered members of an immediately extended moral community and therefore as deserving of equal moral concern. To whatever degree seems reasonable, they should be treated according to either (a) their potential for full agency (and hence as potentially full participants in the moral community, taking into account their past participation, if any) or (b) the degree to which their behavior and capacities approximate what is generally considered to be characteristically human (that is, typically the case at maturity, given normal development) and

the extent to which their behavior and capacities permit full participation in the moral community.

This benefit-of-the-doubt principle might be looked on by critics as speciesist, but it seems to me that charity, benevolence, humaneness, and prudence require such an extension and that it is not inconsistent with a theory of morality that makes rights and autonomy central or, more important, with the way we in fact treat such cases in everyday life. Finally, dealing with these cases in the way I have suggested here, if properly labeled speciesist at all, is not unacceptably so; for extending the moral community to take account of exceptional cases does not exclude other species in principle from being treated in a similar manner or bar them from full membership in the moral community if they so qualify. So-called borderline cases or marginal humans—those where we are unsure whether to call something a human being or person or where our moral principles come under severe strain—are notoriously difficult to deal with. There seems to be no justification, however, for condemning a theory holding persons (not species) to be the central focus of moral concern on the grounds that it favors *Homo sapiens* over other known species in fringe areas where the applicability of our usual moral categories is bound to be far from clear-cut.

SUFFERING AS THE CENTRAL CONCEPT OF MORALITY

We have seen what is wrong with ascribing rights to animals. Before we can rest content with the view of morality based on autonomy, however, the utilitarian position on animals must be considered further. According to this outlook, the capacity to experience pleasure and to suffer, along with the desire to seek the former and avoid the latter, is a sufficient foundation on which to construct the notion of a moral community. It would be foolish to deny that the capacity to suffer and to experience pleasure is one of the characteristics which members of the moral community share; one reason why some acts are judged to be right and others wrong is their consequences in terms of pleasure or suffering for those affected by them.

Any creature that can experience these feelings has an interest in avoiding suffering and in seeking pleasurable (or at any rate neutral) experiences in their stead. According to the utilitarian, whether or not an animal is conscious of having such interests, it is also entitled to equal consideration where they are at stake. From this standpoint, then, all animals are morally equal, since humans' interests do not automatically carry greater weight, simply because they are possessed by humans, when we balance out the pros and cons of particular courses of action. But it does not follow, utilitarians argue, that all animals (including human beings) must be treated identically, for each species has capacities and needs that are peculiar to it and deserve to be taken into account. The same is true of individual humans, they would also hasten to point out, and therefore morality does not require that we always treat each fellow human being identically in every situation, but only that we accord each equal consideration of interests when deciding on courses of action that will affect him or her. This means heeding differences as well as similarities among individuals.[19] In the utilitarians' view, the same general principle applies to animals in relation to humans.

One of the hallmarks of the hedonistic utilitarian approach is that states of conscious awareness are the only things that can be meaningfully spoken of as intrinsically good or bad. Everything else is instrumentally good or bad, that is, good or bad solely insofar as it produces pleasurable or painful experiences, respectively, or insofar as it is a means to these ends. Adherents of the theory generally assert that pain is an "intrinsic evil,"[20] by which they mean it is inherently bad, disagreeable, and distressing. This makes it easy to proceed to argue that "given magnitudes of pain and suffering are equally evil in themselves whenever and wherever they occur,"[21] in other words, to whatever sentient creature experiences them.

This seems to me nonsense. The difficulties involved in arriving at an assessment in the human sphere of the relative effects of acts in terms of pleasure and suffering are legion. Imagine the additional complexities introduced by the requirement that we compare relative levels of human and animal pleasure and suffering! Does the quantity of human pleasure generated by eating meat sufficiently offset the suffering of the animal that supplies the meat? Is the knowledge of benefit to humans likely to be gained from a given experiment significant enough to outweigh the suffering of a given number of laboratory animals? These questions, although neither wholly avoidable nor unimportant, seem imponderable; and if pretenses to precise measurement are introduced (as in the preceding reference to "given magnitudes of pain and suffering"), their resolution becomes totally impracticable. In addition, the issue can only grow more intractable when we introduce considerations of short- versus long-term pleasures and sufferings and of the relative quality of pleasures and sufferings. But if we pursue moral issues along the lines of utilitarianism, this is precisely what we must be prepared to do.

As John Stuart Mill was the first to note, a distinction has to be drawn, not just between degrees, but also between different kinds of pleasure if, in utilitarian fashion, we are to regard the pursuit of happiness as the goal of life. Some pleasures have to be acknowledged as better than others (just as some pains are worse than others), not only in degree but also in kind. What Mill did not seem to realize, however, is that if this is so, utilitarianism is a deeply inconsistent theory, as it now appears that moral obligation cannot be derived solely from considering the potential of different acts to maximize pleasure and minimize suffering for those affected by them. We also need to take into account the qualitative dimension of pleasures and pains. But if so, then we move immediately beyond the simple capacity to experience pleasure and pain and in fact arrive back where we started. Essential reference must now be made to the other sorts of capacities considered earlier to account for the diversity which we discern among pleasures and displeasures. Thus once again we shall find ourselves forced to conclude that both moral agency and full membership in the moral community are strongly dependent on other capacities than those to experience pleasure and to suffer (that is, the capacities that constitute autonomy).

Another way this can be demonstrated is as follows. Utilitarians commonly maintain that there is no characteristic universally possessed by human beings that enables us to separate ourselves from other species as beings whose interests deserve higher consideration than those of animals. If we seek among human beings for a lowest common denominator—some attribute shared by all members of our species without exception—this will prove to be nothing other than the capacity to experience pleasure and pain. Utilitarians then object that since this capacity fails to distinguish humans from animals and therefore to establish the former as deserving of higher moral consideration, any attempt to assign a special moral status to humans on the basis of capacities which we alone possess must be abandoned as futile. However, it may be doubted whether any characteristic is really so clearly universal as the utilitarians assume, including the capacity to experience pleasure and to suffer.

To begin with, physiologists have long known of and thoroughly documented a rare condition known as "congenital universal indifference (or insensitivity) to pain,"[22] which is characterized by complete absence throughout life of any pain-sensing capability. But if the capacity to experience pain is missing, any moral status predicated on it must vanish as well. Perhaps this is not the strongest example, since it is still conceivable that individuals so afflicted might experience psychological distress (that is, suffer).[23] Consider, then, completely anesthetized, hypnotized, or deeply comatose humans. These are individuals who—temporarily at least—lack the capacity to suffer, yet it seems peculiar that they should lose and regain their moral status because of the transitoriness of this capacity, as if such status were something that could switch itself off and on intermittently like a streetlight. But if moral status is linked solely with conscious awareness, we are driven to this conclusion. Now if the position that persons in such states have no rights and hence no moral status is unacceptable, as I argued earlier, it is instructive to see why. The reasons are as follows: (1) Basic moral rights arise from other criteria than the capacity to experience pleasure and pain. (2) What counts in establishing rights must be the characteristics a certain class of beings share in general, even if not universally. It follows that if one attribute that is not strictly universal among humans (the capacity to experience pleasure and pain) may be considered relevant to establishing their moral status, then so may others. Indeed, as we have seen, other attributes must be taken into account to explain why humans are beings with rights and objects of moral concern.

To be fair, it must be pointed out that utilitarians are not so naive as to have overlooked the fact that there is a problem of accounting for a being's moral status during periods of unconsciousness such as sleep, coma, and so forth. But they can only deal with such states ex post facto in terms of the potentiality for conscious awareness (and hence sensation) that the agent possessed all along. (Indeed, how else could this problem be dealt with?) But using potentiality as a reference point for determining moral status lends at least as strong support to the nonutilitarian position for handling the borderline cases discussed in the previous section as it does to a utilitarian approach.

A last objection to utilitarianism, seemingly more fatal still, concerns the possibility of instantaneous, painless death. Briefly, it is this: If the death of an animal (or indeed of a human) could be brought about without accompanying suffering, what, on utilitarian grounds, could be judged morally wrong with such an act? The effects on the individual victim cannot be cited because *ex hypothesi* he does not experience them. If the possible effects of the painless taking of life (on other animals or humans, as the case may be) are brought into the picture, we need only alter the example slightly to that of a solitary, unwitnessed death. Deliberately causing the painless death of another human may be judged morally wrong within the theory of autonomy and rights possession I have set out; it is difficult, however, to see how doing so could be condemned by the hedonistic utilitarian or how the utilitarian could begin to deal with the far less complex case of painless animal death.

Thus the utilitarian position on animals must be counted a failure. We are entitled (indeed required) to take into account other characteristics than the capacity for experiencing pleasure and pain when assessing whose interests take precedence in cases of conflict between the interests of humans and animals. It is these other characteristics that make the lives of humans (and other autonomous beings, if there are any) more valuable than those of other species and their interests of consequently greater importance. Peter Singer, one of the leading spokespersons for the utilitarian approach to the moral status of animals, has even acknowledged this point: "It is not arbitrary to hold that the life of a self-aware being, capable of abstract thought, of planning for the future, of complex acts of communication, and so on, is more valuable than the life of a being without these capacities." [24] However, Singer unfortunately never explains why he says this or how such a declaration can be reconciled with utilitarian precepts. Whether such a reconciliation is possible must therefore remain an open question. [25] I suspect, however, that it is not.

We are now in a position to see even more sharply why this is so and to understand still better why the notion of autonomy plays such a crucial role in comparing humans' and animals' respective moral status.

BEYOND PLEASURE AND SUFFERING

What the utilitarians have failed to appreciate about human nature is that pleasure and pain (or pleasure and suffering, pleasure and displeasure) are not the sole reference points for judging a thing's value or disvalue. Rather, as Nietzsche observed a century ago, it is often the case that an object attained or an activity performed affords pleasure because it enhances our sphere of effective behavior. Autonomous beings engage in activities of different levels of complexity and significance, in accordance with the many possibilities opened up to them by the wide range of characteristics they have acquired during the course of evolution. The exertion required in overcoming an obstacle or in learning, solving problems, gaining understanding, or plotting a course of action is experienced as exhilarating when the effort expended gradually succeeds in realizing an objective. Attaining a goal may be experienced as pleasurable because autonomy and freedom are affirmed and reinforced by such successes. In numerous instances, pleasure is a by-product, so to speak, of the experience of autonomous effort expanding the domain of effective action and control.

Why do the things we do give us pleasure?—not because pleasure is somehow tucked away inside them as their intrinsically valuable feature; not because pleasure is some essence, secret ingredient, or singular feeling, that is our real aim; and not necessarily even because the satisfaction of doing them is a function of the pleasure we derive from such activity. Rather, the things we do may give us pleasure because they pose interesting challenges of one kind or another to our initiative and self-motivation; and in accomplishing the ends we set for ourselves, we derive the satisfaction of asserting our own vitality and active agency. This sense of the efficacy of our actions, which is accompanied by pleasurable sensations or states of awareness (but not by pleasure per se), is central to the very meaning of autonomy and personhood.

In contrast, the sense of agency frustrated, of initiative thwarted, or of effort blocked is often the cause of displeasure or suffering. Robert Nozick remarks, with reference to rationality, free will, and moral agency, that

> in conjunction, . . . they add up to something whose significance is clear: a being able to formulate long-term plans for its life, able to consider and decide on the basis of abstract principles or considerations it formulates to itself and hence not merely the plaything of immediate stimuli, a being that limits its own behavior in accordance with some principles or picture it has of what an appropriate life is for itself and others, and so on. However, this exceeds the three listed traits [i.e., rationality, free will, and moral agency]. We can distinguish theoretically between long-term planning and an overall conception of a life

that guides particular decisions, and the three traits that are their basis. For a being could possess these three traits and yet also have built into it some particular barrier that prevents it from operating in terms of an overall conception of its life and what it is to regulate and guide its life in accordance with some overall conception it chooses to accept. Such an overall conception, and knowing how we are doing in terms of it, is important to the kind of goals we formulate for ourselves and the kind of beings we are.[26]

The conclusion that should be drawn here, surely, is that humans are beings whose lives have greater value than those of animals because they have almost unlimited potential for self-guided development and growth. This also explains why it is even reasonable to say that human suffering is generally of greater concern than that of animals. The number of possible conditions—to which animals are not subject—that can produce the sense of thwarted agency, diminished selfhood, or ineffectualness, from which suffering so often arises, is astronomically high. This is why many philosophers of the past and present have asserted that human beings are not destined to be happy. Even Mill, let us remember, reflected on this problem and said, "It is better to be a human being dissatisfied than a pig satisfied; better to be Socrates dissatisfied than a fool satisfied."[27] If, by being more complex creatures, humans gain significantly more potential sources of pleasure, as the utilitarians too seem prepared to assert, then it follows that they also acquire many more potential sources of suffering. It is because we are the sort of beings that can have a life plan at all and because we can seek ends other than pleasure and the avoidance of suffering, that our potential for suffering (and pleasure) is so great.

The guiding principle or life plan idea also helps reinforce two points made earlier; namely, that moral rights are contingent on the possession of capacities other than sentience and that deficient humans are still quite capable of being included in the moral community. As Arthur L. Caplan has remarked,

> The fact that something can be injured, hurt, or displeasured by various acts seems not to be as relevant a consideration for moral inquiry as is the fact that a being has a degree of mentality sufficient to have wants, desires, and hopes, and to engage in speculations as to how these longings might be satisfied or fulfilled.[28]

Although we might want to regard unfulfilled aspirations and frustrated longings as falling under the heading of "suffering,"

Caplan's point supports my view that the complex cognitive/ linguistic capacities—possessed to some degree by deficient humans— are at least as crucial to establishing a being's moral status as its capacity for experiencing pleasure and displeasure.

WHY CRUELTY TO ANIMALS IS WRONG

The argument thus far has established two points: (1) As a rule, animals lack the capacities essential for rights to be ascribed to them. (2) The fact that they can suffer, although morally significant because it gives animals the status of moral patients or recipients, is not by itself a sufficient ground on which to accord them equal moral status with humans and other autonomous beings, if such there be. From what basis *can* a generalized moral concern for animals be derived? Like many statements of its kind, "Cruelty to animals is wrong" seems patently true and indisputable; yet to justify it satisfactorily, to give reasons why cruelty to animals is wrong, is a more difficult task than we might at first think. This is a topic to which animal welfarists of various persuasions have devoted too little attention and that, when it has been examined, has been treated very inadequately from a philosophical standpoint.

If moral obligations are contingent on rights and their possession by certain beings, then since animals have no rights, humans cannot have correlative obligations toward them. It follows that we have no duty in the strict moral sense to prevent animal suffering. Therefore, if it is wrong to inflict suffering on other sentient creatures, this must be for reasons other than the failure to heed or be bound by a moral obligation not to cause harm. Cruelty or inhumaneness may be defined as the knowing and deliberate causing of unnecessary or avoidable pain to innocent and undeserving sentient beings. (These notions are investigated further in chapter 6.) In the case of humans, cruelty is morally wrong because it violates their right to well-being (or their right not to be harmed), which there is a corresponding obligation to respect. What makes it wrong to be cruel to animals? Perhaps a better question is: Why should we treat animals humanely at all? There are several considerations here. The first three I explore have to do with empathy, a sense of the evolutionary continuity between *Homo sapiens* and other species, and the perspective supplied by the science of ecology.

EMPATHY

Humans identify, often to a high degree, with what they perceive as animals' expressions of emotion. Although the dual dangers of unwarranted anthropomorphizing of animal gestures and facial expressions and of overreaction are always present, much of this natural empathetic response is healthy and psychologically sound. The question how (if at all) we know the contents of other minds has been much discussed by philosophers, and the issue is both complex and perhaps irresolvable. But we are so much farther from knowing the contents of any other species' mind, let alone what it would be like to be that kind of creature, or indeed whether its type of body radically structures the experience it has of the world,[29] that all statements about the mental life of animals—even exceptional individual companion animals—should be regarded with profound skepticism. Questions like "How would *you* like to be an animal that is being experimented on?" make no sense and cannot be answered, because they hinge on the additional complex (and hidden) assumption that I, as a human, can know what it is like to be an animal of perhaps a quite different species. But clearly no one can know this.[30] Nevertheless, suffering in animals is often easily recognized by obvious signs such as cries, grimaces, avoidance and defensive behavior, and the like and does not require unusual moral sensitivity to respond to.

It is worth remembering that indifference to animal suffering and the belief that animals cannot experience pain were once commonplace. Also instructive is the fact that the humane societies movement is just over a century and a half old[31] (though the first anticruelty statute was enacted as early as 1641).[32] Perhaps many of our forebears were not as morally sensitive as we in certain respects, or perhaps religious and other precepts prevented them from developing a conscience in matters of the treatment of animals.[33] Whatever the explanation, there seems little doubt that attitudes toward animals in the West have been changing slowly for the better over the last few centuries.

EVOLUTIONARY RELATEDNESS

One reason why feelings of empathy with other species have become more widespread is the influence of evolutionary theory generally and the scientific study of animals which it has stimulated. As we saw in chapter 2, there are many and often striking continuities between *Homo sapiens* and diverse species, so that it is extraordinarily difficult to believe any longer that sensation, conscious awareness, and related attributes are totally unique to humans. Not only this, but evolutionary theory also brings other animals closer to humans in the sense that we are products of the same natural processes, subject to similar environmental selection pressures, and endowed with similar physical systems and adaptive strategies. Why, then, should animals not be like us in other ways as well, such as how they respond to noxious or disequilibrating stimuli, stress, and so on? In addition, awareness of evolutionary continuity tends to develop in us the sense that animals are not just raw material or fodder for human consumption but have a long history like (and parallel to) our own and are integral parts of a slowly developing, complex chain of being.

Many who have this appreciation of the relatedness of all creatures express it by saying that attitudes of respect toward animals and of reverence for nature are appropriate and that animals have a (natural) right to life. These are understandable and perhaps laudable sentiments, if somewhat confused in their expression. Inasmuch as animals lack rights, they also lack the right to life, and the notion of respecting animals seems anthropomorphic and strained. Reverence for nature is, I believe, a meaningful and valuable sentiment, and I discuss it in the concluding chapter. What may be said here is that the awareness of evolutionary continuity should engender in us an enhanced sensitivity toward other species—their resemblance to us, their needs, and their vulnerability.

Something more should be said here about the role of suffering in establishing our empathetic relationship with animals. There appears to be no structural or functional reason why at least those animals with a central nervous system should be unable to experience pain and, as noted before, considerable evidence exists for saying that they can and do.[34] However, there are those who will debate about anything under the sun, and thus it is not uncommon to hear that animals experience pain less intensely than humans under hypothetically comparable circumstances because they have no ability to anticipate the course of future events, are inured to pain by nature's ordeals, lack a self-concept, have a less complex emotional life, and so on. It has been maintained equally vehemently that animals experience pain more intensely than humans because they cannot place pain in perspective or see it as something that can be endured or triumphed over; have more acute nervous systems, needed in the raw struggle for survival; and so on. However, the long and short of the matter seems to be that we really have no firm basis at present on which to compare or contrast animal and human suffering (and pleasure) considered as subjective states. Nor is it at all clear that we ever will have or in principle could have. Such wrangles must accordingly be regarded as largely speculative and unhelpful. But perhaps we should go further than this and give animals (or at least vertebrates) the benefit of the doubt. We may do this by recording as a standing presumption the belief that animals with a central nervous system are capable of experiencing pain as intensely as we. (The topic of identifying the signs of animal suffering is taken up in chapter 6, second section.)

How will this presumption affect our argument? I think it must be reiterated here that in some sense animals' pain still counts for less than that of beings like humans. The reason is twofold. First, it may be reasonably conjectured that animals do not suffer psychologically as greatly as humans, since their psychological and inner mental life gives every appearance of being far poorer in content, associations, anticipations, memories, and the like, so far as this can be judged. Furthermore, as everyone knows who has performed surgery on animals or treated them for injuries, animals as a rule recover from painful stress much more rapidly than humans. Second, the capacity to experience pain and to suffer may be an important ingredient of moral personhood, but it is hardly sufficient. Therefore, the equivalence in intensity of animal and human pain, if it is ever established as a fact, would not succeed in generating a moral right of animals not to suffer. The most it could do, I think, is cause us to extend by empathy our sense that wantonly inflicting pain on other species is a wrongful act and that causing any kind of suffering must in general be justified. It has been pointed out many times that we cannot both (a) argue that the close and important similarities of animals to humans provide the rationale for experimenting on the former and (b) remain oblivious to the fact that such similarities also compel us to raise and come to terms with tough ethical questions about using animals in this way.[35] Now if the argument presented thus far is correct, such an empathetic extension signifies at most a limited or weak moral obligation, and I think it would be preferable to regard it as analogous to, but not identical with, a strict moral principle.

ECOLOGICAL AWARENESS

Like our awareness of the evolutionary continuum and our natural feelings of empathy with other species, our dawning ecological sense has given rise to an appreciation of the relatedness of all life and to corresponding sentiments. As the still infant era of environmentalism has unfolded, knowledge about the systematic interconnectedness of things has grown at a rapid rate, practical experience has confirmed scientific findings—often bringing home to us the results of our own shortsighted policies in the most unpleasant fashion—and steadily increasing numbers of people have begun to acquire a grasp of and a feel for their place in nature. Some environmental thinkers have even gone so far as to theorize that the earth is best understood as a gigantic organism.[36] The ecological perspective has led many to rethink the merely exploitative or dominionist attitude toward nature and to see its limits; it has also fostered a sense of the frail environmental balance that nurtures and sustains all life. A feeling for our unity with all organisms co-struggling for survival has become not just possible but scientifically respectable as well. With this has developed the ability and open-mindedness to recognize animals' unique traits, needs, and the like, their place in the "great chain of being," and their vital contribution to our own success as a species.

CRUELTY AS DEMEANING

Natural empathy and an awareness of the evolutionary continuity and of the environmental interdependence of species, then, are three good grounds for regarding humaneness as a virtue and wanton cruelty to animals as morally wrong—for extending our moral community or horizon of moral concern to embrace animals. Perhaps together they constitute the major grounds for doing so. But there are other relevant considerations too. One is that inflicting pain or suffering on animals, particularly defenseless ones, is demeaning and degrading to humans. It is important not to confuse this point with an old and still frequently heard argument—first put forward by Immanuel Kant in the eighteenth century—that mistreating animals will lead people to mistreat other humans. Kant wrote, for example, "If a man shoots his dog because the animal is no longer capable of service, he does not fail in his duty to the dog, for the dog cannot judge, but his act is inhuman and damages in himself that humanity which it is his duty to show towards mankind." [37] The implication here is that cruelty toward animals is causally connected with cruelty toward other humans. There is a widespread tendency to assert that this is a truism, as well as the related proposition that benevolent treatment of animals leads to benevolent treatment of humans.

Unfortunately, the facts do not support either generalization. *In Humane Education: An Overview*, by Eileen S. Whitlock and Stuart R. Westerlund, a publication of the National Association for the Advancement of Humane Education in Tulsa, Oklahoma, the so-called transference theory is described. This theory "holds that an individual's attitude toward animals is transferable to his fellow humans." [38] The authors note that "as yet, no empirical data has [*sic*] been gathered to verify this theory." Far from being a truism, then, no evidence has been found to support the views in question, and individual hunches, feelings, and intuitions do not establish the truth of such claims. In spite of their admission, Whitlock and Westerlund continue as follows: "But it [the transference theory] appears sound by virtue of the observations of many qualified and highly respected individuals. Numerous cases are cited in which a history of cruelty to animals is found in the background of persons who commit violent acts against society." Citing a psychiatrist's observations that "cruelty to animals[,] . . . setting fires and persistent bed wetting after age five [are] three indicators of potential criminality," they then conclude, "Thus we see that a history of cruel acts toward animals serves as a warning signal of potential hostility toward society in adulthood. If this is true, *it would appear to logically follow* that a child who behaves kindly toward animals will exhibit the same kind of compassion toward his fellow humans." [39] However, this is an incorrect inference.

From (1)   If childhood cruelty to animals, then adult hostility toward fellow humans (If *a*, then *b*)

it does not follow that

(2)   If no childhood cruelty to animals, then no adult hostility toward fellow humans (If not-*a*, then not-*b*). [40]

In other words, a history of cruelty toward animals may be positively correlated with later antisocial behavior, but from this relationship the quite different correlation between humaneness toward animals in childhood and a compassionate adult personality cannot be deduced. Furthermore, no correlation—however firm—establishes by itself a relation of causality. There may be a causal connection of some kind between early humaneness and later compassion, but in the absence of empirical studies to support this conclusion, we are left with mere conjecture.

I think it is fair to say that humaneness in children is only in part a product of education and of examples set by parents and others whose behavior serves as the most influential examples for their conduct. To a far greater extent and in their healthiest form, humaneness and compassion flow from well-adjusted personalities; they are, in short, characteristics of individuals who have themselves been reared in a loving, caring, and compassionate environment. Those who cite a history of childhood cruelty to animals as the cause of someone's adult acts of cruelty to humans mistake what are essentially the symptoms of a deeper personality problem for the cause of odious behavior. Both later cruelty to humans and earlier viciousness toward animals appear to stem from an impoverished childhood environment. For example, one study of male psychiatric patients at the C. F. Menninger Memorial Hospital in Topeka, Kansas, showed that most of the group that abused animals as children and later abused people "had been severely punished by a person who served as a mother or father figure to them." In addition, "other studies have drawn a link between cruelty to the child, the absence of a father figure or presence of an alcoholic or similarly impaired father, with cruelty to animals."[41] The *Scientists Center for Animal Welfare Newsletter* summarizes the results of the Menninger Hospital study as follows: "A boy who is treated as an enemy of the parent (i.e., physically brutalized) is apt to regard himself as evil and to project maliciousness onto others."[42] It follows that the alleged link between early (childhood) animal abuse and later (adult) people abuse is not a causal one, for both are frequently the effects, so far as can be surmised, of pathology created in children who have been brutalized by the adult world. We should therefore look primarily at the parent-child relationship for an explanation of cruel and aggressive behavior in adulthood, as this would appear to be the root of the problem (see also chapter 7, third section).

We may assume, then, that in the absence of evidence to the contrary, cruelty to animals does not necessarily lead to cruelty toward humans. It is possible that there is some crossover effect in some cases, and perhaps this furnishes an additional precautionary reason for regarding cruelty to animals as wrong or as something that is detrimental to human moral character; but it would be unwarranted to designate this merely possible effect as a main reason, much less as *the* reason.

What I wish to argue instead is that cruelty is inhuman (unhuman-like) and in this sense beneath human dignity. One who causes unnecessary and unjustified suffering to animals sinks below some ideal standard of behavior (or virtue) for which human beings should strive. In some sense, the cruel individual damages his moral character, not in the way Kant contended, but inasmuch as he lets himself be insensitive, unmindful of morally relevant similarities between himself and the animal(s) concerned, unkind, merciless, sadistic, or whatever. In short, he gives expression to the worst side of himself. To say that such people debase their moral character is, at least in part, to make an empirical claim that, I grant, is very difficult to establish, though moral psychologists from Plato on have portrayed the effects of evildoing in just this way. So perhaps this argument should not be pushed too hard. Suffice it to say that whether or not the behavior of inhumane people debases their moral character or affects how they treat anyone else, abusers of animals (or humans) permit themselves to lose control, to act in a purely instinctual manner, and to give expression to what is less than the best in themselves.

Another interesting way of looking at this is in terms not of the effects of evildoing on the moral character of the agent but by reference to the judgments others pass on such behavior. In the course of an exposition of Arthur Schopenhauer's moral theory, Richard Taylor comments,

> What men do morally condemn is pure malice, and this is the only thing that unfailingly stamps an act and its agent with the deepest moral opprobrium. That a man should trample on others from the selfish egoism of his nature is not incomprehensible. It is a natural and inevitable part of social life. But that a man should, from no egoistic impulse at all, and even at considerable trouble and expense to himself, make the suffering of another the very object of his will—this, and this alone, morally outrages. Nor does it make the slightest difference whether the suffering thus wrought is the suffering of a rational being,

or of a dumb and helpless animal. The moral character of the agent is the same in either case, for the motive is the same, and that motive is malice.[43]

Here the perspective has shifted from the subject of the action (the doer) to the observer who judges; but the sense of the moral condemnation is the same.

SELF-INTEREST

Finally, there is a factor of enlightened collective self-interest that also contributes to our judgment of the wrongfulness of cruelty to animals. Simply put, this means that acts of cruelty may (though they need not always) lead to unfavorable consequences for humans. For instance, cruelly treated animals often turn vicious themselves; animals that are mistreated may become unhealthy and hence less useful or companionable; and the systematic practice of cruelty or insensitivity may also result in the decimation or extinction of animal populations that play an important part in the ecosystem or on which the lives of certain human groups depend in a most intimate way. (A typical example of this latter predicament is the wholesale slaughter of African elephants by poachers interested only in ivory, by means ranging "from sub-machine guns and automatic weapons to fruit poisoning with car battery acid.")[44] This aspect of our assessment goes beyond mere considerations of prudence in our use of animal resources; for when the actions of a few have adverse consequences for many others, such behavior is not only thoughtless but also wrong.

In an important sense, animal welfare is in our interest just as it is in animals' interest. Cruel acts directed at nonhuman creatures can have adverse practical ramifications and also possible deleterious consequences for the personalities of those who perpetrate them. But they may also have a negative effect on those who merely witness them or otherwise allow them to occur—that is, the rest of us—in the sense that we experience varying degrees of disgust, discomfort, anger, shock, disapproval, shame, guilt, or the like in the face of wanton cruelty. Therefore a strong motivation to eliminate cruel acts can be found in this dimension of self-interest as well, namely, our desire to be free of these kinds of unpleasurable emotional states.

ANIMALS AND THE MORAL IMPERATIVE

These five considerations—empathy, evolutionary continuity, the ecological perspective, the demeaning nature of cruelty, and enlightened collective self-interest—all contribute to answering the question posed earlier, Why should we treat animals humanely? By appealing to them (and perhaps to other factors), we may grant animals a sort of adjunct moral patient status by reference to which we are able to formulate principles of humaneness.[45]

But the foregoing constitutes only part of the story of how we ought to treat animals, though perhaps the most important part. An account has been provided of the psychological origins of our moral concern for animals, but not of the degree of obligation we may or ought to feel toward them. Earlier I remarked that we have no duty in the strict moral sense to prevent animal suffering. Is there, then, any force to the notion that we ought to do so? Have we any basis for prescribing certain forms of behavior toward animals? I think it must be acknowledged that we do. It is evident that animals do have interests and needs: They have interests of a very basic and uncomplicated sort, because they are sentient creatures. Some probably have a (non-self-conscious) sense of what we call physical health and illness, and they have needs that are prerequisites for existence and well-being (food, water, space, habitat, and so on). It must be recognized that animals do not have interests or needs in the full moral sense in which humans do. The reason for this is that animals cannot (even potentially) (a) formulate a perception of the conditions of their lives and (b) judge these conditions to be either adequate or inadequate. Consequently, they lack the highly complex interests and needs of autonomous beings, as described in chapter 2, and in earlier sections of this chapter. Nevertheless, animals' interests and needs merit some consideration.

To explain this, we must return for a moment to the awareness of our evolutionary continuity and our feelings of empathy with other species. Both of these should provide insight into the natural needs of animals and into their similarity with some of our own. This sense of closeness arises at the level of ordinary experience, even before scientific observations and data come into the picture. Our ability to see animals for what they are—as independently developing creatures with characteristics resembling to a greater or lesser extent those which we associate indelibly with moral status—can scarcely fail to lead to the recognition of a kind of obligation on our part, although a relatively weak one, to accord them humane treatment. The fact that the fate of animals worldwide rests with us and that they are often at our mercy lends additional force to this imperative. This sensibility is sometimes attached to the label *stewardship*, meaning an attitude of care, concern, and wise management.

In other words, although animals do not have even potentially full moral status, they may be assigned a limited moral status in terms of which (a) they may be included within an extended moral community, (b) certain principles of human conduct can be applied, and (c) an appropriate degree of moral sensibility can be generated. Such principles would stem from recognizing the similarities between animals and humans, the unpleasantness of suffering, and the various factors discussed in the preceding two sections.

These principles would be of the following sort: (1) Animals should be treated humanely (cruelty to animals, although not wrong in the strong or strict moral sense of rights violation, is nevertheless wrong in the sense that animals are still proper objects of our moral concern).[46] (2) The natural needs of animals in the care of humans should be provided for. (3) When an animal is killed, the method for doing so should be as nearly painless and instantaneous as possible. These are clearly not as stringent principles as those that might be generated by the moral obligations to which human beings are subject in their dealings with one another. This fact is, I believe, correctly apprehended by the tradition of humane legislation, which generally imposes considerably less severe penalties for cruelty to animals than for cruelty to humans.[47]

ANIMALS' AMBIGUOUS MORAL STATUS

I do not think there is any way to escape the conclusion that animals have an uncertain and ambiguous moral status and that neither conceptual clarification of the kind practiced by philosophers nor wishful thinking nor passionate devotion to the cause of animal welfare is going to alter the fact one iota. New scientific discoveries, however, may have some impact on our assessment of this situation, and for this reason it seems useful to think in terms of a moral spectrum along which forms of life can be arrayed. As I noted earlier, we must be prepared to accept the idea that some animals (such as whales, dolphins, and chimpanzees) may possess capacities very similar in kind and degree to those that constitute moral autonomy, whereas other vertebrates (like dogs, cats, pigs, horses, elephants, pigeons, rats, and snakes) might fall considerably short of this level of development, and many invertebrate creatures (like ants, spiders, and shellfish) would perhaps be placed outside the moral framework altogether. Of those seen as having adjunct moral patient status, their capacities and needs (so far as these can be determined) should be taken into account in deciding how to apply moral principles to them and what sorts of treatment are acceptable.

R. D. Guthrie, a biologist, has argued that "a sliding scale of morally obligatory conduct toward, or expected from, other organisms," like that which we customarily apply to incapacitated or underdeveloped humans, "is operationally unfeasible." Guthrie remarks that "we would have to formulate some sort of discriminatory system which would define the nature and extent of preferential moral treatment. Which organisms would we include in our moral system and to what degree?" He then rejects the notion of "higher" and "lower" organisms as "nebulous" and "interlaced with teleological overtones that are rejected by virtually all evolutionists."[48] Guthrie also suggests that phylogenetic proximity to *Homo sapiens* is an unacceptable criterion for differentiating among animals and points out that individual variation within species cannot be ignored.

I do not find the difficulties raised by Guthrie to be insurmountable, much less a *reductio ad absurdum* of the moral perspective advocated here. (Guthrie, I believe, has fallen victim to the common but erroneous assumption that evolutionary continuity among species is antithetical to an anthropocentric view of ethics.) It is not my intention to suggest that precise differences among species or individuals within species of capacities, pain thresholds, and the like can be ascertained and used to establish their respective moral status. But note that in practice decisions of the kind rejected as arbitrary and unworkable by Guthrie are routinely made by reputable scientists. For example, a widely observed rule for experimentation is that all things being equal, a lower (less complex or evolved) organism should be used in preference to a higher one.[49] If this procedural principle were merely arbitrary, there would be no moral reason in a given instance to use, say, an insect or even a microorganism in place of a chimpanzee, a cat, or a horse (or, for that matter, a human being). If its application were genuinely impracticable, then (contrary to fact) the decision could not be made at all.

Individual variation within a species group would also appear to present no real problem. As in the case of humans, typical behavior and capacities of the mature members of the species are what we cite when making judgments about species' moral status. If this were not the case, highly intelligent or responsible humans would deserve superior moral status to ordinary people and the notion of equality would go out the window.

Finally, ethologists (scientists who study animal behavior in natural surroundings) have argued in recent years that comparative ethology is a desirable and attainable objective.[50] Some have even gone so far as to call for the construction of an "ethogram" or behavior inventory specifying the principal normal behaviors of a given species, to be used as a standard by which artificial environments may be made more humane and behavior in the laboratory setting assessed more accurately.[51] Decisions about the relative moral status of different species are difficult to make, and if a demand for precision is pressed, may be made arbitrarily. But it seems plausible that our present rough ideas of an evolutionary hierarchy of certain qualities like consciousness, adaptability, intelligence, language, and so on is not without foundation and can in fact be sharpened by further ethological findings.

SOME OBJECTIONS AND REPLIES

At this point some miscellaneous objections may be considered and put to rest.

IF FISH COULD JUDGE . . .

One objection goes as follows: the judgment that human life is more valuable than animal life is a purely anthropocentric one. If animals could express their views on the matter, they would certainly have a different story to tell.

I have already explained in chapter 2 that, of course, all judgments of preference are human centered and why there is no possibility of altering this locus of valuing. But just because judgments of this kind are purely human, they are not arbitrary or discredited. We must either refrain from making any value judgments at all or accept the fact that they are inevitably made relative to human interests and preferences.

George Gaylord Simpson, reflecting on the meaning of evolution, offers a nice knockdown argument against this objection. Simpson writes,

It has often been remarked ... that if, say, a fish were a student of evolution it would laugh at such pretensions [i.e., humans' belief in their superiority] on the part of the animal that is so clumsy in the water and that lacks such features of perfection as gills or a homocercal caudal fin. I suspect that the fish's reaction would be, instead, to marvel that there are men who question the fact that man is the highest animal. It is not beside the point to add that the "fish" that made such judgments would have to *be* a man![52]

Perhaps we should emend Simpson's final phrase and say that the fish would have to be a person. His point, nevertheless, is well taken. An animal can no more imagine or conceive of what it would be like to be a human (without actually becoming one) than we can envision what it would be like to be an animal without divesting ourselves of all those characteristics that make for autonomy—including, of course, our ability to reflect critically on our own condition. The difference is that we have not only our own experiences but also the accumulated historical experience and observations of humankind to draw on to reach the judgment that a life reduced to sheer animality would be far poorer and less valuable, whereas the animal has never reflected on its state, nor does it possess the conceptual apparatus necessary to gain an inkling of the life of autonomy.

Earlier I cited Mill's famous remark that "it is better to be a human being dissatisfied than a pig satisfied; better to be Socrates dissatisfied than a fool satisfied." Readers familiar with this passage will recall that he immediately adds, "And if the fool, or the pig, is of a different opinion, it is because they only know their own side of the question. The other party to the comparison knows both sides." Mill no doubt exaggerates. But in spite of his colorful prose, it is not difficult to grasp his reason for saying this.

Another aspect of this same issue is that many of us assume that animals want the same things we do. This is why we worry so much about incarcerating them, say, for the purposes of research. But *Homo sapiens*—as a species and as individuals—develop more complex and exotic wants only when their basic needs have been fulfilled. Animals in the wild, by contrast, seldom have time to do much more than look after their most rudimentary needs. Reaching the plateau where basic needs are satisfied, however, has often required of humans great expenditures of energy and considerable sacrifice. If animals can meaningfully be said to "want the same things we do," must we not assume that if they had the choice, they would be willing to make similar sacrifices to attain the same goals? If so, then can we be sure they would not gladly forfeit their freedom to roam the savage wilds in exchange for the good health and care they generally receive within the human sphere, even if the trade-off involved some pain or an "unnatural" death? Mark Sagoff has remarked, "Nature is a war of all against all, as Hobbes said, and man and beast alike prefer the safety and comfort of an artificial environment." [53] Perhaps if animals could judge, they would set us straight on this matter as well.

THE PLANET OF THE APES PROBLEM

A second objection may be stated: If humans may justifiably use lower sentient beings for food, as subjects for experimentation, and so on, may not species superior in capacities to *Homo sapiens* (if such there be) justifiably use us in the same ways? [54]

We may think of this dilemma graphically as the Planet of the Apes problem, after a well-known 1967 Hollywood film of that title in which humans become slaves and experimental subjects on an alien planet. Very briefly, I think the answer to this objection is that we may relax, at least so far as the question of moral justification is concerned. If morality is truly universal in the dual sense that certain precepts and principles are clear to and accepted by rational, responsible, sentient beings generally[55] and that some characteristics or capacities are recognized as compelling grounds for ascribing full moral status to beings, then the Planet of the Apes problem should not arise, even in a state of mutual hostility. Even if we suppose our hypothetical extraterrestrials might have a different conception of morality than we in some respects, there is no reason to think that their most fundamental moral precepts would diverge greatly from our own. Of course, this is not to deny that beings more advanced technologically than ourselves could overpower and enslave us if they chose to. But they could not do so without committing a moral transgression (in their own eyes) against us, which as superior rational beings they would presumably feel enjoined from doing. This may be cold comfort to us in such an eventuality; but remember that the only issue before us at the moment is whether it would be morally permissible for hostile aliens to use humans in the same manner in which it is morally permissible for us to use lower animals. To this question the answer is no.

THE BEASTS AMONG US

A third objection can be framed in the following way: Some members of our own species have, through their consistent brutality toward their fellow humans, shown themselves to be deranged, beyond redemption, and unfit to remain in society. Can we seriously entertain the view that the lives of a Hitler, an Idi Amin, or a Mafia-hired killer are more valuable than that of a gentle and intelligent animal and the former more deserving of inclusion in the moral community and of rights?[56]

This objection overlooks a simple but vital distinction, namely, that between the value of the life of an autonomous being in general and the worth of an individual's particular life as he or she has chosen to fashion it. It is one question to determine why (if at all) the life of an autonomous being is valuable as such. This has been addressed in the present chapter. But it is quite another question whether any given individual's life is worthwhile.[57] Furthermore, because individuals are autonomous beings—however cruel and inhuman—they do not through cruel behavior lose standing in the moral community. For if they did, no moral judgment could be brought to bear on them and no form of punishment justified. (We do not punish animals—"beasts"—for moral transgressions. See "The Position of Animals vis-à-vis the Moral Community" in this chapter.)

NONINTERFERENCE IN NATURE

Here is a fourth possible objection: Most of the species that populate the world have been around much longer than *Homo sapiens* and have established their own regular rhythms and patterns of existence and their own place in the scheme of things. What right do we have to interfere with nature, killing animals for food and using them for other ends of our own?[58]

Now there is no question of our having or not having a right to do so, as I have already indicated in the introduction. Since we have no obligation not to do so, such action is morally permissible. The onus is on those who wish to extend the concept of rights to demonstrate that theirs is not a misuse of rights talk. Besides, modern humans and their direct lineal ancestors have been interacting with nature in this same basic way for millions of years. Is it accurate, then, to speak of interference in this context at all? To do so seems to lose sight of the fact that we are ourselves part of nature. Practicing a policy of total noninteraction with nature is imaginatively impossible. Granted, there are kinds and degrees of impact which our species may have, and it is a large task to decide which are justifiable and where to draw the line. But to suppose that the impact on nature of so populous and widely dispersed a species as *Homo sapiens* could be arrested or dramatically curtailed is naive in the extreme.

A second facet of the noninterference-in-nature argument is that we should avoid harming any living creature. Here we confront the reverence-for-life principle face to face. This principle—central to Buddhism, Jainism, and the Christian outlook of Schweitzer, for example—is considered in more detail later (see the first section of chapter 7). It is obviously derived from a deeply held religious or spiritual conviction and is therefore not subject to refutation by argument or by the assertion of a rival imperative. But by the same token, such an unqualified assertion carries only the force of an article of faith with which we may agree or disagree and which we may choose to accept, modify, or reject. I suspect that for most of the world the concept of reverence for life remains an ideal that is unknown, ignored, found impossible to adhere to, hypocritically observed, or adapted (as in Schweitzer's own case) to the practical and complex realities of everyday life.

THE CASE OF THE SCREAMING PLANTS

A final objection: What if plants could feel pain? Various efforts have been made to show that plants have feelings, make anguished sounds when cut, and even manifest, when threatened, a type of electrical output similar to humans' galvanic skin response (measured in lie detector tests).[59] Suppose these bizarre hypotheses proved true. Would we then be compelled to assert not only the equality of all animals but of all organisms, animal and vegetable as well? Then what?

If all organisms were equal, we would obviously encounter a moral dilemma about the sacrifice of any living thing in the interests of human survival. If it could not be resolved (and quickly!), then we would find ourselves in the extreme position of being morally obligated to share our homes with plague-ridden rats, allow rabid foxes to roam free, and starve ourselves to death, the logical outcome that was indeed followed by an Eastern religious figure I once read about, acting on his version of the reverence-for-life principle. (The Jains of India carry brooms to sweep the path before them, lest they inadvertently step on a bug and kill it, and also wear face masks to filter out organisms they might destroy by normal breathing. But even they—since they opt to stay alive—realize that a line must be drawn somewhere!)[60] In fact, however, almost no one believes we are obligated to die in the name of the moral equality of all organisms. It is instructive to note that even Peter Singer, who has inspired so many to advocate the cause of the equality of animals, writes, "If we must inflict pain or starve, we would then have to choose the lesser evil. Presumably it would still be true that plants suffer less than animals, and therefore it would still be better to eat plants than to eat animals."[61] This reveals a commitment to the greater value of human life than to that of other forms of life and to a human right to survive that overrides that of other species. So much for the moral equality of animals (and, in the imaginary scenario, plants)! But what if plants did suffer as much as animals? Under such hypothetical circumstances, Singer's underlying commitments would no doubt emerge all too clearly.

The answer to the original question—If plants could suffer, would we be obliged to assert their morality equality?—is no, we would not. The reason is that the capacity to suffer does not by itself establish moral equality. There would still be an evolutionary hierarchy even if plants could suffer (as Singer tacitly acknowledges); and although the lesser-of-evils argument has force, relative evils are to be weighed by the impact of acts on beings according to all the capacities they possess (or lack) that might be considered relevant to our moral assessments. As we have seen, much more than the capacity to suffer is essential in this connection.

CONCLUSION

The general outcome of this chapter is that it is morally permissible for humans to use animals for their own ends. Some animal liberationists have argued that humans' possession of autonomy does not by itself justify using animals for their own ends. But beings that

are more valuable because they have the attributes that identify them
as full members of the moral community may use less valuable
species, which lack some or all of these traits as means to their ends,
for the simple reason that they have no obligation not to do so. As I
have consistently asserted throughout, however, it does not follow
that humans may use animals in any way they wish, that animals are
merely means to our ends, or that animals' capacities and interests
need not be taken into account by us when we act. Indeed, I hold that
they should be.

Chapter 1 argued that animals' lives lack intrinsic value and
therefore possess value only in the instrumental sense, that is, in
relation to the uses to which we put them or the valued experiences
we derive from interacting with them in diverse ways. Many hold,
on the contrary, that animals' lives have intrinsic and not just
instrumental value. This viewpoint is expressed in one of two forms:
(a) Animals' lives are of equal value to those of humans. (b) Animals'
lives possess intrinsic value, but their value is less than that of
humans' lives. It can be seen readily that anyone who holds view
(a) cannot consistently justify any infliction of suffering or any
deprivation of animals' lives for the satisfaction of human ends. Since
animals, being nonresponsible (nonautonomous) creatures, are incapable of acting in morally culpable ways, we commonly regard them
as "innocent." (They cannot "deserve" to suffer or to die at our
hands.) Hence, for someone accepting (a), inflicting suffering on
animals or depriving them of their lives would seem to be defensible
(if at all) only in terms of the benefits likely to be received by a
particular animal or by other animals. It is doubtful, however,
whether the proponent of (a) could even argue consistently for these
sets of interventions since he or she cannot consult the animal or
animals concerned to discover what its (their) wishes are in the
matter; there is no possibility here of informed consent, which is a
crucial ethical requirement in human experimentation and medical
treatment. Nor could the advocate of (a) consistently hold that all
animals' lives are of equal value, but that some may be sacrificed for
the sake of others. Among other undesirable consequences, this
would seem to rule out as unjustifiable even progress toward the
alleviation of animal suffering through veterinary medical research.
Because of implications like this, few thoughtful individuals—in
Western society at least—are willing to commit themselves to a view
as uncompromising as (a).

Those who subscribe to position (b) would experience no logical difficulty in maintaining that it is sometimes permissible to inflict suffering on animals or deprive them of life. Thus, for example, one or more animals may be caused to suffer in the interests of a large class of animals, as in veterinary medical research aimed at discovering disease-preventing vaccines; and severely injured or ill animals may be euthanized to stop their suffering. It would appear that people holding view (b), unlike those advocating (a), could also maintain consistently that animals may be caused to suffer or be deprived of life for human ends. This is where the inherent weakness of position (b) reveals itself, however. The adherents of (b) often argue that although animals are not our moral equals, they are deserving of (or perhaps have the right to) equal consideration of interests when our intended actions will likely affect them. But as I have illustrated in the previous section, using the example of Peter Singer, those who argue in this way set aside the intrinsic value of animals' lives and the principle of equal consideration of interests when things like human survival or human lifesaving research are at stake. There is, then, an apparent inconsistency in this position too: Although its proponents are unwilling to regard animals' lives as of merely instrumental value, they are prepared to consider them merely instrumentally in certain circumstances, leaving intrinsic value and equal consideration aside. But it seems to follow from this that the intrinsic value assigned to animals' lives is not what it appeared to be at first. Rather, it is something that can be meted out in varying degrees to different entities and either revoked or overridden when it is convenient to do so. More intelligible, I think, is the view that assesses the moral issues of animal suffering and the taking of animals' lives in relation to the instrumental value (benefits) derived by humans from the use of animals, that is, in relation to a broadly anthropocentric ethical framework.

If this position be regarded as speciesist in spite of the various cautions and qualifications I have set out, so be it. Speciesism or species chauvinism in its full-blown form is unacceptable from an ethical standpoint. I have acknowledged this although it has not yet been shown convincingly that speciesism is wrong. (For example, the alleged analogy between speciesism and racism/sexism, on which the case has thus far been based, will not survive critical scrutiny, as we have seen earlier.)[62] It seems almost inescapable, however, that in this age of marketing and instant information a label will be invented by someone for the view I have advanced and defended. Given this fact, I suggest that it be called "autonomism."

4

Animals in Research: Understanding the Context

THE SCALE OF ANIMAL USE

The case in favor of using animals for human ends has been stated in general terms in the preceding chapters. A careful consideration of the nature of *Homo sapiens* and other species as well as of their relative moral status shows, as we have seen, that common objections to our use of animals either are ill considered or may be overridden by more compelling counterarguments. We have not yet, however, examined the question of how well our actual practices correspond to the principles of humane treatment for which we established the grounds at the conclusion of chapter 3. Given that humans may use animals for their own ends, for which ends and under what conditions? It is clear that an attitude of "anything goes" is incompatible with a humane outlook and is therefore morally unacceptable. Our sense of what is better in ourselves and our knowledge of and sensibilities toward the rest of nature (sentient beings in particular) should incline us away from cruelty and exploitation and toward kindness, caring, thoughtfulness, prudence, and proportion in the use of resources of all kinds.

I consider in this chapter a few examples of biomedical and behavioral research, two of the major areas of animal use today and by long tradition the most controversial. My purpose here and in chapter 5 is to show the following: (1) Most research of this kind, contrary to its most vociferous critics, is morally acceptable. (2) It is not possible to judge the ethics of animal use without reference to the larger context in which research takes place. (3) In the final analysis, some form of peer ethics review system, widely adopted at research institutions today, is the most appropriate and workable mechanism for ensuring that humane standards in experimentation are observed and enforced. (4) Much opposition to research involving animals stems from ignorance about the nature of that research and of scientific inquiry in general.

It is important to have a working notion of the total number of animals required yearly for research of all kinds, even if we cannot be expected to comprehend fully the vast scale on which it is conducted. According to the most recent survey published by the Institute of Laboratory Animal Resources (ILAR), a United States government agency that compiles figures on the use of animals by the scientific community, a combined total of 28,776,323 warm-blooded animals were acquired in 1978 by nonprofit U.S. biomedical research organizations (postsecondary schools, hospitals, research institutes, and laboratories) and nonprofit, commercial, military, Department of Health, Education, and Welfare, and other federal organizations.[1] (This represents, incidentally, a 40 percent reduction in animal use since the previous survey year of 1968.) In Canada 2,840,514 vertebrates were used in experiments during the year ending April 1974,[2] and in Great Britain the UK Home Office reported that in 1978, 5,195,409 experiments were performed on animals by licenced experimenters.[3] However, the full magnitude of animal use world-wide can only be guessed at. Robert A. Brown, executive director of the Chicago Anti-Cruelty Society, estimates that laboratory animal science "consumes in procedures rarely benign some two hundred million lives each year."[4]

Is the very large number of animals "consumed" by research morally acceptable? I think it is, but this is not the sort of question to which a simple yes or no answer is either possible or meaningful. The position I shall take is that since human life, health, and happiness are more important than animals', and since we are not morally obliged *not* to use animals as means to our ends, research using animal subjects is morally permissible as a general rule even if it causes suffering. Obviously, there are limits to the degree of suffering that is warranted or morally acceptable, that is, to the claim that human goods outweigh the comfort and well-being of animals. There is room for much debate here. But the need for limits does not invalidate the claim that the potential alleviation of a considerable amount of human misery and the gaining of knowledge that will promote human health and welfare or prolong human life sanction conducting painful or stressful experiments on animals—as do the beneficial effects of many of these same experiments for the health and well-being of animals themselves. The large number of animals used in experimentation is, as I note later, a function of both the magnitude of current research efforts and the statistical requirements for significant results in science.

FOR AND AGAINST ANIMAL RESEARCH

It is very easy to find extreme statements for and against experimentation on animals, and because animals evoke strong, even uncontrolled emotional responses, the nature of the dispute over research often contributes significantly to hardening opposing positions and tends to obscure the real issues it generates. In *Slaughter of the Innocent*, Hans Ruesch, a leading radical antivivisectionist, contends that "there doesn't exist one single important therapeutic discovery indisputably due to vivisection [i.e., animal experimentation]." He also maintains that "the researchers' entire ingenuity focuses on this project: To get hold of healthy animals and to create in them experimental diseases and injuries. Which, being inflicted deliberately by arbitrary interferences, from the outside, are inevitably entirely different from any disease or injury that arises spontaneously or occurs by accident."[5] Thus animal experiments are decried as purposeless, sadistic, and totally unproductive. At the opposite end of the spectrum, publications like Frank Stilley's *The $100,000 Rat and Other Animal Heroes for Human Health*[6] tend to paint a glowing picture of animal experimentation as untainted by inhumane practices and motivated by the pure selfless desire to better the human condition.

Polarization of opinion over the use of animals in research can only lead to an adversarial confrontation on important issues and a fruitless round of hostilities in which all concerned—including the animals themselves—stand to lose. This outcome can be avoided, however, if the great majority in the middle inform themselves and bring their considerable influence to bear on legislators and other decision makers concerned with the practical resolution of the problems of animal welfare.

To begin, let us consider two questions: (1) Why are animals used in research at all? (2) What has animal-based research accomplished?

F. L. Marcuse and J. J. Pear have summarized quite succinctly the reasons why scientists use animals in research.[7] These are as follows: (a) Animals have "a much simpler life space" than humans; they are less complex in many ways—both constitutionally (that is, as organic systems) and psychologically. (b) "Animals usually have a shorter life span," a factor of great importance where the transmission of genetically determined traits is of vital interest. (c) "One can control the animal's environment more easily than that of the human," reducing the number of variables that we have to take into account. (d) "One can use larger numbers when one uses animals as compared to humans." (e) "One can use animals for critical experiments," that is, experiments which it would be unethical to perform on people. An additional important reason related to (a) and (c) but not specifically mentioned by Marcuse and Pear is that (f) One can use animals as models for human systems and their responses. In sum, animals resemble humans to varying degrees according to species and in relation to the system or type of reaction under investigation. Many animal diseases are closely related or identical to their human counterparts.[8] We can also set up a situation for testing some reaction where the immediate cause, relevant influences, and irrelevant or extraneous factors can be strictly controlled. (Some of these characteristics are examined in more detail in the next chapter.)

In more general terms, we might say that animals are used in research to study living systems according to the requirements of scientific study to understand such systems and to apply this knowledge to alleviating human and animal problems, specifically diseases and behavioral disorders.

To answer the second question, experimentation on animals has indisputably yielded a great range of benefits, some of which the following statement summarizes clearly:

> In pharmacology there can be little doubt that the traditional and basic procedure of animal experimentation has been central in the development of drugs used in the treatment of diseases of known etiology— drugs such as antibiotics, antiparasitics, antiallergenics, and others. It has also led to the development and validation of drugs useful in the treatment of diseases of unknown etiology—drugs such as antiinflammatories, pain relievers, and drugs for nonspecific disorders such as heart

and renal diseases. The whole field of nutrition has its foundation firmly rooted in animal experimentation, which has led to the discovery of diet essentials [such as all the known vitamins], the understanding of deficiency diseases, the interrelationship of diet and cardiovascular disease, and such recent mass programs of disease prevention as fluoridation. The literature shows that advanced surgical techniques (cardiac surgery and organ transplants to name but two of the more recent and glamorous, which will in their time move to the classification of routine), the control and management of hemorrhagic shock, the development and use of nuclear medicine, and even the conquest of space would not have been possible under concepts of research different from those that have evolved from centuries of efforts using animals as the basis for experimentation and observation.[9]

The central role of animal experiments in the discovery and development of immunizations against a wide spectrum of diseases has been highlighted frequently. Some of the most noteworthy landmarks in the history of preventive medicine can be included here, such as vaccines or antitoxins to combat rabies, cholera, diphtheria, tetanus, pneumonia, polio, measles, and viral hepatitis.[10]

The productive applications of animal-based biomedical research to both human and animal well-being has also received special emphasis in various writings on the subject. For example:

General medical research has provided the basis for important improvements in the care, feeding and protection from infection of domestic animals. It is also significant that a large proportion of the medicaments, procedures and materials used in human medicine form the basis for, or are identical to, those widely used in veterinary medicine. Laboratory animal technology which has done much to advance the health of experimental animals, particularly when allied to statistical analysis, also has led to significant reductions in the numbers of animals used.[11]

As for the benefits to animals, another author has observed simply that "virtually everything learned for the benefit of man through animal experimentation is of the same benefit to animals."[12]

A further area in which animal-based research promises far-reaching advances is genetic engineering. Developments in this field are occurring with such rapidity that it is difficult for any survey to remain up-to-date for very long. In one typical experiment scientists accomplished the successful transplantation of rat growth hormone genes into mice, producing mice twice the normal weight that could pass on the new genes to their offspring.[13] This represents a small but significant step toward the mastery of techniques that may eventually make possible the elimination of genetically inherited diseases in humans and animals.

In the past few years animal research has, in addition, led to progress in understanding the physiology of pain—and thus toward the control or eradication of pain itself. I am referring to the discovery of natural opiates in the brain and of specific sites where these substances concentrate.[14] Here we have an example of a breakthrough with potentially profound consequences, which came about as a serendipitous by-product of brain research that had been headed initially in a different direction. (We also confront a challenging paradox: the use of animals in painful experiments, one object of which is to bring an end to pain in both humans and animals.)[15]

In relation to behavioral research, effective techniques have been developed out of the experimental study of animal behavior for the eradication of phobias and obsessive-compulsive neuroses, and for the treatment of retardates, autistic children, and those with other serious mental disorders that are difficult to manage.[16] In both areas definite advances have been made over traditional psychiatric approaches to these problems. The benefits of these same techniques for handling animal behavioral disorders has also been pointed out.[17] Indeed, one pioneering researcher in this field has gone so far as to state that "in all respects in which comparisons have been made human clinical neuroses have the same attributes as those experimentally induced [in animals]."[18] Other experimental psychologists have argued, in defense of their discipline, that "significant recent developments in the treatment and understanding of such problems as phobias, obesity, drug addiction, brain disorders, ulcers, depression, enuresis, and childhood autism are tied directly or indirectly to the results of animal experimentation."[19] Neal Miller, a distinguished dean of experimental psychology, has recently written:

> Such lab research provides a scientific foundation for a variety of behavioral treatments—psychotherapy, assertiveness training, meditation, and relaxation training with or without biofeedback, which uses measuring instruments to guide the therapist and help the patient know how well he is succeeding in relaxing various muscles.
>
> Behavior therapists have found that a significant number of patients who continue to have physical complaints for which no organic basis can be found are actually being rewarded for the types of behavior that cause them to be considered sick. Discovering the conditions that are

rewarding the symptoms and changing the environment so that healthier, independent behavior is rewarded has produced dramatic cures. Bio-feedback has also proved useful in helping patients suffering from neuromuscular disorders, such as those produced by accidents or strokes, to learn better control of their hands and feet.[20]

Finally, and speaking most generally, a Canadian psychologist states that "if one were to compare a psychology textbook of 50 years ago with one of today, the major conceptual developments that have occurred in our understanding of human nature and experience are quite apparent, and they are based in no small measure on animal research."[21]

In spite of this impressive record of achievement, there is no denying that laboratory animals are sometimes subjected to unpleasant procedures and manipulations, of which the following are major examples: burn injuries, electric shocks of varying intensities, radiation, brain stimulation by electrical means or by the injection of drugs, stress (including the induction of seizures, fear, social isolation, and so on), eye damage, and battering trauma. From published reports it appears that some potentially painful or stressful experiments are carried out without using anesthetics (for example, neurological procedures in which anesthesia would suppress the response being tested for or aversive conditioning); and in cases where anesthetics are used (as in experimental surgery), mention is seldom made of the postoperative use of analgesics (painkillers)—although most contemporary ethics codes for animal experimentation prescribe them. The employment of muscle relaxants or paralytics (curariform agents) in place of anesthetics is also quite common, particularly in brain stimulation experiments in which they ensure that the subject animal will remain conscious and alert throughout, though unable to move, struggle, protest, or escape. (They are prohibited, however, by certain professional codes of ethics, such as that included as an appendix to this book.) In addition, many procedures involve the use of restraining or immobilizing devices, for instance, harnesses or constricting boxes of various designs.

Reading through discussions of research conducted under these conditions is a chastening experience for the uninitiated, and we often feel that the experiments summarized in them are morally dubious as well as of questionable practical significance. It is not my purpose here to offer a survey of such cases, particularly as this has been done copiously (if one-sidedly) elsewhere.[22] In any event it is clear to me that little can be gained by reading secondhand condensations of scientific papers—especially if prepared by those deeply biased against experiments using animals, for these easily mislead us into making unwarranted judgments about the nature and value of the original research.

Still, we get the feeling when reading or hearing about a variety of psychological and biomedical experiments that too many of the procedures on which they depend are unnecessarily stressful and pain producing and sometimes just plain cruel; that is, they often seem morally unjustified in view of the small and apparently insignificant bits of new information they yield. But emotional appeals aside, this is an exceedingly difficult matter for laypersons to judge, particularly since they seldom have a grasp of the larger context of ongoing research within which a given experiment is conducted. Furthermore, they have little understanding of the pursuit of scientific knowledge and only a faint inkling of how the results of research slowly accrue. They have no notion of how many bits and pieces of knowledge have to fall into place before practical applications become feasible, of the number of hits and misses that characteristically pave the way, or of the significant role that serendipity plays in scientific progress. Even an examination of published accounts of experiments in professional journals will not provide much insight, as these are not written with a view to persuading a critical, skeptical, sometimes hostile public of the merits and moral justification of some piece of research. If lay readers then turn instead to popular presentations, they are most likely to run across antivivisectionist literature that is anything but balanced and objective or, at the opposite extreme, to be snowed by progress reports offered for their consumption by journalists or PR people in the scientific community.

To illustrate the obstacles that stand in the way of assessing the value of a piece of scientific research using animals, consider the following two examples. I recalled seeing somewhere a picture of an experiment in which a mouse was held submerged in a chemical liquid for an extended period of time to see if it could acquire sufficient oxygen from this substance to survive. The procedure seemed, on the face of it, a pointless exercise in satisfying scientific curiosity. (Many antivivisectionist accounts of experiments provide just the amount of descriptive material I have given here and then condemn the research as merely gratifying sadistic impulses and inquisitiveness run riot.) When finally I located the place where this experiment was reported scientifically, I found quite another story— one about the search for a universal chemical blood substitute.[23] This research is aimed at developing "perfluorochemical emulsions" and testing their properties as carriers of oxygen in place of blood. As the article I consulted notes, there are not only serious problems world-wide in maintaining adequate blood supplies but also in storing and in supplying blood rapidly when and where it is needed. Rare blood types present even greater predicaments. Furthermore, "blood supplies for animals are virtually nonexistent." I learned, in addition, that 90 percent of the blood of dogs and 100 percent of the blood of laboratory rats had been replaced by one of these artificial fluids without ill effects. A subsequent report on this ongoing research revealed that the lives of several human beings with rare blood types had been saved by the first clinical use of blood substitutes in Japan.[24] In a time in which there are ever-increasing worries over the spread of hepatitis and AIDS (acquired immune deficiency syndrome) via blood transfusions, the problems that originally called forth this research are compounded still further and would appear to make it even more urgent.

What of the mouse I had first seen in the photograph? "After an hour's immersion the mouse was inverted to drain the liquid from its lungs, and is now alive and well." [25]

The second example concerns the way in which popular antivivi-sectionist or animal liberationist publications almost invariably tell only half the story of research involving animals. In so doing, of course, they deliberately cast all research in the poorest light. Both Richard Ryder and Peter Singer report an experiment in which a monkey was blinded by a brain operation.[26] Ryder concentrates on describing how the animal later bumped into objects and fell into a pond, whereas Singer dwells on the fact that the researcher left the monkey in a small cage after the operation for ten months while he completed his thesis. Ryder also claims, without documentation, that when the monkey was killed subsequently and its brain examined, it emerged "to the embarrassment of the scientists concerned . . . that the experimental injuries to her brain were not quite those that had been intended." What neither author tells us, however, is that the monkey in this experiment, which had its visual cortex surgically removed, was trained to see again, to discern small objects, negotiate around obstacles, and so on. They fail to mention how retraining included regular walks in a large woods and free movement in an indoor arena. They also neglect to inform their readers how "the knowledge and subtle techniques of this unique experiment are now being successfully applied to human patients, whose cortical blindness has previously been considered irremediable." [27]

Clearly, then, to form a reasonable judgment about the moral justification of an experiment, it is essential to move beyond superficial summaries and first impressions and attempt instead to appraise it in relation to the larger body of research of which it forms a part. When we do so it often becomes much more difficult to be sure that a given experiment or research program, which appeared at first to be inhumane and morally unacceptable (that is, to cause greater suffering than its positive benefits offset), really is so. The following examples, selected because they continue to generate controversy, illustrate this point.

EXAMPLES OF ANIMAL EXPERIMENTATION (I): BEHAVIORAL RESEARCH WITH NOTORIETY

"LEARNED HELPLESSNESS" AND DEPRESSION

At a conference I attended not long ago, one speaker, eager to impress on his audience the evils of inhumane research, told disapprovingly of an experiment in which dogs under restraint were given electric shocks until they became totally helpless and incapable of escaping from further shocks when subsequently allowed the opportunity to do so. I later found out from him that he was referring to a research project carried out over a number of years by University of Pennsylvania psychologist Martin Seligman and various associates. Anxious to discover whether this research was indeed as cruel and pointless as it had been made out to be, I looked up some of the original papers in which the studies were reported, as well as a book by Seligman and some discussions by other authors of his work and its importance. [28]

What I found was that the experiments did indeed cause considerable suffering, and the experimenters make no attempt to hide this fact. As Seligman relates, more than 150 dogs were strapped into hammocks and subjected to painful electric shocks, which they could not accurately anticipate, control, or escape. Typically, sixty-four shocks of five seconds' duration each were used to prepare the dogs for an experiment. The experiment proper consisted of placing each dog in turn into a "shuttle box" in which it again received electric shocks. In the shuttle box, however, the dogs could escape the shocks by jumping a partition into a safe (no-shock) area. Seligman observed that compared with a control group of unpreconditioned dogs, which almost invariably and rapidly learned to escape the unpleasant stimulus, fully two-thirds of the preconditioned dogs simply gave up and lay down, whimpering and passively accepting shocks until they ceased. The state of the latter group Seligman labeled one of "learned helplessness."

This description, taken by itself, may make Seligman's work sound little more than sadistic. The appropriate question to ask, then, is whether his investigation has accomplished anything of lasting value and importance. It turns out that it has. To begin with, learned helplessness has proven to be an illuminating animal model for depression in humans. The learned helplessness model has been tested on people,[29] and it is believed that many situations in which we become depressed bear a close resemblance to this phenomenon. For example, an individual undergoing a traumatic experience beyond her control (such as the loss of a loved one) may become passive, convinced of her own inability to influence the course of events and hence unable to cope with life situations. Because she senses a loss of control over the important aspects of her life, she feels ineffectual, hopeless, and depressed. The value of having a reliable animal model of depression lies in (a) the relative ease with which depression can be investigated under controlled and less complex and variable conditions and (b) the fact that "depression" is a poorly defined clinical concept. The refinement of a model of depression, therefore, can lead both to the exclusion of certain phenomena from this classification and the inclusion of others. The formulation of a more solid and precise definition of depression makes it possible to sort out conditions previously lumped together unhelpfully under a vague rubric. This is important because a clearly defined set of symptoms is, obviously, most readily amenable to treatment.

Seligman and his colleagues have already discovered that learned helplessness in dogs (and rats) can be eradicated if the animals are forcibly dragged from the shocking area of their box to the safe zone. Though this may have to be done as many as fifty times, the dogs eventually learn that their own escape attempts will be rewarded by an alleviation of shocks, and consequently normal escape behavior is restored. This shows that learned helplessness may be unlearned, and it may therefore be said that within the limits imposed by the experimental situation a cure for it has been found. The pathbreaking idea that depression can be therapeutically undone by assisting a patient to overcome the sense of being ineffectual through encouraging direct, self-assertive actions—actions designed to influence events and to obtain gratification—predates Seligman's work in the laboratory. But owing to his studies of learned helplessness, such techniques can be tested for effectiveness, refined, and their underlying principles better understood. Finally, some suggestive ideas about the possible prevention of depression have also been derived from this research.

How much does it all matter? Is depression enough of a concern to warrant the continuation of such stressful and painful research? The following statistics, though they do not by themselves settle this issue, make it evident that depression is a health problem of gigantic proportions:

> Each year, 4 to 8 million people in the United States suffer from debilitating depression, which is possibly the most common major mental disorder. Many people recover from depression, but unlike most other forms of psychopathology it can be lethal. One out of every 100 persons afflicted by a depressive illness dies by suicide. . . . The economic cost is also enormous. Loss of productivity and cost of treatment among adults in the United States amount to between $1.3 and $4 billion a year.[30]

Seligman has described depression as "the common cold of psychopathology." If it were possible to develop a "behavioral immunization" against depression, it would be very difficult to argue that his research is unjustifiable.[31]

SOCIAL ISOLATION AND DEVELOPMENT

One of the favorite targets of criticism for antivivisectionists, animal welfarists, and other individuals concerned with animal suffering is the work of University of Wisconsin psychologist Harry Harlow and his colleagues on the effects of maternal and sibling deprivation on young rhesus monkeys. Over a period of twenty years or more before his retirement, Harlow, his wife, Margaret, and numerous graduate students and collaborators studied the development of infant monkeys reared from birth in total social isolation, without even human contact.[32]

In one of Harlow's best-known experiments, monkeys separated from their mothers within a few hours of birth were placed in isolation cages equipped with two "mother surrogates," one soft, cloth covered, and heated and the other bare wire mesh. The infant monkeys spent most of their time clinging to the cloth "mother" even when the wire one was the supplier of milk. Monkeys have been isolated for periods of three, six, and twelve months and the effects of maternal deprivation and isolation observed and recorded. All monkeys kept in isolation exhibited a marked fear response when exposed to their peers for the first time. After a month, monkeys raised in isolation for three months became fully socialized. Those isolated for six months, however, were unable to form bonds of affection and their social interactions were minimal at best. They played mostly by themselves and passively accepted aggressive attacks by other members of the group. Monkeys isolated for as much as twelve months and then placed in a social situation were unable to display aggression, though this is normal for their age. In addition, they failed completely to participate in playful interaction with their peers and proved to be the most passive of all, crouching and cowering in the face of physical abuse from other monkeys. As Harlow notes of this intractable group, "We have been unable to test them in the playpen beyond a ten-week period because they are in danger of being seriously injured or even killed by the others."[33]

Harlow's experiments, in the judgment of most observers, rate about the highest in terms of the levels of stress and suffering caused to the animals used. In the opinion of some scientists I have talked to, it is even doubtful they would pass muster before today's ethics review committees (which by itself tells us something important about positive change within the scientific community). Both mothers and babies have been forced to experience the effects of separation which, given the extremely social nature of monkeys and their evolutionary proximity to humans, we must assume to have been devastating.[34] Furthermore, in some of Harlow's investigations, monkeys were placed in inescapable narrow pits until they became totally withdrawn and depressed through lack of stimuli or social contact. Isolated monkeys generally crumple themselves pathetically into a ball, hiding their faces in their paws, and constant rocking movements and self-directed aggression (clawing and biting their

own skin) are not uncommon behaviors. Female monkeys reared as
social isolates and having no interest in mating have been restrained
so that they could be impregnated by normal males. These unwilling
mothers frequently batter their own infants brutally. In some
instances, maladaptive forms of behavior have been observed over a
period of years in individual monkeys to ascertain the long-term
effects of social isolation.

Yet even these nightmarish and regrettable experiments, offensive
as they are to normal sensibilities, are not without redeeming features
of considerable importance. Harlow's work is discussed and cited in
virtually every textbook on the psychology of child development,
and by all accounts has contributed in a major way to the advancement of knowledge in this field. John F. Travers notes that Harlow
"studied a range of affective systems in monkeys: maternal, peer,
heterosexual, and paternal," and his method of inquiry was characterized by "a wide range of experimental devices plus cautious
conclusions."[35] E. Mavis Hetherington and Ross D. Parke, authors
of a leading textbook on child psychology, describe Harlow's
research as "one of the most thorough and systematic attempts to
investigate the effects of early environmental deprivation on later
development." His work comprised "carefully controlled experimental studies," which "permit quite refined statements about cause-
and-effect relationships. By comparing these experimental findings
with the nonexperimental data yielded by the studies of institutionalized children, firmer conclusions about the impact of variations
in early experience on human development may be possible."[36]

One of Harlow's notable discoveries derived from his observation
of isolated infant monkeys' preference for soft, cloth-covered mother
surrogates even when they were not the providers of food. Harlow
reasoned that what he called "contact comfort" was a crucial factor in
the formation of a relationship of attachment in the infant monkey. It
has been remarked that "these studies indicate that satisfaction of the
hunger drive does not singly promote and nurture the infant's
attachment for the mother, a belief held for years by many psychologists."[37] The full impact of this finding comes out in the following
comment:

> Harlow's landmark research contains the seeds of a radically different
> view of the nature of infant attachment. Implicit in Harlow's view is the
> idea that certain behaviors have been preprogrammed from birth—even
> such complex behaviors as clinging, smiling and vocalizing. These

preprogrammed behaviors are believed to be intimately involved in the development of attachment and subsequent social and emotional development.[38]

There are other significant ramifications of Harlow's research. One of these has to do with the long-standing controversy over the extent to which human behavior contains an instinctual component. Child psychologist Jere E. Brophy writes, "Until these [Harlow's] studies were conducted and publicized, it was generally believed that animals (and perhaps humans, too) engaged in a complex of behaviors that we call mothering (and perhaps also fathering) for basically instinctive reasons. They apparently did not need to be taught these behaviors." However, this prevailing belief, rich with implications for society in a feminist age, "is called into serious question by the data from monkey studies conducted by the Harlows."[39]

In addition to his deprivation research, Harlow studied the question of whether the effects of early social isolation could be reversed. He and his associates found (as noted earlier) that three-month isolates could be rehabilitated fairly quickly by interaction with a normal peer group. They also found that six-month isolates could regain normal social behavior by interacting with nonisolated three-month-old monkeys, which posed less of a threat than their normal peers.[40] A similar procedure has subsequently proven effective in rehabilitating twelve-month-old isolates.[41] This research has, according to Hetherington and Parke, "strongly challenged" a widely held "critical-period view of development, which postulates that certain periods in development are of particular importance and if the individual does not receive the appropriate experience during this phase, permanent deficits will result."[42] One significant application of these findings relates to the growing problem of child abuse. Brophy remarks,

> Child abusers are not individuals who somehow are lacking in appropriate maternal or paternal instincts for biological reasons. Instead, they are individuals who, for a variety of environmental and reversible reasons, have learned to take out their frustrations by abusing their offspring. Just as with the Harlows' motherless mothers, this behavior pattern can be eliminated and replaced by more appropriate parenting.[43]

Finally, Harlow's rehabilitation studies have been suggestive in other ways as well, for they tend to show that "attachment to a single mother figure appears not to be necessary for normal social development" and that "human children, like young monkeys, probably need the companionship of peers for normal social development." [44]

Though we must always observe caution in applying the results of animal studies directly to humans, it seems generally agreed that Harlow's work is momentous and enormously stimulating for the field of human developmental psychology.

Behavioral (or psychological) experiments of the sort considered in the preceding two examples are atypical; the majority of experiments performed by behavioral scientists are far less open to charges of cruelty or inhumaneness than Seligman's and Harlow's procedures. But the experiments I have described are not entirely exceptional either, since there are many others that resemble them to one degree or another, and this is what has made psychology and its methods so vulnerable to negative judgments by outside critics. In cases where experimental procedures comparable (from the standpoint of suffering) to those of Seligman and Harlow or procedures of somewhat lesser severity are used, antivivisectionists are always quick to condemn the scientists who carry them out, especially if it is believed that the studies they conducted have provided little benefit to humanity or show a very low potential for doing so. However, as we have seen, to perceive the possible applications of research requires a wholly different perspective from that usually adopted by protesters against experimentation. The value of research must be judged cumulatively and contextually, not independently of a meaningful frame of reference; not simply in terms of a simple opposition to inflicting suffering on nonhuman creatures. If experiments like Seligman's and Harlow's can be said to have produced useful results and important knowledge that perhaps could not have been acquired otherwise, that is, to be significant enough to cause us to reflect on our initial rejection of them as ethically unacceptable, consider how much more likely it is that experiments involving procedures that are not so questionable from a humane standpoint can be justified by their offsetting benefits.

It is in this manner that most experiments—whether in the behavioral sciences or in the domain of biomedical research—should be critically assessed. This requires, of course, that those conducting the assessment have knowledge of the larger context, which requires in turn that peer review—the method normally followed in science—be the basic vehicle for decision making about justifying, funding, and conducting experiments, a topic which I explore later.

SEXUAL RESPONSE IN DESENSITIZED CATS

A *cause célèbre* among animal rights advocates a while ago was a series of experiments designed to study the physiological mechanisms affecting sexual arousal, performance, and development as well as mating patterns in cats, conducted at the American Museum of Natural History in New York by Lester R. Aronson and his associates.[45] Aronson was at the time of this publicity (1976) chairman and curator of the museum's Department of Animal Behavior and also adjunct professor of biology at both the City University of New York and New York University. The experiments in question were carried out over a period of more than fifteen years and received grant support totaling more than $400,000 from the U.S. National Institute of Mental Health and National Institute of Child Health and Human Development. Aronson's research involved procedures such as desensitization of the glans penis in male cats by surgical means (denervation or severing of penile nerves) or by topical anesthesia, the attachment of electrodes to penile nerves, and olfactory bulbectomy (surgical destruction of the sense of smell). According to Aronson, his penile operation was minor compared with some of the "drastic surgical procedures" performed by forerunners in the 1930s and 1940s. Furthermore, he wrote, "healing was always rapid and uneventful, and the males were ready for testing the following week."[46] Between 1965 and 1976, 350 cats had been tested.[47]

Word of Aronson's experiments leaked out to the public and press and an avalanche of protest followed, with crowds of up to two hundred people picketing the museum during the summer of 1976 carrying signs reading: "Jail These Perverted Sadists! Stop Their Obscene Torture of Animals!" "What Weirdos in Our Government Granted Money to These Obscene Perverted Sadists?" and "Castrate the Scientists!" The "cat crisis" naturally received full media coverage and even sparked an inquiry by two New York congressmen, responding to voluminous mail from their constituents. (As many as 1,500 letters of protest were received during the month of August

1976—the height of the controversy. Some thirty congressmen ultimately got into the act.)[48] For his part, Aronson was unable to carry on with his work for several months and even received a number of death threats.[49]

After a considerable period of stonewalling, the museum finally allowed reporters to talk to Aronson and visit his laboratory on August 17, 1976. Statements had previously emanated from Aronson and his colleagues via museum spokespersons emphasizing the potential human applications of the cat research. One statement noted that "small lesions in specific parts of the human brain are believed to cause sexual aberrations, and that such lesions were being duplicated in the brain of the cat" to study their effects.[50] (Cats were being used, it continued, because they are relatively complex organisms and the quantity of data available on their brain and nervous system is vast.) In his interview with the press, Aronson was more circumspect and realistic: "We are not looking so much for a solution to human problems yet because we must first understand how sexual mechanisms work." In the article containing this interview, his work was said to have shown that "cats became disoriented and gradually lost interest in sexual activity after removal of nerves in their genitals and that the loss of smell had no effect on sexual activity." It was also reported that the "experiments had resulted in significant contributions to veterinary medicine, including the study and testing of remedies for urinary problems such as kidney stones and bladder infections that commonly affect cats and other animals."[51]

Were Aronson's experiments inhumane, sadistic, and cruel?[52] Here it seems as though the evidence is clearly on the side of the researcher. His laboratory and methods of investigation were repeatedly and carefully inspected by various bodies concerned with preserving the credibility of science or upholding standards of humaneness in experimentation and animal care, none of which reported negatively. These included the National Society for Medical Research (NSMR), the National Institutes of Health (NIH) Animal Welfare Office (under the Office for Protection from Research Risks), the Animal Welfare Committee of the American Museum of Natural History, the Animal and Plant Health Inspection Service of the U.S. Department of Agriculture, the Division of Laboratories and Research of the New York State Department of Health, and the ASPCA. Aronson's experiments, according to the NSMR and the museum, were conducted in conformity with humane standards established by the NSMR, the U.S. Department of Health, Education, and Welfare, the U.S. Animal Welfare Act, the American Physiological Society, the American Psychological Association, and the American Humane Association.[53] In the course of all this assessment, William Sadler, head of the population and reproduction branch of NIH, stated after the completion of his agency's inquiry that "a number and variety of allegations were made [against Aronson and his coworkers] without the identification of a single individual who claimed to have observed any wrongdoing."[54] Thus, the massive outcry occasioned by this research project appears to have been out of proportion to the suffering caused to the research animals.

Did Aronson's preoccupation with cats' sexuality have a discernible payoff that would make it ethically defensible? The question is not easy for an independent inquirer to answer, and indeed the picture is less clear than in the two cases previously discussed. Thomas D. Nicholson, director of the museum that employed Aronson, stated in the *New York Daily News* that

> Dr. Aronson's past and present studies of the endocrinological, neurological and psychological factors controlling sexual behavior contribute importantly to the basic knowledge whereby we come to understand and alleviate stressful human problems, such as sexual disorders, impotence, frigidity, infertility and over-population as well as more general problems of nervous disorders and endocrine dysfunctions. His work also contributes to the solution of certain veterinary problems and problems in breeding livestock.[55]

According to the NSMR *Bulletin*, "The experiments hope to clarify the problems of hypo- and hypersexuality that affect humans. . . . Cats are being studied because of the similarities between the brain and nervous system of the cat and humans." The *Bulletin* continues, "Reviews of Dr. Aronson's research have shown his experiments with cats to be relevant to medical research." In addition, the Experimental Psychology Study Section, Division of Research Grants for NIH reviewed the project four times after 1961 and assessed it as having "such scientific merit and worth to warrant continuous funding."[56] In an article in *Science* magazine, Nicholas Wade raised some questions about the actual contribution of the cat experiments to ongoing research in physiology on the basis of the low rate of citations of Aronson's results in the relevant scientific literature. However, he also added that this may have been due to the fact that most experiments on sexuality focus on other species. In any case, Wade noted that "peer review committees [such as NIH's] are composed of the nation's leading experts in the field and it is difficult to second-guess their judgment." [57]

Postscript: Aronson's retirement in August 1977 terminated the cat research. The museum continues to this day with animal experiments, but has abandoned using domesticated species. No further protests, to my knowledge, have been heard from animal protectionists.

STRESS AND HEALTH

The late Hans Selye's experiments on the nature of stress, its causes and effects, and the prevention and treatment of stress-related diseases are world famous. A pioneer in basic biomedical research, Selye wrote some 1,500 articles and thirty books which have been translated into thirty-four languages, making him "the most widely read medical author of our time." [58] Yet the experiments conducted over a period of more than forty years by Selye and his research team at the University of Montreal's Institute of Experimental Medicine and Surgery (which he directed) have been bitterly attacked. Hans Ruesch, for example, contends that among other things, Selye was responsible for tormenting laboratory animals on an unprecedented scale and that the principal fruit of his scientific labor was a concept of stress that is ill defined and hence of little value in the understanding of human health and disease. [59]

Selye's use of animals indeed reached unparalleled proportions. By his own reckoning, in a typical year "we used about 1,400 rats a week for research." [60] Selye was naturally somewhat defensive on the subject of the use and abuse of animal experimental subjects, and in his classic work, *The Stress of Life*, spent some time justifying his research program. In doing so, he claimed that "every effort is made to diminish pain to the absolutely unavoidable minimum" and that "not one of them [i.e., the rats] was exposed to unnecessary pain because of carelessness." [61] It is reassuring to know that Selye's animals were handled by competent staff and were not exposed to extra risks and dangers through ignorance or sloppy procedures. But the larger question remains, namely, the degree of intentionally inflicted suffering considered to be necessary for the success of stress experiments.

It would seem that Selye, if he were still alive, would in all candor have to admit that the suffering caused by his experiments was very considerable, as these were designed to expose the animals' physiological systems to challenges of varying degrees of severity to see how they respond. According to Selye, "stress is the nonspecific response of the body to any demand made upon it" or "the nonspecific (that is, common) result of *any* demand upon the body." [62] Drawing on the fundamental notion that each bodily system acts to maintain its own specific state of equilibrium or homeostasis, he noted that when the balance is upset the organism reacts in certain identifiable ways to restore its normal level of functioning and in addition often faces the requirement to readjust or adapt itself to a new environment or situation. Thus in humans, circumstances as far removed from one another as the death of a spouse and winning a lottery can cause significant levels of stress. To learn about the nature and biological mechanisms of stress, Selye had to duplicate conditions in the laboratory that resemble injuries or traumas to which humans are subject and to create others that would produce measurable demands on the physiological system of experimental animals whose properties as living organisms are well known. This is why it is impossible to avoid the conclusion that Selye over the years caused an enormous amount of suffering in his animal subjects.

Selye produced several massive compendia of various sorts of stress research containing abstracts of experiments performed by those working in this field, and anyone who peruses the entries bearing Selye's name will discover that procedures of the following kinds have been used to induce stress: surgical injuries (such as removal of adrenal, thyroid, pituitary, or other glands or organs); prolonged exposure to cold; starvation for forty-eight hours or more; restraint (sometimes for lengthy periods); forced exercise; inadequate diets; toxic doses of various chemicals and drugs (atropine, morphine, formaldehyde, hormones, corticoids, phenothiazines, histamines); spinal cord transection; skin pinching with a hemostat; and production of quadriplegia. [63] These stressful events have in turn caused gastrointestinal ulcers, ovarian atrophy, cardiac hypertrophy, myocarditis, hypertension, nephrosclerosis, hypoglycemia, acute appendicitis, and not infrequently death.

Once again, however, we must ask what these experiments have achieved. Selye's research has had a far-reaching impact on our whole way of thinking about disease and injury. It has wide applications in cardiology, endocrinology, immunology, surgery, rehabilitative medicine, psychiatry and psychosomatic medicine, gerontology, sports medicine, and many other fields, as well as important implications for our conception of physical fitness and general physical and mental health. Selye is responsible for first articulating the concept of the "general adaptation syndrome" (GAS), a three-phase biological process (alarm reaction, stage of resistance, stage of exhaustion) that is triggered by a wide variety of stressors and has become the cornerstone of subsequent stress research.[64] The biochemical analysis of the GAS, in which Selye was instrumental, constitutes a breakthrough that identified the role of specific agents in the syndrome. He has, for example, distinguished between and studied the effects of "syntoxic" hormones (ACTH, cortisone, cortisol, STH, aldosterone, DOC), which "facilitate coexistence with a pathogen, either by diminishing sensitivity to it or by encapsulating it within a barricade of inflammatory tissue" and "catatoxic" hormones (ethylestrenol, spironolactone, certain cyanosteroids), which "enhance the destruction of potential pathogens, mostly through the induction of poison-metabolizing enzymes in the liver."[65]

Selye has also established that events that cause marked changes—whether beneficial or harmful to the organism or psyche—are stressful and take a certain toll. The organism must use its energy reserves to adapt, readjust, or cope and to restore the equilibrium of its systems. In addition, and perhaps most important, his investigations on animals showed that a certain amount of stress is necessary to prepare an organism to meet the challenge of unexpected and uncontrollable changes and hence to maintain its well-being in the face of adversity. Many experiments have substantiated Selye's belief that animals whose physical systems are toughened by exposure to low-level stressors are much better able to withstand the effects of more intense stressors.[66] Selye has effectively demonstrated in rats that "even the tissue damage induced by prolonged total interruption of the circulation can be prevented by [prior] systemic stress."[67]

Like many other areas of scientific inquiry where animals are used, Selye's stress research has often been confirmed by other investigators in subsequent observations of human responses and performance.[68] In some of his more systematic and technical books, Selye reviewed synoptically the vast literature on stress, painstakingly detailing the process by which bits of evidence, accumulated slowly from research on animals, eventually crystallize into a coherent picture of the mechanisms of disease and resistance.[69] He thereby provided much of the rationale and justification for stress research by illuminating the connection between basic and applied science. Anyone who has doubts about the usefulness of basic research involving animals or who is interested in how scientific knowledge slowly accrues over time should examine some of these writings.

INTERIM CONCLUSIONS

What the foregoing discussion shows, I believe, is that many experiments that appear at first to manifest inhumaneness or cruelty and little else—to be examples of research whose aim is merely to satisfy scientific curiosity at animals' expense—can be seen in quite a different light on closer examination. Though it is perhaps an unfortunate truth, valuable information has frequently come out of experiments that strike the layperson, who usually gives them only passing attention, as the most odious. To decide whether such investigations are morally justifiable in relation to their resulting benefits for humans (or animals) is no easy matter. No simple formula will give us the answer. Indeed we often cannot even attempt to give an answer without considering the larger context of ongoing research of which the experiment is a part and the slowly developing applications of basic biological and behavioral knowledge to the larger questions of human (and animal) life and health. Once we penetrate beyond superficial media reports, antivivisectionist outcries, and skeletal outlines of research procedures published in specialist scientific journals—for example, by listening to scientists explain their work or reading their books and by reading the more accessible science magazines—previously puzzling and jumbled bits of information often fall into place to form a coherent picture, helping us make a more reasoned and cautious evaluation. With this proviso in mind, even the brutalizing experiments of Harlow described earlier may be morally justified (if only in retrospect) by being weighed against their truly enormous range of applications.

Some critics of this kind of research argue that no knowledge, however fruitful, is worth the agony to which the test animals have been subjected, even if the number used is quite small. They would cite the sorts of considerations that arose from the Nuremberg trials, which gave rise to codes of ethics governing human experimentation, and contend that certain procedures are too horrible to inflict on any living, sentient creature, for whatever purpose. This is not the place to discuss experimentation on humans (though I briefly consider the Nuremberg trials and Nazi concentration camp experiments in chapter 5). We may note, however, that those who debate the ethical aspects of experimentation generally agree that one important principle relevant to judging the moral acceptability of a piece of research is that its (actual or potential) benefits must be directly proportional to the amount of suffering it entails. In the case of very stressful experiments, such as Harlow's, the benefits must be considerably in excess of the harm caused. As I indicated earlier, it is not at all clear, whatever our initial reactions might be, that the monkey isolation procedures are unacceptable when viewed in this light.

Scientific research using animals is most often defended by those who conduct it in one or both of two ways: (1) by appeal to the probability that it will have an important bearing on a human (or animal) health problem of significance or (2) on the grounds that the same procedures involving human subjects would be morally unacceptable. The background assumption of the latter is that the experimentation is the only way, if not also the best way, to attain the desired results. In the opinion of some scientists almost any piece of research using animals can be judged permissible on these grounds, though in appealing to (1) the possible application of a piece of research is sometimes acknowledged to be fairly remote. There is, however, far from universal agreement on the acceptability of individual research projects even within the scientific community. Some are turned down by granting agencies on scientific grounds, whereas others are blocked or amended by ethics review committees, usually at the researcher's home institution. Within the granting agencies, "study sections are instructed to consider proposals on their scientific merit alone." But "in practice, study sections do turn down experiments that surpass a certain combination of harshness and triviality." [70]

However, in spite of this screening process, experiments sometimes receive funding that are either lacking in scientific merit or dubious from a humane standpoint, though estimates of their frequency, number, and proportion vary widely. Nor is there agreement among scientists who recognize this problem on the best way of attacking it. (I have more to say about so-called wasteful research and the question of unnecessary or excessive suffering in the next chapter.)

For twelve years Harry Harlow edited one of the leading scholarly publications in his field, the *Journal of Comparative and Physiological Psychology*. On stepping down from this position in 1962, in which he reports "having passed judgment on about 2,500 original manuscripts," Harlow expressed the view that "most experiments are not worth doing and the data obtained not worth publishing."[71] In spite of the somewhat jaded and sardonic tone of this editorial pronouncement, it would probably not be amiss to construe Harlow's words as a warning to his colleagues to clean up their act. More than two decades have passed since then, and during this time better animal welfare legislation has been enacted, procedures for ethics review have been dramatically tightened or introduced where they were previously nonexistent, animals for research have become more expensive (some, such as primates, very restricted in supply as well), and funding has become more competitive. Nevertheless, concerned individuals can readily cite instances of research projects that seem inessential and unwarranted even by the standards of someone (like myself) who subscribes to fairly liberal attitudes toward experimentation.

For instance, consider the area of experiments on learned helplessness in which Martin Seligman did the research described earlier. We may concede that it is important to guarantee that results of the kind found by Seligman and his associates are capable of replication and are generalizable to humans by seeing whether they also hold for species other than dogs. But over how many species must this testing range? Seligman's work has been repeated on mice, rats, cats, chickens, other birds, primates, and even cockroaches and goldfish![72] These experiments have in turn been duplicated by still other observers under varying conditions to see whether the same results can be obtained. Different procedures, including administering psychiatric drugs, have been tested with a view to reversing or alleviating the effects of learned helplessness in animals. In one such experiment, dogs were first rendered helpless by Seligman's method and then subjected to a series of six electroconvulsive shocks (ECS), one every ten to fourteen hours.[73] Their recovery from helplessness was measured by the reappearance of efforts to escape from shocks in the shuttle box apparatus. The dogs' response after ECS was taken as further evidence of the close resemblance between learned helplessness and depression, which when severe in humans is also sometimes treated by ECS (so-called shock treatment). Whether this small additional contribution to knowledge offset the cost in suffering to the animals, however, seems open to question.

Another case in point is an experiment that arose out of Harlow's own social deprivation experiments. In a paper entitled "Effect of Bilateral Frontal Lobectomy on Social Preferences of Rhesus Monkeys," Harlow and his coworkers attempted to determine whether lobectomized monkeys prefer the company of other lobectomized monkeys or of normal ones and which are preferred by normal monkeys.[74] It was learned that there were differences in the social preferences of lobectomized and normal monkeys and the following weighty comment concludes this research report:

> It is obvious that monkeys are quite capable of discriminating among monkeys that look the same to a human observer and, moreover, they apparently have good reasons for making the choices they do. The suggestion is that in some ways monkeys are probably more knowledgeable observers of monkey behavior than are humans—which need not be taken as a blow to an experimenter's pride. After all, they have had a bit more experience than we.[75]

DETERMINING THE SIGNIFICANCE
OF CURRENT RESEARCH

It is relatively easy (at least for someone in the field) to answer questions about the fruitfulness and humaneness of experiments that are in the past and those whose methods and results have become part of the public record. But what about research that is currently under way or has yet to be undertaken? The great majority of experiments performed today are supported by granting agencies that operate in accordance with the dual screening procedures mentioned previously: ethics review at the researcher's home institution (under guidelines stipulated by the granting agency, the government, or some other body) and peer review under the auspices of the funding agency to determine the potential scientific value of the research proposal. Only if the project passes both these stages of assessment can it receive support. Clearly, then, some judgment has to be made in advance about its potential merit, relevance to important human concerns, and the like.

For a layperson to acquire a sense of how ongoing research in a given discipline is likely to pay off in potential dividends at some unspecified future time is no mean task. This is just as true in the sciences as in nonscientific fields of research and scholarship. Yet it is precisely this sort of question to which peer review committees must address themselves and which they must resolve on a routine basis. To try to fill this gap in our understanding of research, and specifically of the role of animals, I offer some examples of research in progress and how it relates to larger concerns. What we find here can also be applied to proposed research.

EXAMPLES OF ANIMAL EXPERIMENTATION (II): CURRENT BIOMEDICAL AND BEHAVIORAL RESEARCH

BIOMEDICAL RESEARCH

While gathering background material for this book, I was given a unique opportunity to observe some aspects of research in progress and to discuss procedures, pertinent moral issues, and potential applications with scientists at Toronto's renowned Hospital for Sick Children. I was briefed on the entire range of research projects being conducted at this center by Dr. Aser Rothstein, director of its Research Institute, and Dr. Carl Grant, a member of the Department of Surgical Research and chairman of the hospital's animal care committee.[76] A wide-ranging research program was outlined, involving animals in experimental work in the areas of embryology and fetal development, surgery, cardiology, immunology, pathology, pharmacology, virology, bacteriology, endocrinology, nutrition, nephrology, and otolaryngology. Among the achievements of this program are the fabrication of a portable artificial pancreas (then in the developmental stage), a spinal pacemaker to correct scoliosis (then in the clinical testing stage), and a special respiratory oscillator, a device that has applications in cases of emphysema, respiratory insufficiency in the elderly, and respiratory distress in infants, where it may replace conventional respirators that can cause lung damage during the prolonged surgery required to correct this condition. Noninvasive (nonsurgical) techniques have also been developed to look at cardiac functioning (replacing catheterization), and progress has been made in the study of ways to improve and accelerate joint healing by mechanically induced slight constant joint movement (rather than the conventional immobilization of joints). The Hospital for Sick Children, finally, is the major center in Canada for pediatric immunology, where animal models have been developed to study immune deficiencies and thymus growth.

As a result of my discussions with these hospital personnel, I selected four projects that seemed on first hearing to be, from the standpoint of humaneness, most clearly in need of ethical scrutiny. I then arranged to interview the researchers engaged in these projects, and on two occasions observed the experimental surgery and other procedures associated with them. I also had an opportunity to see some of the animals during and after recovery. I wish to emphasize that no one tried to give me biased information, nor was I placed under pressure to write this account from any particular slant. I was free to ask anyone any questions I chose to. My account was checked for scientific accuracy but in no way censored by those whose names I mention. A description of the experiments and my observations follow.[77]

Burn Research

The first thing I heard about this hospital's research program was that pigs were used in research relating to the treatment of burns. I was naturally alarmed as it was obvious burns would have to be inflicted on these animals in the course of such experimentation. I easily conjured up images of blowtorches causing hideous burns on hapless immobilized creatures who then lay about groaning in agony. I was not only put off by the idea of this research, to put it mildly, but also quite prepared to find it morally objectionable. However, after talking to Dr. Ronald Zucker, principal investigator in the project, and his coworker, Dr. Grant, I formed quite a different impression.

Zucker, a plastic surgeon skilled in microvascular surgery, explained to me that burns are the most severe injuries that humans can sustain and still survive, particularly in view of the physical problems that often ensue. Immediate problems are loss of blood and other body fluids, consequent weight loss, organ system failures, shock, and infection of exposed surfaces. Subsequent to healing, burn patients may have to contend with immovable joints, physical deformities, and psychological traumas (what Zucker labeled "the gross stigma of being burned"). Children have the best chance of surviving major burn injuries, but are also most severely affected psychologically and functionally.

The main difficulty in treating burns, Zucker stated, is how to replenish missing skin to prevent infection, avoid the complications just mentioned, and enhance the healing process. If a significant amount of the body's surface area is burned, not much of the victim's own skin will be available for grafting, and owing to the rejection phenomenon the skin of other people or animals can be used, if at all, only temporarily. An alternative is to employ a method developed by Grant in which a small patch of the patient's own skin is excised at the time of admission to hospital and expanded under controlled conditions in an incubator.[78] To this end the burn experiments on pigs, of which I had previously heard, were undertaken. (Pigs are used because of the close similarity between their skin and that of humans.)

In these experiments a 5 cm² patch of pigskin is first removed using the same techniques applied to humans for obtaining skin grafts. This tissue is then diced and cultured into several sheets which can later be "autografted" (allowed to grow without stitches) onto burn sites. Under general anesthesia the animals then receive third-degree burns "of uniform depth and distribution"[79] on their backs from a special device consisting of small square brass plates heated to 120° C. It is a well-established fact that third-degree burns are not a source of subsequent pain since nerve endings in the burn area are destroyed. By the time the burn sites were ready to receive grafts, the cultured tissues were large enough to cover them. The procedures used throughout this experiment are the same as those employed in treating burns in humans, including aseptic surgical techniques and the application of saline solution and antibiotics during grafting.

This burn experiment has been described as having "the potential to provide intact coverage for extensively burned patients in the first few weeks." The cultured tissue "is not a cosmetic replacement for normal skin, but it does provide immediate viable coverage for denuded areas at the time when it is most needed for patients with extensive burns."[80] Zucker estimated that using human subjects alone, it would take as much as a decade to develop the same techniques derived in a short period from animal experiments. He also pointed out that it is possible to use the same animal simultaneously to test the relative advantages of the new technique versus the conventional method of skin grafting and as its own control (that is, certain areas can be left to heal on their own, without any grafting), and thus fewer animals are required. This important feature of the experimental situation could not, of course, be realized ethically in human subjects since it requires that treatment known to be inferior be applied) or, conversely, that superior treatment be withheld) for purely investigative reasons.

Auditory Research

In the Otological Research Laboratory, Department of Oto-laryngology, Dr. Ivan Hunter-Duvar familiarized me with his program of basic research, carried out in collaboration with a group at Detroit's Wayne State University and Henry Ford Hospital. The immediate objective of his project is to learn how the inner ear works, a task that sounds simple but is in fact formidable, as it involves attempting to understand the mechanical and neurophysiological aspects of sound reproduction, the reasons for hearing loss (both temporary and permanent), and related matters. The long-range goal of this research is to develop a prosthetic device that can, by means of appropriate electrical stimulation of the auditory nerve fibers, replace "dead" ears. (It is known that stimulation of these fibers can generate the sensation of noise, but as yet no one knows how to do so in such a way as to produce meaningful noise patterns, like recognizable speech.) It was quite clear to me that this goal, although perceived as lying some distance away, was nonetheless in the forefront of Hunter-Duvar's awareness as a practical end, and for this reason it served a very definite heuristic function in his work.

Hunter-Duvar explained why animals were used in his research in the following way. For obvious ethical reasons we cannot get at the inner ear of living humans to perform experiments on it, since hearing would thereby be destroyed. Even though there are many individuals with impaired hearing, testing alone cannot begin to reveal what needs to be known of changes that take place in the microscopic structures of the inner ear as a result of auditory damage. These changes can only be studied by invasive methods.[81] Nor are the ears of recently deceased humans satisfactory as research material because the sensory cells and other structures in them deteriorate rapidly. (Furthermore, of 18,000 sensory cells in the ear, only 50 percent still remain intact by age seventy.) As is usually the case, the use of animals was justified by the potential benefits of the research to humans. This point was underscored when Hunter-Duvar informed me that in North America more compensation is paid to workers for loss of hearing than for any other job-related disability.

Some auditory experiments have involved the exposure of squirrel monkeys for eight hours a day to the common industrial noise that impairs human hearing in certain known ways. The monkeys were then killed and their inner ears examined carefully for signs of structural damage. In Hunter-Duvar's work chinchillas are the subjects of investigation because they possess an auditory range very similar to that of humans. In one series of experiments chinchillas are first taught to respond to pure sound tones by jumping over a bar when the tones are heard.[82] This makes it possible to obtain an audiogram showing normal hearing thresholds for each test animal. The chinchillas are then exposed to a noise level ("traumatic acoustic stimulus") of 120 decibels. Only one ear is damaged in this manner, the other being protected to serve later as a control for histological studies. Some animals are killed directly afterward to observe the immediate effects of damaging noise, and others at intervals up to ten weeks later. Their cochleae are examined by various means including, most recently, the scanning electron miscroscope. The ear damage revealed in photographs taken at several thousand times magnification by this instrument was quite evident to me as a layperson.[83]

When I raised a query about the humaneness of exposing test animals to damaging levels of noise, I had in mind stress experiments I had read about in which animals have been sent into convulsions and have even died as a result of intense noise. Hunter-Duvar replied that the noise level in his experiments was of the sort that humans find stressful and irritating but not painful (such as that produced by hard rock music, milling machines, and the like) and to which they soon become accustomed with prolonged exposure (the reason why hearing loss is so insidious).

Cardiovascular Research

The circulatory system of a human fetus contains a vessel known as the ductus arteriosus, which although vital during prenatal development, normally closes at birth and subsequently becomes a ligament interposed between the pulmonary artery and the aorta. Dr. Flavio Coceani explained to me the work he and Dr. Peter Olley have done at the Hospital for Sick Children's Research Institute and Department of Cardiology in addressing two important kinds of surgical problems related to the ductus.[84]

First, sometimes congenital cardiac malformations, for example pulmonary valve atresia, will prevent the flow of blood from the right side of the heart to the lungs in the newborn infant. In these malformations the only route by which blood reaches the lungs to become oxygenated is via the ductus arteriosus. When the ductus begins to close, soon after birth, these infants become increasingly short of oxygen and unless some effective intervention takes place they will die. In these instances, the surgeon can create an artificial shunt between the pulmonary artery and the aorta to serve in place of the closing ductus arteriosus. A fairly recent discovery is that certain chemical regulators in the body called prostaglandins control muscle tone in the ductus arteriosus. By administering prostaglandins Coceani and Olley have found that the ductus can be kept open after birth to maintain an adequate supply of oxygen to the infant's body until surgery can be performed. This procedure is potentially life saving for many infants who previously would not have survived long enough for heart surgery to become feasible.

Second, the process by which the ductus arteriosus naturally closes may also fail, especially in premature babies. When this occurs the result is an overload on the heart and lungs, frequently complicated by "respiratory distress syndrome." In such cases the need to close the ductus often arises. The standard procedure for accomplishing this is by surgical ligature. However, a medical treatment is obviously preferable to a surgical one, particularly for the newborn. Coceani and Olley have shown that administering indomethacin, a prostaglandin inhibitor, can hasten the closure of the ductus. Though the success rate has not been so great here as in the former procedure, this technique will almost certainly save lives as well.

I had chosen to investigate this experiment because I had doubts about subjecting lambs (the experimental animal of choice here) to traumatic surgery in the name of basic research. Fortunately, I was able to observe the surgical implantation of electrodes designed to encircle the major heart vessels. After the operation was completed, the leads to these electrodes were encased in a harness around the lamb's chest and the animal allowed to recover. Both the surgery and the postoperative care were exemplary from both aseptic and humane viewpoints. Subsequent testing would attempt to determine the precise effects of certain pharmacological agents on the dilation and constriction of the major vessels. Two weeks later, on completion of testing, the lamb would be killed and a postmortem examination conducted. Further animal experiments of a similar sort were planned to discover more precisely the effects of prostaglandins on the cardiac and respiratory systems, refine the techniques described here, test the safety of long-term administration of prostaglandins, and so on. I concluded that this experiment was well justified.

Perinatal Research

Few painful experiments would be more disconcerting to the layperson than those that might be performed upon human fetuses or newborn infants, which are in the nature of things completely at our mercy. We feel inclined therefore also to take an extremely dim view of such experiments using animal subjects. Consequently, I was ambivalent about witnessing an experiment of this kind, but desirous all the same to see for myself and either confirm or correct my own preconceptions.

On two occasions I observed experiments carried out on rhesus monkey fetuses in utero, one of which was followed by a successful cesarean delivery of a fully developed infant. These experiments were conducted by Dr. F. J. Holland of the Research Institute, Hospital for Sick Children, assisted by Dr. David DiBattista, a psychologist associated with the Primate Laboratory at the University of Waterloo.[85] After administering total anesthesia and under sterile operating conditions, Holland performed surgery on the gravid uterus, which he handled gently throughout and continually maintained in a moist state by applications of saline solution. By touch and sight (aided by illumination of the translucent sac in which the fetus is housed), the two placental discs were located and thereby too the interplacental vessels. The purpose of the experiment was to inject into these vessels chemicals known as releasing hormones to determine, by the analysis of fetal blood samples taken from the same sites before and after the procedure, the precise conditions under which the releasing hormones trigger production of other hormones important for growth and development.

The releasing hormones are peptides normally secreted by the hypothalamus. These act on the pituitary gland, which in turn signals the thyroid to release certain hormones. Up to the point at which I observed the project, measurements had been made in the preceding manner of the release of thyrotropin, leutinizing hormone, prolactin, and growth hormone. For each fetus in the experimental sample, the same procedure was repeated at gestational ages of 90, 130, and 160 days (normal term for rhesus monkeys is 164–168 days), the intervals having been accurately calculated from the date of controlled mating. At the final stage, as previously mentioned, cesarean (sterile) delivery was also part of the routine. (On the occasion when I observed this experiment a normal, robust infant was born—the largest DiBattista had ever seen.)

Despite the fact that each pregnant monkey mother was operated on and her fetus tested three times, I could find no reason to object to this experiment. The animals were clearly given the best of care before, during, and after the procedure just described,[86] and the information being sought is plainly valuable and its implications potentially far reaching. Many human infants suffer from congenital abnormalities owing to hormonal deficiencies of one kind or another. With the advent of amniocentesis many of these abnormalities can now be detected before birth and more are being added all the time.[87] The long-term result of this technological advance in genetic screening seems to be that eugenic choice of infants and elective abortion will continue to increase. However, the basic research in which Holland and others[88] are engaged may hold out the promise of a constructive alternative in at least some cases: the chance to correct detectable hormonal deficits during the gestation period itself. For this reason, and because reasonable humane standards were strictly adhered to, the experiment considered here seems wholly acceptable.

BEHAVIORAL RESEARCH

After these investigations I made further observations of research in progress, this time in the area of behavioral science. I interviewed four members of the Department of Psychology, Queen's University at Kingston, whose work, it was suggested by an adviser in their department, raised ethical issues of the sort that commonly stir controversy and also showed considerable promise of yielding information that will contribute to the alleviation of human suffering. These cases were chosen, not because they were the only ones possessing the two ingredients just mentioned, but because they did so most clearly. I describe the three projects in turn, indicating, so far as possible, how they fit into a larger context of ongoing research, so that some reasonable judgment of their potential benefits (as contrasted with their costs in terms of animal suffering) can be arrived at.

Neuroleptic Drugs, Dopamine Production, and Behavior

In the past two to three decades a strong link has been established between the human brain's production of dopamine, a biochemical essential to transmission in some neuronal systems, and Parkinson's disease, schizophrenia, and "attention deficit disorder with hyper-activity" (also called "minimal brain dysfunction"). Before 1960 tens of thousands of patients with Parkinson's disease languished indefi-nitely in the back wards of mental hospitals. However, with the discovery of low levels of dopamine in postmortem examinations of these patients' brains and the formulation of the hypothesis that Parkinson's disease is caused by premature aging of the dopamine-producing system (and therefore underproduction of dopamine), the treatment of this terrible affliction has been revolutionized. It is now possible for Parkinson patients to lead normal or near-normal lives for an extended period, and it is universally recognized that their illness is organic, not mental.[89]

Evidence has also accumulated suggesting a causal connection between dopamine and schizophrenia, a disorder that affects approxi-mately one person in fifty in the general population and the treatment of which I have heard cited as claiming a greater number of hospital beds than that of any other medical problem. Three pieces of evidence are particularly relevant: (1) Antipsychotic drugs (neuro-leptics) all reduce dopamine activity. (2) Stimulant drugs (such as cocaine and amphetamines) also can produce acute psychotic episodes indistinguishable from those of schizophrenics. (3) Postmortem examinations of schizophrenics' brains (using bioassay techniques) confirm the existence of the link. In each case the connection is just the opposite of that found in Parkinson's disease, for in schizophrenia it appears to be the oversensitivity of the brain to dopamine that produces the bizarre symptoms associated with this illness.

It is widely believed that schizophrenics are incapacitated by an excess of stimuli which the neural network of their brains fails to block or filter out. Irrelevant and confusing sensory messages bombard consciousness, with the result that these individuals experience auditory, visual, and other kinds of hallucinations. In addition, thinking becomes disoriented and organized rational activity frequently impossible. To see whether these incapacities can indeed be explained by the presence of an excess of dopamine in the schizophrenic's brain, various researchers have attempted to design an experimental situation in which the effects of altered levels of dopamine can be clearly observed. Such a situation must be relatively simple so that an unambiguous result may be obtained.

Dr. Richard J. Beninger is a psychologist whose background and experimental work are chiefly in the field of psychopharmacology, the study of the effects of drugs on the brain and behavior.

Responding to the challenge just described, Beninger is experimenting on animals (specifically rats) to see if learning or performance deficits can be noted that correspond to the manipulation of the levels of dopamine in their brains. Beninger points out that the brains of rats and human beings are very similar: Both contain the same systems as constituents, as well as the same chemicals, neural connections, and structures. What differentiates the two brains is principally the enlarged cortex found in humans and the overall respective shapes of human and rat brains. Beninger's intention is to design a series of experiments to enable him to chart the precise effects of different dopamine levels on behavior (in particular, on the performance of certain tasks under controlled conditions). Because of the evident similarities between rats' and humans' brains, he believes it is possible to make direct inferences from these experiments about the causal influence different dopamine levels exercise on human behavior.

In one of Beninger's procedures a group of rats was first taught (conditioned) to press a lever to obtain a food pellet. The rats were then divided into two subgroups—one that received injections of pimozide (a dopamine-blocking chemical) and the controls, which received a chemically neutral injection. All rats were then placed in turn in a shuttle box where they were presented with a tone that signaled an imminent electric foot-shock that could be escaped from by running from the side of the box with the electrified grid floor to the other, safe side. It was observed that whereas undrugged rats could learn to avoid shocks by running away before their onset (on hearing the warning tone), drugged rats could not avoid the shock although they succeeded in escaping from it after it had commenced. One final phase completed the experiment. Since the tone had been associated with shock, the two groups of rats could be tested for conditioned suppression of response to the food lever. It was found that when the rats were returned to the original feeding box, the onset of the same warning tone measurably inhibited the rate of response to the food lever of both groups of rats, indicating that although the drugged rats were unable to behave appropriately in the shuttle box when the warning tone was sounded, they had, in spite of appearances to the contrary, formed the association between the tone and an unpleasant consequence. Beninger and his colleagues concluded, "The results of this experiment indicate that neuroleptic-treated animals, although impaired in initiating responses, are not impaired in associative learning." [90]

The experiment's importance was that it yielded the first clear, unequivocal way of stating this point, which had been (and still remains) the source of much contention among researchers in this field. The finding of Beninger and his associates is suggestive because it indicates that disruption of the normal activity of the dopamine-producing system (and of motor activity dependent on its integrity) does not by itself impair cognitive ability. The truth of this is now abundantly evident in the case of Parkinsonian patients and may also be confirmed by further studies of schizophrenics.

When asked in which direction future stages of his research might move, Beninger replied that he would want to experiment with newer, more selective drugs (those that act more specifically on the dopamine system) to determine the actual mechanisms of dopamine-induced changes in the brain. Other goals are to analyze which drugs have side effects less deleterious than those of classical neuroleptics and to develop further experimental models for testing dopamine-blocking chemicals.

Such experiments as Beninger's do not, of course, by themselves lead to a cure for conditions like Parkinsonism or schizophrenia. Very seldom is it the case that one or even several experiments are this global in their effects. But each helps complete just a little bit more of the picture than its predecessors, helps to chip away at the wall of ignorance that separates us from understanding. (Even those experiments that do not bear fruit often help define the area of investigation more accurately, if only in a negative way, by defining the sterile areas. Those that arouse controversy help focus attention and set up a clash of ideas and approaches that may eventually lead to new knowledge of a useful sort.) A few dozen rats have, it is true, been subjected to drugs and noxious stimuli in the form of moderate electric shocks. But the procedures have been carried out with care, the animals handled professionally by accountable personnel, in accordance with reasonable humane standards laid down by a code of ethics prescribed by a responsible institution. More rats will be sacrificed for future experiments in this series. But the importance of this research is difficult to overestimate, if understood in its proper context. Anyone who has either of the diseases under investigation by Beninger and others or is related to or engaged in treating someone so afflicted will, considering the magnitude of human suffering the illnesses cause, find little to object to from an ethical viewpoint.

Methyl Mercury and "Minimata Disease"

A controversial environmental problem in Canada as elsewhere is the discharge into the environment of heavy metals, such as mercury, cadmium, and lead. Mercury has been used in pesticides, slimicides, and fungicides (for preserving flour grains) and is a byproduct of the mining, chloralkali, and pulp and paper industries; it is also released into the atmosphere by the combustion of fossil fuels. Methyl mercury, created when mercury is methylated (turned into an organic compound) by algae and bacteria or directly dumped into waterways, is absorbed by fish through respiration and ingestion. The metal accumulates in greater concentrations along the food chain and can only be released very slowly by the human body. Large amounts of mercury are clearly known to have toxic effects.

Some of Canada's native peoples—in particular the Cree Indians of northwestern Quebec—depend on fishing for sustenance. The waterways in which they have traditionally fished are now polluted by methyl mercury and many who appear to be suffering from "Minimata disease" (a serious and potentially fatal neurological disorder)[91] contend that their affliction is caused by chronic mercury poisoning.

How is it possible to test this claim? Some would say it does not need to be tested; the cause-effect relationship is self-evident, especially if we compare the population eating contaminated fish with populations that do not. To others this inference is at least not obviously valid. Since the result of this disagreement is a three-way political confrontation among government, industry (which has the task of disposing of mercury and the liability for damages it can be shown to have caused), and the Indians who are the complainants, it became essential to conduct detailed studies of the effects of methyl mercury on the central nervous system. Such an investigation would have to determine with precision how this compound affects the organism and to ascertain whether indigenous factors (such as a hereditary predisposition to neurological disease) and components of the diet other than methyl mercury can be ruled out as possible explanations of the Indians' symptoms.

As psychologist Dr. Nelson Freedman indicated to me, to achieve these ends an experimental situation must be created in which the following variables can be measured precisely: the amount of methyl mercury in the diet; how much actually gets carried to the brain; the extent of the damage caused; the exact location of the damage; and resultant behavioral deficits, if any. Freedman points out that because we cannot measure these factors in living human subjects nor deliberately poison people in a controlled way and then kill them and examine their brains to find out what needs to be known, animal experiments are crucial. Therefore, a colleague, Dr. Ron Weisman, and he have undertaken research on pigeons and studied the effects of methyl mercury on the birds' physical organism as well as on their complex learning and memory. Learning and memory are among the most involved functions in animals and humans and therefore those in which deficits in performance are seen earliest. For this reason behavioral studies of the kind described here have special relevance to humans, in whom the same functions are subject to comparable disturbances under the influence of toxic substances. Weisman and Freedman have found that exposure in brief bouts to high levels of methyl mercury can cause behavioral deficits even before neurological damage is evident. These prepathological disturbances indicate interference with the function of the brain when destruction of brain tissue has not yet occurred. However, they also discovered that high dosages of methyl mercury do not have as potent an effect if there has been earlier exposure to lower levels.

Throughout this experiment methyl mercury was administered in amounts smaller than or equal to those which humans might ordinarily consume in a particular environment. The appropriate actual amounts were determined in proportion to the pigeons' total diet and their normal feeding pattern. The birds were then given a minimum dose of the poisonous substance in bouts followed by a "clearing time" of 30–40 days (to mimic the conditions of human exposure to methyl mercury), and small variations in behavior were observed. Because the experiment was a minimum dose study, gross disturbances could not be expected and only a trained observer could tell that anything was wrong with the birds.

Freedman indicates cautiously that although mercury-induced neurological damage can be produced under laboratory conditions, we cannot necessarily infer from this fact that the same causal mechanisms are at work in the human environment. In other words, mercury poisoning may be a compound problem, a case in which two or more sources jointly cause something and no single factor can be blamed. This point is particularly pertinent in view of the fact that the symptoms of Minimata disease are also associated with other conditions: Tremor, incoordination, and abnormal eye movements have been linked with alcohol and caffeine consumption; sensory loss and abnormal reflexes with thiamine and other nutritional deficiencies and with diabetes.[92] Freedman expressed the hope that his project may offer a greater understanding of the hazards posed by mercury pollution of the environment.

Freedman noted that his attitude to experimentation is that the investigator should always consider whether an alternative procedure is available that might reduce or eliminate stress and discomfort to the animals concerned. He holds also that when there is no alternative, animals should be allowed to suffer only so long as is absolutely necessary for the purpose of the experiment. Thus in the pigeon experiment, a bird showing signs that it was disinterested in eating or was experiencing serious discomfort from its symptoms would be humanely killed.

These candid comments placed the methyl mercury experiment in a different perspective for me, since I had reservations about the morality of what I had envisioned as the slow poisoning of birds followed by the observation of a writhing death agony. Though I did not have the opportunity to see the animals themselves, as in many of the other experiments I have described (the six intoxicated and six controls that were used had already been killed for post-mortem examination), I felt reassured that they had been treated humanely, that the minimum dose approach avoided causing unnecessary suffering. Furthermore, considering the scope of the problem of environmental contamination by heavy metals—which is more widespread than the case of the Cree Indians reported here and other sporadic epidemics of Minimata disease would indicate—the research of Weisman and Freedman seems clearly warranted.

Strabismus, Visual Behavior, and the Brain

Strabismus is a condition in which the eyes cannot be made to focus simultaneously on the same spot. An individual who has this deficit may, in common parlance, be either "cross-eyed" (convergent strabismus) or "wall-eyed" (divergent strabismus). He may also be amblyopic; that is, his eyes may be in part functionally disconnected from the central nervous system. Strabismus and related eye abnormalities affect 5 to 8 percent of the human population. Intermittent strabismus (caused by eyestrain, difficult visual tasks, fatigue, and so on) is believed to be present in 20 to 25 percent of the population. Strabismus is thus a significant health problem.

Dr. Michael von Grünau has conducted experiments in physiological and behavioral psychology to investigate the relationship between strabismus and changes in the brain and nervous system. The cat was chosen for this research because of its easy availability and the close structural similarity between its brain and that of humans. Though strabismus does occur naturally in cats, there are not enough cases to furnish sufficient subjects for experimental use. Therefore, von Grünau has used various procedures to induce strabismus in cats, including surgical cutting of the eye muscles. His early investigations showed that strabismus is correlated with altered neuronal activity, which can be inferred from measurements obtained by means of electrodes surgically implanted in the cats' brains. (This procedure, if properly performed, is painless.)[93]

More recent research has been designed to gain a better understanding of normal binocular vision and the changes that differentiate it from strabismic vision. Von Grünau has studied how cats orient their eyes to the direction and movement of a visual stimulus. Some present procedures are noninvasive; that is, the visual input received by each eye is carefully controlled to produce strabismic vision by external optical means rather than by surgery. For example, kittens born and reared in the laboratory may be allowed visual experience only during periods when they are wearing specially designed goggles with prisms appropriately oriented to create a double image and otherwise confined to darkness. (Eye muscle development is not affected by this device, but the visual effect on performance is the same as with eye muscle surgery.) After several weeks' conditioning, behavioral experiments are conducted in which the strabismic animals (and a normal control group) learn to discriminate between visual patterns. The performance of one eye may be tested against that of the other, and such phenomena as visual acuity and localization response may be measured quantitatively with high accuracy. The cats' behavioral mistakes (inappropriate responses to visual stimuli) may then be related to eye movements and to electrical measurements of neuronal activity in individual brain cells.

Visual experience and the behavior associated with it depend both on the development of inborn capacities and on complex interactions with the environment. Some of the questions von Grünau hopes to shed light on are whether and how the cerebral cortex controls eye movements; whether normal eye movement is necessary for proper cortical development; whether there are crucial periods for correcting defects of vision and what kind of treatment or manipulations might be used to this end. To study the latter, he plans to experiment with eye patching, motor (muscle) exercise, intermittent patching with motor exercise, and the use of frosted lenses to see which gives the best results for different conditions. Another objective is to discover what type of environment to design for correcting visual deficits during the plastic period of visual development. In sum, the general question von Grünau hopes to help answer is how strongly strabismus and related conditions are eye-movement dependent and what additional factors may be involved.

Von Grünau's strabismus research appears at first to raise ethical problems as cats are subjected to procedures that, we assume, would severely disorient humans under the same circumstances, and we naturally suppose that the animals suffer, perhaps excessively relative to the objective sought. I asked von Grünau about this, and he said that just as in human experiments in which the retinal image is systematically inverted for a sustained period of time, animals rapidly become accustomed to their altered vision and behave in ways indicating that they experience little or no discomfort—they eat normally, have no trouble finding food, do not run into stationary objects, pay no attention to their goggles, and so on. Cats on which surgery is performed receive long-lasting anesthesia which, combined with typically faster recovery, makes postoperative analgesics less imperative than in human surgery. As has been noted already, the implantation of electrodes in the brain is not a painful surgical procedure, nor is the recording of impulses during experimentation a cause of suffering.

Two other items of some importance arose from the discussion of this experiment. One is that to ensure that inferences about humans could be made from his research, von Grünau selected a species of animal in which strabismus occurs naturally. The naturally strabismic cats can then be compared with the cats in which strabismus has been induced, and in this way the value (applicability) of the cat model of the disorder can be established and inferences about humans well founded. The other is that, as von Grünau pointed out, a very peripheral system of the brain is being studied in his research project, one that has the same neuronal elements and properties as are found in the corresponding human system. For this reason we can say with confidence that observing the basic properties of the visual information-processing system in cats gives us fundamental insights into the functioning of the human brain.

A final observation on the value of this kind of research may be appropriate. Sir William Paton, a distinguished British scientist, wrote in defense of similar experiments that "the work has already improved the handling of operations on the eye in children. More deeply, the work illuminates the critical adaptive changes going on in early life, and are [sic] important more generally, and relevant to education and development. The experiments cannot be done unless the kittens are healthy and cooperative since they involve behavioural tests."[94]

The Perception of Visual Motion

A distinction is often drawn between basic and applied research in science (though as we shall see in chapter 5, there are good reasons for questioning the validity of this dichotomy). Critics of animal research are always quick to seize on the distinction and to isolate basic, or "pure," research as a target for abuse. Thus basic research, aimed at understanding how processes in living organisms work, has frequently been branded as satisfying mere curiosity at the expense of animal suffering and therefore as trivial, pointless, or redundant. Applied research, however, since it is "mission oriented," or directed by the desire to solve some specific health or technological problem, is looked on much more favorably. There is no cause that can raise funds more easily than the search for a cure for cancer, heart disease, or muscular dystrophy. But it is impossible to have applied research without basic research; much of what goes on under the general rubric of, say, cancer research *is* basic research; and the boundary between basic and applied research is very hazy. These facts, however, are often lost on the critics of animal experimentation.

Dr. Barrie Frost is a physiological psychologist engaged in studying visual mechanisms in the pigeon. Why?—generally, to learn more about how certain parts of their brains work and perhaps to illuminate similar processes in humans. Specifically, Frost's project is an endeavor to understand the detection of visual motion, which in nature "has immense survival value for predator and prey alike."[95] Frost observes that

> in real life a visual stimulus seldom occurs in isolation but instead usually appears in the context of images of surrounding objects. A considerable number of human and animal perceptual and psychophysical studies have shown that these contextual relationships can exert powerful influences on the appearances of size, brightness, hue, orientation, and motion characteristics of visual stimulus patterns. Experiments

on motion perception in particular have suggested that movement of one stimulus pattern relative to another pattern (either stationary or moving) is the prime determinant of perceived motion rather than the absolute motion characteristics in the retinal image.[96]

To investigate the perception of visual motion, Frost has spent considerable time studying "directionally specific neurons" (nerve cells that detect motion) in the optic tectum of the pigeon brain.

I observed one complete trial in an experiment that is part of an ongoing series, and describe it briefly here. A pigeon was anesthetized deeply by injection, tested for reflex responses to make sure it was totally insensate, and then carefully placed in a stereotaxic apparatus—a precision-made immobilizing device in which the bird's body is supported while its head is aligned exactly along certain axes and then fixed in position. A supervised research assistant then gently made an incision in the skin and membrane covering the skull and pulled them back to expose an area of the skull. A tweezerlike instrument was used to pick a small hole through the skull (which is filled with tiny air pockets for lightness and strength). When the brain was reached and certain preparations made, the experiment began. (During the entire several-hour trial, the pigeon showed no signs of pain or any other conscious sensation, and its brain was constantly kept moist with sterile saline solution.)

A previously prepared microelectrode, made from a thin glass rod in which a very fine tungsten needle had been embedded, was inserted gradually into the optic tectum. This electrode was advanced and retracted by a "stepping motorized hydraulic microdrive system with digital readout,"[97] a very precise electrical instrument which, when activated by a switch, sends liquid through a tube attached to the implanted electrode, altering the depth of the needle's penetration by extremely small amounts (measured in microns). The exact position of the needle electrode at any given moment appears on a digital display mounted on the wall. In this manner electrical activity in a variety of adjacent brain cells (neurons) can be recorded.

While the electrode is implanted, different visual stimuli are presented to the pigeon. (Even though deeply unconscious, cells in the eye and many of the visual areas of the brain are still active and capable of registering visual input.) These consist of patterns juxtaposed against a different background, either or both of which may be put into motion by the experimenter in phase with each other (synchronously) or moving in opposite directions (asynchronously). The differences in neural activity levels when various sorts of stimuli are presented can be transmitted from the microelectrodes to an oscilloscope and computer and graphically represented on paper.

Frost's physiological work on pigeons is almost a paradigm of what many antivivisectionists and animal welfarists take strong exception to: what they perceive as using animals as mere machines, or investigating their purely machinelike properties. They see scientific interest directed not to animals as functioning wholes but only to small parts that perform equally well in the absence of the normal condition in which the animals show their natural species characteristics. They would also object to the stereotaxic device, which has been portrayed by critics (and indeed pictured numerous times in the media) as some kind of hideous torture apparatus.

Now no scientist would pretend that minute levels of electrical activity in a few brain cells are all an animal reduces to—or, for that matter, all that animal vision reduces to. (Indeed, Frost has published purely behavioral studies that corroborate his physiological findings; and other projects of his, such as the development of artificial ears for the deaf, clearly constitute applied research.) However, inasmuch as knowledge of the part contributes immeasurably to knowledge of the whole, investigations of this kind have a rationale and a justification. Certain questions can only be answered at the micro level; the issue, then, is only whether answers to such questions should be sought. Although a researcher may not be viewing an animal holistically because of the orientation he or she adopts in a particular experiment, the animal as a functioning totality is taken for granted; indeed, the results would hardly make sense otherwise, since what is being investigated is the way in which a physiological subsystem guides the entire organism. As for the stereotaxic device, it need only be pointed out again that animals so immobilized are fully aesthetized or unconscious and that the pigeons in Frost's experiment are in any case never allowed to regain consciousness (they are killed by another injection at its termination). No cruelty, callousness, or indifference was observed in the handling of these animals or in attitudes toward them (quite the contrary); nor is there any reason to believe that either the procedure itself or the equipment used fosters inhumaneness.

CONCLUSION

In this chapter I have considered several examples of research using animals and tried to place each in some meaningful scientific and ethical perspective. It is doubtless true that in the biomedical and behavioral sciences there is a constant risk of animal abuse, against which great vigilance is required. The extent and frequency of abuse is bound to be much debated, especially since judgments on this matter depend on our general ethical position concerning animals, our knowledge of scientific procedures, and our assessment of the relative benefits and harms of which animal experimentation is the source.

When are the limits reached? When does an experiment reach a level of pain or suffering so that it becomes unacceptable on humane grounds? These questions are explored further in chapter 6. The problem, however, is that critics of experimentation often seem to desire a simple formula for answering these and similar queries; but the situations in which the questions arise unfortunately give us no general rules for arriving at definitive judgments. Take the case of Harlow's social isolation experiments with monkeys, discussed earlier. These experiments shock and even revolt many of us; and yet they have yielded wide-ranging benefits in terms of knowledge and insight into human relations, development, and behavioral maladjustments. Sometimes our natural feelings of shock and revulsion spring from sensibilities to which we should pay heed. But they are not infallible guides, and we should always be on guard against the sway of unreflective emotion. (Photographs of aborted fetuses, for example, may raise but do not settle the issue of the morality of abortion, however negative our reaction to them might be.) Has Harlow's work revolutionized the world or made it a better place in which to live? Probably not, though this sort of question is overgeneralized to the extent that we cannot be sure how to respond. Nevertheless, the results of his work are quite tangible and, in the opinion of many experts, of great importance and value. To require that any experiment or experiments be justified only in terms of a profound impact on civilization as a whole is to put forward a demand that is impossible to fulfill and hence inherently unreasonable. It betrays a serious lack of understanding about the nature of scientific research itself.

The experiments I have personally observed and described here are more typical of what actually goes on today in biomedical and behavioral research. As I have argued, it is very difficult to fault them on the grounds of either pointlessness or cruelty when once we appreciate the context in which they occur. In every field or profession we can find examples of abuse of codes of morally accepted conduct, work that is of substandard quality, and people who take advantage of the system. This is no less true in laboratory animal science. There will always be the odd case in which even an eminent researcher is found guilty of mistreating experimental animals.[98] But such incidents are anomalous. Indeed, it seems entirely plausible to suppose that research scientists, whose training is rigorous, whose work has to conform to exacting standards, and whose findings must stand up to the constant public scrutiny of their peers (at conferences, in journals, in grant applications, and so on), are considerably less likely than most other professionals to be able to get away with carelessness or unethical behavior.

In the absence of much better arguments and examples than have been offered thus far by the opponents of research, we may conclude that scientific procedures using animals are in general ethically acceptable and conducted in accordance with reasonable standards of humaneness. In chapter 5 I clarify further some of the requirements of scientific inquiry to extend our understanding of laboratory animal research and to lend further support to these conclusions.

5

Some Observations on Scientific Inquiry and Related Matters

INTRODUCTION

Discussions by nonscientists of the ethics of animal use in experimentation generally reveal an inadequate understanding of science and the requirements by which the results of research can be judged to be genuine and significant contributions to knowledge. In chapter 4 some of these requirements have been indicated, particularly in relation to the description and justification of selected ongoing research projects. To obtain a more complete picture, however, it is necessary to correct certain misapprehensions about animal experimentation and to clarify some important principles of scientific inquiry. In this chapter I examine four main considerations especially relevant to animal experimentation: (1) the probability of success in scientific ventures; (2) the need to manipulate variables under controlled experimental conditions; (3) the requirement that scientific experiments be repeatable; and (4) the notion of the statistical significance of experimental results. In addition, I give some attention to what may be called the politics of funding research and finally to the widespread tendency among critics of animal-based research to equate or draw comparisons between laboratories where biomedical and behavioral experiments are carried out on animals and Nazi concentration camps where hideous medical experiments were performed on humans.

THE PROBABILITY OF SUCCESS IN SCIENTIFIC
VENTURES: BASIC VERSUS APPLIED RESEARCH

As I have already noted, antivivisectionists and animal welfarists often denounce experiments that cause animals to suffer as "pointless," "worthless," "trivial," motivated by "mere idle curiosity," and so on. The trouble with these charges, however—even if sometimes accurate—is that they totally fail to take account of the fact that we cannot always predict with confidence whether a given experiment or experimental approach will lead to a result of lasting significance, much less to a breakthrough of colossal importance to humanity. This is, of course, no less true in the physical sciences than in the biomedical or behavioral sciences, and the history of science is littered with the remains of wrongheaded (but often ingenious) experiments and incorrect hypotheses that seemed at the time to their inventors and others to have been adequately confirmed by observation. There have also been many discoveries that initially appeared (and perhaps appear even now) to have no practical applications. It is easy enough to judge something as useless or wrong with the benefit of hindsight—the same gift that makes everybody an invincible general after the battle or a brilliant postgame quarterback. What cannot so easily be done is to foretell when and where some crucial advance in our understanding of nature will occur. Experiments that seemed very modest in their objectives have led to results whose importance extends far beyond even the wildest expectations of the scientists conducting them. Time and again researchers have stumbled upon important discoveries, crucial in their benefits to humanity as it later turns out, without themselves realizing it then or perhaps even during their lifetimes.

A number of impressive examples of serendipitous scientific inquiry have been collected by Julius H. Comroe, Jr., a medical educator and researcher who has served for many years as director of the University of California's Cardiovascular Research Institute in San Francisco. In his book *Retrospectroscope: Insights into Medical Discovery*,[1] Comroe shows not only that many important discoveries were accidentally made by people investigating something other than what they eventually found but also how the significance of what is discovered is often overlooked at first and how discoveries sometimes have valuable applications and benefits that are quite far removed from those that were envisaged (if in fact any were envisaged at all).

Comroe and Robert Dripps, with the assistance of consultants, studied "the ten most important clinical advances in cardiovascular-pulmonary medicine and surgery" between 1945 and 1975. Out of 4,000 scientific publications they selected 529 "key articles" ("a key article was defined as one that had an important effect on the direction of subsequent research and development, which in turn proved to be important for one of the ten clinical advances"). Comroe notes, "Our analysis showed that 217 of the 529 key articles (41 percent) reported work that, at the time it was done, had no relation whatever to the disease that it later helped to prevent, diagnose, treat, or alleviate."[2] Numerous classical examples also bear out this finding. The French physiologist Claude Bernard has been credited with performing the first cardiac catheterization in animals. Comroe writes,

> Bernard wanted to settle a then-controversial matter: Was animal heat produced in the lungs by the chemical reactions involving exchange of O_2 and CO_2 (as Lavoisier maintained) or was it produced by combustion occurring in all tissues of the body (as Magnus maintained)? Bernard decided to learn whether the temperature of left ventricular blood (that had just passed through the lungs) was greater than that of right ventricular blood. In 1844, he passed a long mercury thermometer down a carotid artery of a horse into its left ventricle and one down the jugular vein into the right ventricle and settled the matter in favor of Magnus. In 1847, Bernard passed a glass tube through the right jugular vein of a dog and measured right ventricular pressure.[3]

As Comroe goes on to remark, "None of this [from Bernard to early twentieth-century investigators] . . . was clinically oriented; it was all done to solve basic physiologic problems." Another case Comroe cites is that of the first direct measurement of arterial blood pressure, which was

> made in 1733 by an English clergyman, Stephen Hales. He used a 9-foot-long glass tube attached by a brass connection to a flexible windpipe of a goose and measured blood pressure in the femoral and carotid arteries of horses. Why did he do it? . . . In brief, Hales was curious about nature. [He had previously measured the sap pressure in trees.][4]

As an instance of missed opportunities and delayed application of basic research the history of anesthesia is instructive:

Laughing gas parties were common in the early 1800s and Humphry Davy, who repeatedly inhaled nitrous oxide in his experiments of 1799, even suggested its use as a general anaesthetic agent. But no one deliberately gave it to prevent pain until 1844. . . .

Michael Faraday suggested in 1818 that ether be used to prevent surgical pain, and ether jags were a common form of social entertainment in the 1830s and 1840s; but no one gave it deliberately to prevent surgical pain until 1842.[5]

Case studies of the sort written up by Comroe reveal that science can progress only if considerable encouragement and support is given to basic or "curiosity-oriented" research. Only in this way will there be a fund of ideas and information for subsequent researchers to draw on. Without such a pool of contributions, the dramatic breakthroughs would become impossible and science itself would atrophy.[6]

In contrast to the serendipitous successes of which Comroe speaks, it also frequently happens that experiments that looked initially as if they would yield great benefits have been dashed to ruins by subsequent research. Such, for instance, was the fate not too many years ago of the niacin therapy proposed as a cure for schizophrenia and the vitamin C treatment for the common cold. For every breakthrough or significant piece of scientific knowledge acquired, the price to the scientific community as a whole is months or years of relatively fruitless search, determined effort, trial and error, and redoubled persistence. This is the dialectical nature of the advance of human knowledge, governed as it is by the inherent limitations of our capacities, and there is no reason to expect that it will ever be otherwise. As Mahlon B. Hoagland, a distinguished American biochemist, has observed,

By far the greater number of experiments scientists do are failures. We learn from our failures, and design better experiments that may eventually give us a new insight. . . . Most ideas are wrong, and one is very lucky to have a few good ones in a lifetime.[7]

The question whether the desire simply to understand something or to comprehend how something functions is enough to justify a person's engaging in a certain kind of inquiry, and even to receive money for so doing, can be raised throughout the entire range of human disciplines. What, for example, is the value of doing philosophy or of studying history, the classics, and literature? How worthwhile is it to inquire into the origin of the universe or of our own species? Of what use is it to know why bees dance or trees change color in the fall? Perhaps these questions have no other answer than that human beings perennially ask Why? of anything and everything.

We are accustomed to thinking that value questions about human endeavors are difficult to answer when nonpractical disciplines are under consideration and self-evidently answerable when practical activities such as engineering, technology, or business are being discussed. But it is valuable to know how to build a bridge from A to B, to send a payload of a certain size into outer space, or to maximize profits in a given sector of the economy only if we have good reasons for wanting to do these things; yet our reasons may be no better or stronger than the reasons we have for wanting to know about prehistory, the wisdom of ancient Greece, or the world as seen through the eyes of Dostoyevsky. The latter sorts of knowledge may tell us just as much about ourselves—who we are and where we are going—as the former, and hence may prove equally valuable in the long run. In a way, they are like basic research, which may have remote and subtle applications and a kind of practical significance that was not initially apparent.

To return to science for a moment, it is worth noting one of the most fascinating examples in Comroe's *Retrospectroscope*, that of John Tyndall, a nineteenth-century British physicist, who became pre-occupied with the apparently useless question of what makes the sky blue. In a brief account of his research, Comroe shows how Tyndall's experiments designed to answer this question (which he did) also provided "(1) the final blow to the theory of [the] spontaneous generation [of germs], (2) proof of the defense mechanisms of the airways against inhaled particles, (3) quantitative tests of air pollution and of clearance of particles from inspired air, and (4) the first observations of the antibacterial action of *Penicillium*."[8]

This brings us to the crux of the matter, that basic research is not really goalless at all,[9] unless we arbitrarily choose to designate knowledge and understanding as valuable only when they have immediately foreseeable practical benefits. If we do so, however, much of what has always passed for worthwhile human endeavor—in the arts, the humanities, letters, and science itself—must be relegated to the trashbin of idle and useless activity.

I have so far deliberately left out of account the view that the search for knowledge and understanding does not need any justification, that the domain of pure inquiry is self-justifying, or that knowledge is an end in itself. Many would reject this view of knowledge for knowledge's sake, though probably an equal number have defended it, a few even to their deaths. Still, most of us would probably want to draw the line where absolutely undisciplined curiosity or unfocused inquiry is responsible for the sufferings of sentient beings. But most research reviewed unfavorably by the critics of animal experimentation is not of this sort. Indeed, it is only by concentrating on the minority of manifestly pointless or un-redeemably cruel experiments and making them appear to be typical that a wholesale condemnation of laboratory animal science can gain plausibility.[10]

THE NEED TO MANIPULATE VARIABLES UNDER CONTROLLED EXPERIMENTAL CONDITIONS

There is no doubt that much can be learned about health and disease from simple observation and recording of organisms' natural and spontaneous responses to their environment, whether those responses are normal or pathological. But a point is often reached in scientific inquiry at which progress can only be made by ceasing merely to observe objects in their natural setting and bringing them into the laboratory. The great advances brought about by the natural sciences over the past three centuries have been products of the refinement of methodology and the standardization of procedures for obtaining reliable data under controlled experimental conditions. It may be entertaining to think of Newton lounging under an apple tree and receiving inspiration from the blow delivered to his head by an overripe fruit. But this apocryphal episode yields a misleading picture of science, which on a day-to-day basis is the painstaking accumulation of bits of information gleaned from innumerable, more or less intelligently contrived experiments. Likewise, medical science and psychology can learn only so much from observing humans and animals catch-as-catch-can in natural or clinical settings and from studying cadavers. Where do we go from there? The answer must be: to controlled experiments performed under standardized conditions in the laboratory. Now some of these experiments can be done on human subjects; but most people would agree that if much pain or serious risks to health or life are involved, it is better to experiment on animals than on humans. Hence, animal experiments are the only scientifically and ethically acceptable choice in many instances. Because of the sorts of problems posed by the use of alternatives (see chapter 6), animal experiments are often also the best choice.

The chief reason why scientific advance relies so heavily on controlled and well-designed experiments is that in the natural world there are potentially (and often actually) so wide a variety of factors affecting a given process or result that it can be enormously difficult to ascertain which are crucial and which not (recall the methyl mercury experiment recounted in chapter 4). In other words, there are many variables, and to find out which play a significant role in producing the phenomenon under investigation and which do not, the only conceivable way to proceed, given a finite amount of time, is to isolate and control the variables one by one, so far as this is possible. Further, the essence of scientific proof is being able to demonstrate which variable or group of variables is the operative factor in producing the state of affairs we seek to understand and explain. These objectives can be achieved solely under experimental conditions in which natural situations can be reproduced on a smaller or simpler scale, simulated, or modeled. To discover whether a particular substance in the diet is carcinogenic, for example, we must compare subjects that have it in their diet with those that do not and compare cancer rates in sample groupings of roughly equal size from each class. If no natural human communities can be found that afford a meaningful comparison, then a laboratory population of animals can be used. Animals are generally used in such cases because (a) the amount of the substance in the human diet may vary considerably from individual to individual and (b) it cannot be assumed that other dietary factors (which are not easy to control) are irrelevant to the outcome of the investigation. Similarly, to learn the function of a particular endocrine secretion, we may compare a group of animals in which it has been inhibited or eliminated surgically with a control group of otherwise identical animals and note the results after a measured period of time.

These are very elementary, almost schematic examples, to be sure, but they are intended to illustrate that reliable, scientifically acceptable results are a function of researchers' ability to manipulate a carefully designed, controlled situation in which extraneous influences have been minimized or excluded. The more and better this is done, the greater the degree of confidence we may have in the results.

Some animal rights advocates are concerned about the virtually universal tendency among experimenters (especially behavioral psychologists) to refer to their animal subjects as "models." The critics' worry, apparently, is that speaking of animals in this way will reinforce an attitude toward them in which they are seen as mere means to an end rather than as living, sentient, sensitive beings. This problem is addressed in chapter 6; for the moment, however, simply note that although an animal cannot be thought of as a model in the direct, literal sense in which a miniature aircraft mock-up in a wind tunnel can be, there is an important reason for using this term. Animals are not exact copies of humans, nor even copies in all important respects. But they are in significant ways surprisingly closely related to us (as we saw in chapter 2). In addition, they are generally less complex (for example, neurophysiologically) and the functioning of their organisms is better understood. Therefore, animal systems, although not necessarily identical with those of humans, are quite similar and may, under certain special circumstances, be taken as analogues or models for the purposes of research. There are, of course, instances in which there is virtually no difference at all. A nerve cell has the same structure and function in the human brain and in the brains of a wide variety of other species, and anyone who contends that it is inappropriate to speak here of an animal model of a human system is simply out of touch with the facts. (See also chapter 4, the section on strabismus, visual behavior, and the brain.)

THE REQUIREMENT THAT SCIENTIFIC EXPERIMENTS BE REPEATABLE

Opponents of research involving animals sometimes object to what they perceive as redundant and therefore pointless experiments. Now there are undoubtedly cases in which researcher Y replicates the procedures of researcher X without being aware that he has done so and when further confirmation of X's findings is scientifically unnecessary. Here it would be appropriate to state that Y has added nothing new to our fund of knowledge and that if the animals he used in his experiment suffered, they did so needlessly. It might even be pertinent to remark that Y should have done his homework more carefully before beginning, to discover whether someone else had already performed the same experiment and what had been learned from it. The exponential growth of scientific research in all fields over the past few decades makes it almost inevitable that replications of this sort will occasionally occur, even with frequent conferences, monthly research indices, and computerized bibliographies at everyone's disposal as vehicles for monitoring the latest developments in each area of specialization. But it is erroneous to suppose that this situation is commonplace. Most university and other institutionally based research (including that using animals) is supported by grants from outside agencies. For a researcher's grant application to be successful in open competition, he or she must demonstrate to the satisfaction of a peer group (those who have expert knowledge in the same field) that the proposed program of investigation is original and will likely contribute to the advancement of knowledge in some significant way. It is not sufficient that an investigator simply call him- or herself a researcher, have professional certification, a notable reputation, or even be a previous grant recipient.

There are, of course, situations in which a scientist knowingly replicates experimental work done earlier by him- or herself or by others to see if the results obtained previously are valid. This might be especially likely where a controversial conclusion has been drawn from the earlier research (where it goes against the conventional wisdom in the field) or where the previous effort failed to yield an unequivocal result. Thus it would be justifiable to repeat the same experiment, *under exactly the same conditions* described by the original investigator, to determine whether correspondingly uniform conclusions (or less equivocal conclusions) can be drawn. Only if experimental results are shown to be repeatable can an item of scientific knowledge be established; confirmation by independent researchers is the acid test of an experiment's validity. To cite Hoagland again,

> Scientists must repeat their experiments in different ways to be sure there is no possibility of error. They will seek out colleagues and ask them to find flaws in their ideas and experiments; they will attend scientific meetings and present their findings to audiences of critical colleagues. And finally they will publish their work in sufficient detail so that the international scientific community can learn about and repeat the work. Most scientific discoveries become widely accepted as truth only after the experiments have been confirmed by several scientists. Only then does the meaning our ideas give to observations become truth.[11]

This essential feature of the scientific method represents one of the hallmarks of a genuine science as opposed to a pseudoscience like astrology. It also differentiates science from a legitimate field of inquiry like parapsychology, which is in a prescientific phase of development owing to the lack of repeatable results.

An experimenter might, in addition, want to duplicate a previous study under slightly varied conditions to see how far, if at all, the results formerly obtained can be extended and hence to increase their generality. This is quite an important function of research that is oriented toward eventual applications to humans. Inferences from lower animals to human beings often must be legitimized by showing that the phenomenon we seek to understand can be found and explained according to a uniform set of principles across a diverse range of species. Given this understanding, it is curious that those who question the wisdom of making inferences from animal research to humans are often the same individuals who protest most loudly about the alleged redundancy of such experiments.

STATISTICAL SIGNIFICANCE OF RESULTS OBTAINED FROM EXPERIMENTS

Statistical significance is an important criterion for well-established results in scientific inquiry. As science has progressed, and in particular as it has begun to explore the realm of subatomic particles and to probe the causes of human behavior, new methods have had to be invented for analyzing data and extracting conclusions from them. D. H. Smyth has remarked that "biological observations and measurements never have the same consistency and reproducibility as physical measurements, and this is something the biomedical scientist has to live with. In fact, the science of statistics started in order to cope with the problem of variability in biological measurement."[12]

Classical physics was able to operate within the domain of universalizable principles and laws, such as Newton's three laws of motion, Kepler's laws of planetary motion, and the three laws of thermodynamics. Generally speaking, if all the factors governing the occurrence of a given phenomenon are known, then an exceptionless (universal) law can be formulated, to the effect that whenever all these conditions are present the phenomenon will occur. For example, all gases when heated expand. To apply this simple law, all we need to know is whether the substance before us is (has the properties of) a gas. If we then heat it, we need only observe the result. The same holds true of other such laws: All metals are conductors; acids and bases neutralize each other; and so on. Of course, nature is not everywhere so uniform that exceptionless laws can be stated, even where biological systems are not the objects of study. For instance, all liquids except water contract when cooled to freezing temperatures. Here the law retains its absolute generality by absorbing the exceptional case into itself. This law, then, is no less universally applicable than those given earlier, owing to the qualifying clause contained within it.

But what if the critical factors governing the incidence of a given phenomenon are not all known? Sometimes this is the case when the number of variables on which the occurrence of the phenomenon depends are too great or their possible interactions too complex to be readily calculated. Thus, for example, the connection between smoking and lung cancer is far too intricate for anyone to say with certainty under what precise conditions smoking will lead to cancer. We can say only that smokers have a greater probability of contracting lung cancer than nonsmokers and that the probability increases with the amount smoked. It cannot be predicted in a particular sample or population which smokers and which nonsmokers will develop cancer (and why), which will not (and why not), nor can the exact causal process be traced (if it could we would be able to formulate a universal law with precise predictive power, rather than having to rely on a statistical correlation). The much greater risk faced by smokers is amply documented and can be stated in the form of a statistical probability or long-run relative frequency, which yields a generalization that can be uniformly applied (at least within a given population) but does not state an exceptionless connection between the presence of certain crucial conditions and a given type of phenomenon in the manner of a universal law.

In physics, where nonliving systems are dealt with, we suppose that the situation might be otherwise. But this is not the case—and not by reason of the incompleteness of our knowledge; for "some basic laws of science as we now know them are essentially statistical."[13] So whether we like it or not, statistical methods of studying and explaining occurrences in nature are here to stay, and therefore criticism of scientific methodology in a given field must presuppose an understanding of the basic principles that govern the collection and mathematical analysis of data.

Two such principles with wide applicability to experimentation involving animals, whether in medical research, psychological studies, or product testing, concern variability, or the reliability of experimental results obtained from trials conducted under varying conditions, and generality, or the legitimacy of extrapolating results from a limited sample of experimental animals to other, larger populations of animals.

With respect to variability, suppose an experimenter wishes to determine whether a given result is due to the presence of a particular factor introduced into the experimental setting—for instance, she wishes to know what substance in a new cosmetic preparation is producing a rash on her animals characteristically associated with a type of skin cancer. To do this, she will have to ascertain, first, that the result is not occurring by chance, that it *is* caused by the cosmetic application and does not simply appear at a rate that is normal, under nontest conditions, for the species in question. Then, to discover the ingredient that is carcinogenic, she will have to eliminate the chemicals that comprise the compound one by one. If she has reason to suspect a particular chemical rather than some others in the compound (say, because of past experience), she must establish that the rash is actually produced by that chemical and not by some other component of the compound or by a completely different factor present in the experimental setting (such as the animal's diet). Obviously, this will require many trials under varying conditions until the experimenter is satisfied that the chemical ingredient under suspicion has been shown to be the critical variable. Also, all such trials require control groups—animals to which the particular test procedure has not been administered—for comparison. To be sure that her results are conclusive, the experimenter may have to run a series of tests on the same animal, on different animals, compare results obtained over a period of time, and so on.

How does a researcher know when to stop? No simple answer can be given. However, the number of animals used is not governed by the arbitrary whim or purely subjective judgment of the scientist, but rather by theoretical, mathematical considerations. Standard rules of statistical analysis determine the number of tests that will have to be run to obtain a significant result, in other words, an acceptable degree of security that the analysis is correct. The experimenter will have at his disposal a variety of different experimental designs which he may use for a given purpose. There will therefore be some flexibility in the number of test animals he must use; but beyond this, purely mathematical requirements will set a lower limit to the number needed for a given experimental design. For only a certain spread of measurements can assure the statistical significance of a given outcome.

Generality, on the other hand, pertains to an experimenter's license to draw inferences from part of a population (the test animals) to the whole population (all animals of that type). It goes without saying that we cannot test all mice (or even, usually, all mice of a given genetic strain) to find out whether they can, say, run a certain maze with a particular part of their brains removed or functionally impaired. How, then, do we know what inferences about the total mouse population can be drawn about the correlation between brain impairment and behavior of this sort? The answer lies partly in being able to generalize from a subgroup that is taken to be representative of all mice. If all mice were genetically and environmentally exactly alike, carbon copies in every respect, a random sample would be perfectly representative (indeed, any one mouse would be). But this ideal is in fact never realized even though genetically identical strains of mice (more than 126 varieties, born by cesarean section and reared in a sterile environment to guarantee that they are disease free) are available for experimentation.[14] For this reason, and because in other ways (such as age and sex) populations are characteristically non-homogeneous, the experimenter must ensure that he begins with a sample that is genuinely representative. This is especially important if he has reason to believe that the responses of the test animals may be different because of the factors that make them nonuniform. He will then make sure that all such factors are present among the sample being used for testing. Since the usefulness of experiments depends on the validity of the inferences that can be drawn from it (the degree to which the results can be extrapolated with confidence), the larger the number of animal subjects used, the more solid is the inference base on which the experimenter may rely. A greater inference base also means that the results will be more useful and more independent of the constraints imposed by a particular experimental setting.

Clearly, the fact that experimental results can be generalized to an animal species as a whole does not guarantee that the same generality also extends to *Homo sapiens*, and the applicability of animal experiments to humans is recognized to be a serious problem by both researchers and their critics. It is frequently pointed out, for example, that the drug thalidomide passed standard animal tests only to maim thousands of human babies subsequently and that if penicillin had been tested on guinea pigs (on which it has a highly toxic effect), it would have been judged unsafe for humans. What these examples show is that in proportion to the degree of risk for humans, animal experiments should incorporate as great a degree of generality as possible and probably one that is greater than that generally prevailing in certain areas at present (for example, the testing of pharmaceuticals). Recognizing that the potential for grave consequences can be very high, the U.S. Food and Drug Administration (FDA), a regulatory agency that comes as close as any to setting world standards for new consumer products, requires that both the safety and the efficacy of new drugs be proven, and further will sometimes direct testing to be done on three species (invertebrate, vertebrate, and primate) before clinical testing on human volunteers and eventual licensing for sale.[15] (For more on product testing, see chapter 6.)

Whether animal experiments are conducted for the purpose of testing new products or for behavioral or biomedical research, it should be evident from the foregoing discussion that a very great number of animals are needed by scientists if society wants to benefit from the results of their research. This fact should be borne in mind whenever we encounter mind-boggling figures on the number of animals used annually or in a given year by experimenters, such as those cited in the first section of chapter 4. Some new scientific developments hold out the promise of being able to reduce markedly the number of animals used in research (this topic is considered later), but a substantial number will probably always be needed. None of what has been said here, of course, rules out the possibility that refinements in experimental procedure and in the artful application of statistical methods to animal research may also tend to reduce the number of organisms needed for scientific work in the future, at least in certain areas.[16]

THE POLITICS OF FUNDING RESEARCH

Among the critics of animal experimentation, there is seldom an adequate appreciation of how research of the sort I have been considering—most of which is done at universities—comes to be funded. Believing that this research is for the most part fundamentally worthless or ethically unsupportable, Hans Ruesch and Peter Singer (to take but two examples) declare that it continues principally if not solely because of the ease with which grants can be secured, the tendency of grants to perpetuate themselves or lead to new grants, and the competitive need on the part of scientists to keep busy and appear to be doing something valuable to society. Thus Ruesch and Singer are directing attention to what allegedly goes on behind the scenes to sustain animal experimentation, or what we might call the politics of funding research.

Ruesch states bluntly that "vivisection would have been abolished long ago if it were championed only by the vivisectors, whose motives are all too transparent."[17] What are the true motives of experimenters? According to him they are greed (the desire to corner research funds in ever-greater amounts), fame, and honor, however achieved. So corrupt is the funding process, Ruesch maintains, that "it wouldn't be possible to spend the billions of dollars the U.S. government gives to medical research at home and abroad if the researchers didn't constantly think up new experiments, besides repeating the old classical standbys. In other words, *first* there is the money, *then* means must be found to spend it."[18] Singer, less cynical and more moderate and reflective, writes,

> Researchers, even those in psychology, medicine, and the biological sciences, are human beings, and are susceptible to the same influences as any other human beings. They like to get on in their careers, to be promoted, and to have their work read and discussed by their colleagues. Publishing papers in the appropriate journals is an important element in the rise up the ladder of promotion and increased prestige. This happens in every field, . . . and it is entirely understandable and in itself hardly worth criticizing. . . .
>
> Once a pattern of animal experimentation becomes the accepted mode of research in a particular field, the process is self-reinforcing and difficult to break out of. Not only publications and promotions but also the awards and grants that finance research become geared to animal experiments. A proposal for a new experiment with animals is something that the administrators of research funds will be ready to support, if they have in the past supported other experiments on animals. New nonanimal-using methods will seem less familiar and will be less likely to receive support.[19]

Most of this research, Singer contends, is not only inessential (relative to important human needs) but also conducted without concern for the welfare of laboratory animals by individuals who are basically indifferent to their fate. Again, the impression is generated that almost anything goes in the fantasy world of research: granting agencies dole out ample funds in knee-jerk fashion, only too happy to play yes-men to the tune of self-serving scientists.

These characterizations fortunately are remote from the truth. Most animal experimentation does depend on grants from private and corporate foundations and from government bodies like the U.S. Public Health Service's National Institutes of Health or the Medical Research Councils of Canada and Great Britain. These official patrons, although well endowed, are not in the business of giving away money irresponsibly to support harebrained schemes conjured up by individuals who lack both scientific competence and moral scruples. During the same period in which the number of scientists has increased, the world economic situation has deteriorated, governments have adopted more frugal science policies, and the general level of awareness of ethical issues in research has been raised, granting agencies have become increasingly rigorous in their demands. As a consequence, a large proportion of a research scientist's time is now spent preparing grant proposals for submission and less than ever can he or she afford to present an ill-conceived or meretricious project for objective scrutiny. To place this whole issue within a more meaningful perspective, the following U.S. statistics may be helpful:

> In general between 50 and 60 percent of grant applications submitted to the NIH [National Institutes of Health] are approved, and in fiscal year 1972 roughly 60 percent of those approved were funded. (The funding ratio has ranged from 75 percent in the early 1960's to less than 50 percent in recent years.) . . . The NSF [National Science Foundation] panels vote to approve or decline a grant (the ratio between the two is about half-and-half). . . . The National Institute of General Medical Science, which is a major supporter of basic research, was recently funding only the top 15 percent of grants assigned to it.[20]

Experiments to be conducted with the aid of agency funding must be justified from the standpoint of their likely contribution to knowledge as well as their humaneness. The U.S. National Institutes of Health's 1979 statement of "Policy on Humane Care and Use of Animals," for example, states,

Proposals shall indicate whether animals are involved in the proposed activity and the rationale for using animals. Information should be provided to confirm that the species and numbers of animals are appropriate, that unnecessary discomfort and injury to animals will be avoided, and that analgesic, anaesthetic, and tranquilizing drugs will be used where indicated to minimize stress to the animals.

The National Cancer Institute of Canada issues the following instruction in its "Checklist for Applications for Research Grants": "If experimental animals will be involved, provide a rationale for their use and comment on the steps that will be taken to avoid unnecessary suffering." A skeptical reading of this stipulation would no doubt lead many to remark that the word *unnecessary* provides a convenient loophole for the experimenter and hence an obvious pathway to unethical conduct in the laboratory. They would argue that it is not difficult for a researcher to come up with some rationale that will satisfy a peer review committee already favorably disposed to the position that whatever way animals serve humans is legitimate. However, this again is contrary to the facts. In addition to the peer review assessment of a research proposal aimed at determining its suitability for funding, most research institutions also require that protocols (detailed descriptions of procedures to be followed) pass a second peer evaluation by an ethics review committee, usually at the local level, and inspection of work in progress is also often stipulated by such panels.

After a piece of research is completed, investigators must submit reports on the results of their experiments to date when applying for further funds from a granting agency. It is true that in a sense grants tend to beget additional grants; it is a wiser use of resources to continue funding a researcher who is a known quantity and who has produced fruitful work than to appraise a new candidate's submission. But the onus is always on the applicant to demonstrate to the satisfaction of the granting body that his or her project is worthy of continuing support. Such approval is far from automatic, and it is not uncommon for competent and even eminent scientists to have applications for grants or for grant renewals denied. Furthermore, granting agencies try to be equally fair and open to new proposals and applicants.

ANIMAL RESEARCH AND NAZI DEATH CAMP EXPERIMENTS

A number of works critical of laboratory animal science have invoked a comparison of the procedures carried out in these facilities and the unspeakable atrocities visited upon human prisoners in the name of medical research within Nazi concentration camps. It is also a commonplace in public discussion of animal rights. I include a brief glance at this aberration here because those who use this emotional appeal to denigrate laboratory animal research demonstrate not only a lack of knowledge of scientific inquiry and its motivation but also of history and of the difference between the use of animal and human subjects in studies that cause suffering.

Ruesch, whose view is that the "vivisectionist" training that is universal in medical schools today inevitably corrupts physicians' ethical and humane sensibilities, writes, "The German doctors tried in Nuremberg by the Allied court for experimenting on prisoners explained that since they had practiced animal vivisection, it was 'logical' that they wanted to experiment on human beings as well."[21] Other authors attempt to forge the connection between animal experimentation and Nazi torture in less direct ways, but the point is still the same. Thus, quoting a character in a novel by Isaac Bashevis Singer who says that "in their behavior toward creatures, all men [are] Nazis," Tom Regan comments, "A harsh saying, this. But one which, on reflection, might well turn out to contain an element of ineradicable truth."[22] Peter Singer meanwhile writes, "You cannot write objectively about the experiments of the Nazi concentration camp 'doctors' on those they considered 'subhuman' without stirring emotions; and the same is true of a description of some of the experiments performed today on nonhumans in laboratories in America, Britain, and elsewhere."[23] Finally, Richard Ryder observes, "It is often argued that the British law [regulating animal experimentation] is so much better than its equivalents in other countries that it needs no improvement. This is patently a false argument. It is rather like arguing that the concentration camp at Belsen was more humane than the one at Dachau."[24]

To arrive at the correct view of the matter, it is necessary to examine some of the particulars surrounding the practice of and training for medicine under the Third Reich. To begin with, however, bear in mind that the concentration camp doctors' "criminal work was known to thousands of leading physicians of the Reich, not a single one of whom, so far as the record shows, ever uttered the slightest public protest."[25] Some of the findings for which these remorseless and demented experimenters labored so diligently were even presented to their professional colleagues in civilian life at conferences where discussions occurred but no criticisms or ethical reservations were voiced.[26] Corpses supplied from concentration camps were also knowingly used in experiments reported in respected medical journals of the time.[27] Can these bizarre and odious forms of behavior be traced to training in the methods of animal experimentation? Such an inference is not at all in line with what the evidence suggests about the mind of Nazi war criminals. Henry V. Dicks, a psychiatrist who conducted extensive interviews with imprisoned war criminals, writes, for instance,

> In MO [a doctor convicted of war crimes] there is exemplified the tragic confusion of strands of motivation between duty and deep hate, of obedience to incompatible systems of affiliation and loyalty. Of these the least potent is the medical, Hippocratic code, displaced by his identification with the race-hygienic and totalitarian-manipulative assumptions of the Party and the SS, idealized in the name of the greatest good for the ruling in-group. . . . It is not surprising that in the setting of the emergent Third Reich a person with MO's values could here find a congenial field for externalizing his high authoritarian character traits scarcely softened by any human warmth.[28]

Almost without exception, those who have studied the psychological traits of Nazi war criminals have told an identical story—of authoritarian, obedient personalities, immersed in racist mythology, in which simple human decency is overwhelmed by the call of duty to the fatherland. This set of dynamics has nothing to do with training in animal research, for the diagnosis is the same whatever profession or position in the Nazi hierarchy we choose to examine.

For doctors, the social and political milieu is far more telling than their medical training. Transcripts of the Nuremberg trials of German war criminals indicate that "the totalitarian structure of the Nazi State demanded fundamental subordination of all principles of medicine to National Socialist population policy and racial concepts."[29] As a routine part of their education, young physicians were thoroughly brainwashed to instill in them the mythology of race purification and of Germany's sacred mission to exterminate "inferiors." Courses in such subjects were given at the Fuehrer-School of German Physicians at Altrehse in Mecklenburg. "There physicians were indoctrinated in the National Socialist point of view and way of life. . . . These courses finally became compulsory and had to be attended for several months annually." Furthermore, only "Aryans" were selected as suitable candidates for medical studies, and during training, "the students' entire course of study was constantly interrupted by the demands of the various party organizations to which they were forced to belong. A student whose knowledge of the racial theories and Nuernberg laws was not sufficient would fail his medical exams."[30] Is it any wonder that German doctors became butchers?[31]

We might expect and hope that physicians, educated to serve as healers, would be the last group to be dissuaded from compassionate attention to suffering humanity, much less to inflict wanton injuries themselves. It is a sad commentary that such was not the case in Germany, but this only shows how powerful race hatred can be when officially sanctioned and reinforced and what cruelties individuals are capable of once they accept the division of humankind into two classes: persons (superiors) and nonpersons (inferiors).[32]

It is worth adding too that although the atrocities committed by Nazi doctors (which are documented fully in many places)[33] were perpetrated in the name of science, the judgment of history is that they in fact had nothing to do with science:

> Nothing came of Nazi science: nothing could have come of it because it was not science. Science is the establishment of fact on the evidence. The Nazis were only interested in establishing the evidence to prove their assumed fact . . . the doctrine of race superiority.[34]

> The German scientists had become immoral and dishonest, therefore their achievements were of a pseudo-scientific character. . . . The experiments performed added nothing of significance to medical knowledge.[35]

> The Nazi methods of investigation were inefficient and unscientific, and their techniques of research were unsystematic. "These experiments revealed nothing which civilized medicine can use. . . . The experiments were not only criminal but a scientific failure."[36]

Those who equate animal research with Nazi experiments on humans show an apparent bias toward compassion for the plight of animals and a relative indifference to human misery. But this should not surprise us since similar attitudes are unfortunately entirely commonplace, as we saw in chapter 1. We must conclude that people who see little or no difference between animal experiments and Nazi butchery in the name of science cannot be fully aware of what went on in the concentration camps and should inform themselves properly. But they are also guilty of inconsistency; even if they argue that animals are in some sense deserving of equal consideration in moral contexts (as I have argued they are not), most accept the view that human life is, in the final analysis, more valuable than animal life. If so, then the torture and murder of human beings should be of much greater relative concern than they make it. Perhaps there is no moral insensitivity involved here and the greater value placed on human life is more than merely notional; but the writings referred to earlier leave us with a disturbing feeling and many unresolved questions.

Even more unsettling are the remarks of individuals who claim they would rather see humans used as research subjects than animals. This is exactly what Hitler's mentality dictated. M. H. Pappworth has written, "It is interesting to note, as recorded by the distinguished physician who was an important medical witness for the prosecution at the Nuremberg trial, that Hitler when he first assumed power issued an edict making all animal experiments illegal. But this he followed up by ordering the mass murder of inmates of mental hospitals."[37] Speaking for myself, it is difficult to imagine a more frightening example of compartmentalized thinking.

6

Unnecessary Suffering and Alternatives to Animal Experiments

THE MEANING OF *CRUELTY* AND *INHUMANENESS*

Throughout the foregoing discussion the words *cruelty* and *inhumaneness* have been used to describe the treatment of animals objected to by those interested in the cause of animal welfare generally as well as by those committed to reasonable standards in the care and handling of animals within the context of experimentation. If we wish to make some progress toward setting the limits beyond which inflicting suffering on other species for our own ends is unnecessary and hence ethically or morally unacceptable, these key terms must first be carefully defined, particularly since much misunderstanding has been generated by applying them inappropriately.

According to *Webster's Unabridged Dictionary* (Third International Edition), *cruel* means "disposed to inflict pain especially in a wanton, insensate, or vindictive manner: pleased by hurting others: sadistic: devoid of kindness." *Inhumane* is rendered as "devoid of compassion, sympathy, or consideration for other human beings or animals: lacking the qualities of mercy, pity, kindness or tenderness: cruel, barbarous, savage." The *Oxford English Dictionary* defines *cruel* as "disposed to inflict suffering; indifferent to or taking pleasure in another's pain or distress; destitute of kindness or compassion; merciless, pitiless, hard-hearted." The *OED* explicates *inhumane* by contrast with *humane*, which means "marked by sympathy with and

consideration for the needs and distresses of others; feeling or showing compassion and tenderness toward human beings and the lower
animals; kind, benevolent." Behavior that is inhumane, then, is that
which is not humane; destitute of compassion for misery or suffering
in humans or animals.

It would seem to follow (but for *Webster's* final attempt at defining *inhumane*) that the two terms are not synonymous and that *cruel*
conveys a greater sense of disapprobation than *inhumane*. For people
are inhumane if they lack compassion for the suffering of sentient
beings, but they are properly described as cruel only if they are the
deliberate cause of this suffering and are either indifferent to or take
positive delight or satisfaction in the suffering. Therefore, individuals
(or their acts) may be inhumane without being cruel, but not the
reverse.

The reader may be wondering whether anything of importance
can be learned from these distinctions or whether we are, rather,
merely playing with words and splitting hairs. The answer is that
something of importance is indeed revealed by these definitions—
namely, that if we use our language correctly, only those individuals
and actions that display an intention to cause suffering, more or less
as an end in itself, are rightly labeled cruel. If this is the case,
however, then except for a few rare instances, what should concern
us in laboratory animal research is not cruelty but the actuality or
possibility of inhumaneness. It has not infrequently been claimed
that all (or at any rate most) experimental scientists using animals
are unfeeling, uncaring brutes and sadists; but to anyone who has
taken the trouble to observe the work of such researchers and to
discuss it with them open-mindedly, this characterization is remote
from the truth. The great majority of scientists today are sensitive
to the ethical issues generated by their work, and even where
humaneness does not exhibit a particularly high profile, we seldom
find evidence of downright cruelty.

Although it is best to be on guard against abusing language, the
fact remains that people often do use *cruel* and *inhumane* as if they
were synonymous. We should avoid the temptation to succumb to
this tendency. But at the same time, we must acknowledge that
when words like *cruel* and *inhumane* are invoked in discussing the
treatment of animals, they point us toward the problem of unnecessary suffering or the inflicting of pain, deprivation, discomfort, and
so on that exceeds some commonsense and more or less intuitively
understood and agreed-on standard. That is, treatment designated as

either inhumane or cruel is, in a rough and ready sense, that which surpasses the boundaries of what we judge morally acceptable. Let us now see if it is possible to refine the concept of unnecessary suffering.

ON KNOWING WHEN AND HOW MUCH ANIMALS ARE SUFFERING

I assume it is not necessary to prove to anyone that animals are capable of feeling pain or of suffering. As I noted in the introduction, the belief that animals could not suffer was once deeply entrenched in Western thought. Because of this, many authors have supposed that they had first to convince their readers that animals can and do suffer before they could address the ethical problems of animal use. (Peter Singer, for instance, devotes a full six pages to establishing this point in the opening chapter of *Animal Liberation*.)[1] However, assuming that no one seriously wants to argue that animals lack the capacity to suffer, it must still be said that numerous researchers have injudiciously downplayed the painful experiences of their experimental animals. A common observation offered by their critics is that this seeming absence of concern is inconsistent, given the fact that much research (especially of the behavioral and neurological varieties) is premised on the natural, even measurable sensitivities and pain-avoidance tendencies of animals. If so, then we cannot ignore the signs of suffering when and where they occur or the ethical implications of being the cause of this suffering.

But how do we tell when and how much an animal is suffering? To some, an answer to the question When is an animal suffering? is obvious and only the obtuse or perverse could pretend not to know. We simply have to look at an animal and see whether it cries out, moans, snarls, struggles, grimaces, manifests rapidly increased palpitations, looks fearful or forlorn, acts aggressive, tries to avoid or escape from a certain stimulus, guards or continues biting or licking a particular area of its body, shivers or displays bristling hair or fur, defecates or urinates uncontrollably, acts listless, shows loss of appetite, and so on. However, as Marian Stamp Dawkins, Mary Snow Fellow in Biological Sciences at Somerville College, Oxford University, points out,

> We do not know infallibly what the mental experiences of other animals are like, particularly those of animals that are structurally very different

from us. And, if people feel that it is important to try to change the laws about the treatment of animals, they must have more to go on than just their intuition. "Suffering" must be recognizable in some objective way. Otherwise the laws which emerge are almost bound to be arbitrary and might even fail to improve the lot of animals much, if at all.[2]

(Dawkins, it should be noted, has no particular ax to grind, and was motivated to write a book on the subject of animal suffering in part out of humane considerations.) Animal suffering and well-being, like that of humans, must be measured in both physical and mental (or psychological) dimensions. The key question raised by Dawkins concerns the latter; for how (or whether in fact) we can quantify and assess the subjective experiences of animals is a serious method-ological problem of behavioral science and has great implications for what she calls "the science of animal welfare."

Though a great deal of experimental work at the present time is aimed at gaining insight into the underlying physiology of painful and pleasurable states of consciousness,[3] these phenomena are as yet very inadequately understood. However, it is well established that the neurological basis of pain sensations is closely similar in animals and humans. It would seem to follow that the more grossly observ-able signs of severe pain are comparable and hence more readily identifiable in species that are relatively close to *Homo sapiens* on the evolutionary scale. Behavioral manifestations such as those listed earlier are reasonably reliable indicators of pain due to stress, injury, or disease. We can expect fairly widespread agreement in such situa-tions. However, Dawkins observes that a distinction must be drawn between more straightforward pain of this kind and various degrees of psychological suffering for which we do not have equally evident signs, and consequently she focuses our attention on two problems. The first is that "there are reasons for thinking that not all mental suffering is necessarily reflected in such obvious signs of physical debilitation"; the second is how "to decide how much (that is, how intense, or how prolonged) of an unpleasant emotional state consti-tutes 'suffering.'"[4]

Dawkins reviews several criteria that are commonly appealed to by those concerned with animal welfare to assess whether animals are suffering "despite an external appearance of good health." These are (a) the behavior of the same species of animal in the wild; (b) physiological measurements (heart rate, hormone levels, blood and urine composition, and so on); (c) whether the animals' behavior is "normal" or "abnormal"; (d) what the animals do when given "the opportunity to *choose* for themselves which environments they prefer and to show what they find positively or negatively *reinforcing*"; and (e) analogies drawn from the human situation.[5] Without dismissing any of these outright, Dawkins carefully demonstrates the difficulties inherent in too great a reliance on any one criterion. Taken in concert, these bits of evidence may offer a useful indication of animals' subjective states of awareness, but the limitations of each when looked at in isolation are also manifest.

The behavior of animals in the wild is only partially relevant here because animals are subject to many sources of suffering in their natural environments. In addition, domestic or laboratory-reared animals have never experienced an alternative environment and are (more likely than not) the unique genetic products of careful selective breeding. Finally, Dawkins observes, "there is no evidence that a difference in the behaviour of free and restricted animals *in itself* shows that the restricted ones are suffering."[6] Physiological measurements are also equivocal as testimonies to animal suffering because they change from moment to moment during the stresses of ordinary daily life, and reactions to similar situations may vary from species to species, from animal to animal within the same species, and even within the same individual animal on different occasions.[7] Part (though not all) of the explanation of these phenomena is that stress, which is a catch-all term for whatever physiological adaptations an organism is challenged to undergo, is to some degree beneficial to an animal's general health, resilience, resistance to disease, and so forth. It is not clear therefore that the presence of stress per se (caused, for example, by fear of an aversive stimulus, frustration of drives, or conflict between drives that cannot simultaneously be satisfied) means that an animal is suffering or that if it is, this is detrimental to its health or well-being. It has been shown, for example, that monkeys trained to press levers to see photographs or films often continued to select those that evoked acute fear responses (ears laid back, urinating) on first viewing. This appears to indicate that they may choose to expose themselves to stress. Moreover, "complex emotions that come under the heading of 'suffering' are not easily related to the simple physiological measurements that can be made at the moment."[8]

As with physiological measurements, the problem in using abnormal animal behavior patterns as an indication of suffering is one of degree; that is, since some forms of behavior that are frequently labeled abnormal also occur in the wild, in situations where suffering does not appear to be present, it cannot be said that this behavior always accompanies suffering. We must therefore learn to judge what level of repetition or persistence of the given behavior is to be taken as a sign of suffering caused by artificial conditions. Some kinds of abnormal behavior, such as severe tail or limb biting, are obvious symptoms of distress in confinement, but as Dawkins remarks, "other behaviour which has also been described as abnormal is part of the animal's natural repertoire"[9] (for example, aggressive displays of various sorts). A different approach, which holds promise but has not yet been sufficiently refined through research, is to offer a choice between environments (say, a cage or a free outdoor space; a smaller or a larger cage) and between procedures or situations (different forms of reward and punishment) to see which ones animals opt for. However, Dawkins cautions, "preference by itself is not an indicator of suffering. To show that preference does indicate suffering in the less preferred environment, we have to find out not merely what the preference is, but how strong it is. . . . So far, attempts to do this have yielded unsatisfactory results."[10]

In the end, all attempts to ascertain what animals are feeling must refer back to human experience, and they must proceed by inference from analogies with our own emotional responses. There are two ways open to us here. One is monitoring our empathetic reactions to an animal's appearance, behavior, and vocalizations and attempting to gauge its states of awareness on the basis of those palpable signs we can identify with. The other is trying to feel ourselves into an animal's situation, so to speak, to appraise this from this animal's standpoint. However, both these approaches are fraught with difficulties. As Dawkins notes correctly, "To judge an animal's environment in terms of what we ourselves like or dislike is a well-meaning but misguided standard."[11] (For instance, Dawkins cites studies that show, contrary to confident predictions, that greater stress indicators are present in sheep sheared in isolation from their flock than in sheep being slaughtered with their flock; that hens reared in battery cages, when given a choice, preferred fine-gauge wire mesh floors to other sorts thought by welfarists to be obviously more humane.)[12]

The upshot of Dawkins's preliminary but thorough and pioneering study of the criteria for recognizing and evaluating the degree of animal suffering is that "there is no single method which, by itself, can tell us about the emotional experiences that animals might have. . . . What is necessary is a synthesis of the pictures given by all methods." Thus her approach may be seen as a plea for greater knowledge of animals as sentient organisms, of the range of animal behavior both in the wild and in captivity, and for a redoubled effort to develop a more sophisticated understanding of what she calls each species' unique "vocabulary of suffering." [13] The latter is especially important in those cases where animals bear only a distant anatomical, physiological, and behavioral resemblance to ourselves.

In view of the many uncertainties in estimating the quality and degree of animal suffering, it might well be argued that scientists using animal subjects in experiments ought to adopt as a matter of course what may be called the benefit-of-the-doubt principle: that when behavioral and other pieces of evidence are equivocal, it should be assumed that an animal is suffering even if it appears not to be or that it is suffering more than it appears to be. Naturally, some antivivisectionists would try to push this principle to what they might consider its logical conclusion, namely, that all experimentation on animals should be abolished because we can never be certain how much suffering we are inflicting and therefore must always assume that it is more than appears to be the case. However, as Dawkins shows, in my view convincingly, we are not completely without criteria for judging these matters. Furthermore, the antivivisectionists themselves plainly operate on the assumption that they can judge, and so must also concede that there are usable criteria for making such decisions. (In any area of experience or evaluation, the existence of borderline cases does not negate the fact that there are clear-cut cases to which decision criteria can be applied with confidence; indeed, the great majority of cases will normally be of this type.) Finally, the argument for using animals in research has already been given; and if it holds at all, it holds notwithstanding the inflicting of suffering on animals. The benefit-of-the-doubt principle applies therefore in searching for ways to make animal experiments more humane and to guard against certain excesses, not as a vehicle for eliminating experiments altogether.

WHEN SUFFERING IS UNNECESSARY

Even if we can determine, in a given case, that an animal is suffering as a result of some condition or procedure for which human beings are responsible, this does not solve the problem of whether its suffering should be alleviated or eliminated. Many would hold that good reasons can often be given for the deliberate infliction of suffering upon animals and that it is frequently defensible in terms of certain ends we want to achieve. One obvious sort of end that might offset a certain amount of animal suffering is animals' own long-term good (for example, innoculations against contagious diseases or research aimed at the development of veterinary rabies vaccine). It is also commonly asserted that purely human ends may legitimately be served by means that cause animal suffering. Our humane concern for animals requires of us that any defense of this position must take into account both moral and practical matters—both the ethical grounds for using animals for the ends in question and the availability or lack (in the case of experimentation) of reasonable alternatives to the use of live animals. These considerations bring us face to face with the problem usually referred to as that of unnecessary suffering.

If suffering can be labeled "unnecessary," then this is presumably by contrast with suffering which is deemed to be "necessary." What kind or degree of suffering is properly regarded as necessary? Within the context of laboratory animal research, the most general answer would seem to be whatever kind or degree of suffering has to be produced to obtain a particular statistically significant result within the framework of a given, ethically acceptable experiment. I have argued at length in chapter 3 that it is morally acceptable and even necessary for humans to use animals for research even when it causes pain or suffering. It was also suggested earlier that to say animal experiments are in general morally permissible does not mean that we may do to other species whatever we like. Most researchers, I am certain, would agree. What, then, are the limitations a reasonable standard of humaneness would impose on animal experimentation?

As I strived to make clear in chapter 4, the specific (as opposed to the general or theoretical) moral case for experiments on animals must focus on their salient benefits to humans or animals; and from the discussion of the nature of scientific research in chapter 5, we may infer that benefits can legitimately be taken to include adding significantly to the overall fund of knowledge about the physiology and behavior of organisms. Any research that (because it causes suffering) raises moral issues and does not meet this requirement, then, may be said to be unacceptable from an ethical standpoint.

In addition, it seems reasonable to require that any proposal for a morally satisfactory research project also include some effort to show that the methods or procedures to be used constitute either the only way to attack a particular problem or test a key concept or theory or the best way of all those available. If it is contended that these methods are the best way, then it would be vital to consider the relative costs of the alternatives, their reliability, the time likely to be consumed by each, and similar factors to gain a full picture. These factors might be judged to outweigh the suffering likely to be caused by the research method in question. This, of course, raises the whole issue of alternatives to experimentation on live animals, which is taken up later in this chapter. It should be noted here too that determining that a particular procedure to be performed on animals is the only or best way to conduct an experiment also should require some indication that for moral or practical reasons such a procedure cannot be performed upon human subjects. This is most often assumed to be the case without argument, though a sizable number of reports of experiments published in professional journals do at least allude to this consideration.

Finally, an adequate moral justification of procedures in animal research should take into account possible modifications of experimental technique that might reduce animal suffering noticeably without affecting the viability of the inquiry. This would include such things as increasing the amounts of anesthetic or analgesia employed, reducing the number of animals used, reducing the number of trials run, altering the animals' diet or housing conditions, shortening the length of time an aversive stimulus is administered or a pathological state is allowed to persist, and changing the method of euthanasia. Ethics committees that review and approve research protocols in advance of an experiment are frequently quite diligent and helpful in this connection.

Clearly, then, an experiment that entails animal suffering and that contravenes the principles inherent in these categories of ethical or moral assessment may be said to produce unnecessary suffering. A scientist who conducts such a piece of research may be judged to be acting inhumanely and to be responsible for causing unnecessary suffering, especially if he or she has deliberately chosen to disregard available means to reduce suffering that perhaps would not impair in any way the efficiency of his or her work or undermine the significance of the results.

To sum up, suffering is unnecessary when it is morally unacceptable, meaning excessive or preventable. If feasible alternatives to the use of live or "higher" animals have not been explored carefully by researchers, suffering may be preventable in the sense of being dispensable. Suffering is *preventable* when they fail to take advantage of measures (compatible with their experimental objectives) aimed at reducing either the number of animals used, the number of trials run, or when they overlook or ignore modifications to their experimental design or procedures that are in the interests of minimizing pain and stress. Suffering may also be unnecessary if it is *excessive*, that is, not likely to be offset by practical benefits to humans or animals, or else by a contribution to scientific knowledge which most informed persons would judge significantly proportionate to the amount of suffering in question.

CAGING AND HANDLING

One of the areas of greatest concern from a humane standpoint is the housing and care (or caging and handling) of animals in the laboratory setting. These components of the research context do not normally receive as much attention from animal protectionists and the media as experimental procedures themselves, but nonetheless they represent aspects of an animal's life in the laboratory into which unnecessary suffering can easily and often unintentionally be introduced. By the same token, education, careful thought, and judicious planning for proper caging and handling can help minimize the suffering to which research animals are subjected.

A number of agencies that fund laboratory animal science have drafted guidelines for animal housing and care and in many jurisdictions there are laws regulating these matters.[14] The laws, obviously, must be obeyed, though the problem of enforcement is serious in many places because of the lack of adequate personnel to perform routine inspections of research facilities. However, prosecutions of experimenters on the grounds of maintaining substandard animal housing and care are not unknown, even under general anticruelty statutes.[15] But even if such laws are obeyed, they may be so vague, incomplete, or qualified that they offer animals at best only partial protection against unnecessary suffering caused by their laboratory environment. To fill the gap, numerous manuals and other documents have been generated by the scientific community itself, mindful of its ethical responsibilities and accountability to both legislators and society at large. Researchers can still attempt to ignore or bypass the recommendations contained in such publications. But they do so at their peril; virtually every granting agency now requires com-

pliance with a set of ethical guidelines governing not only experimental procedures but also the maintenance of animals while in the
research facility. An investigator who fails to conduct his or her
work in accordance with such guidelines, then, will clearly risk not
getting a grant in the first place, having a grant revoked or terminated early, or having an experiment halted while still in progress
(for example, by a local animal care committee). It hardly needs to
be said that any of these outcomes would constitute a severe blow
to the researcher in view of the high cost of the animals, personnel,
equipment, and the like it takes to run an experiment and in terms of
his or her scientific reputation.

One of the most comprehensive publications on the caging and
handling of laboratory animals is the *Guide for the Care and Use
of Laboratory Animals* produced by the National Research Council
for the National Institutes of Health, the largest funding body for
animal research in the United States.[16] The *Guide*, which was first
published in 1963, is also undoubtedly the most widely consulted
manual, some 250,000 copies of the first three editions having been
distributed. This reference work covers every aspect of the "proper
management of laboratory animal facilities," which it defines as
"any system of housing and care that permits animals to grow,
mature, reproduce, and behave normally and to be maintained in
physical comfort and good health." Some of its considerations
relate to (a) the animals' basic environs and needs (temperature,
light/dark cycles, space, sanitation, disease and vermin control,
avoidance of unnecessary restraint, and so on); (b) exercise; (c) feeding; (d) maintenance of accurate records and identification systems
for animals; (e) provisions for evening, weekend, and holiday care;
(f) adequate standards of veterinary care (including surgical procedures, anesthesia, analgesia, euthanasia); (g) reuse of the same
animals for different experiments; (h) qualifications and personal
hygiene and health of animal care personnel; (i) handling of hazard-
ous materials; and (j) design and construction of research facilities.
As the *Guide* notes, "Rarely are the animal housing requirements
incompatible with the requirements for research." In addition, it
points out that "animal husbandry is an important factor in research.
Husbandry procedures, although generally considered to be routine,
can significantly affect research data."[17]

Any measures that tend to increase the quality of animal care
in the laboratory, then, will make a major contribution to the
prevention of unnecessary suffering. The close supervision of all

experimental procedures by well-qualified scientists and veterinarians, a mandatory requirement that all routine handling of animals be done by certified laboratory animal technicians, and more regular and stringent inspection of research facilities would all help in this endeavor.

THE PROBLEM OF DESENSITIZATION
TO ANIMAL SUFFERING

Living in the age of the "global village"—of instant communications via satellite—an abundance of suffering from every part of the world is brought home to us each day. Social commentators have observed with increasing frequency that the general population has become alarmingly habituated to violence and suffering—so much so that indifference to suffering has occasionally reached tragic proportions. There is a genuine cause for concern here, even if exaggerated by the media; overexposure to the sufferings of others does seem to dull some people's sensibilities and cause them to react in inappropriate ways when their fellow beings are in need of aid.

The same sort of concern has been aired by those who are parties to the animal welfare debate. Thus Richard Ryder, a clinical psychologist who abandoned animal research, has written from the antivivisectionist viewpoint,

> So it is when a young aspiring scientist finds himself in an animal-experimentation laboratory. He does not dare question convention; to be successful he must conform. His natural feelings of compassion for the laboratory animals and also any feelings of squeamishness are quickly suppressed. After a few months or years, he can no longer feel them, he is hardened, habituated, de-sensitised and unlikely to repent.[18]

Although theological language of repentance—not uncommon in the history of antivivisectionist thought—and the dogmatism of Ryder's remarks are impossible to overlook, others perceive an important problem here too. George K. Russell, a biologist who for many years has been in the forefront of humane research, raises the same issue from the perspective of one who regularly experiments on animals:

> In my view, undergraduate animal experiments often inflict unnecessary suffering on animals; they also have a hardening and desensitizing effect on the students required to perform them at a time when the development of a sympathetic attitude toward the natural world may be just as important as the teaching of actual scientific knowledge.[19]

The reality of the problem addressed in these two sets of remarks, then, is something on which fairly widespread agreement can be found.

A word or two might be added here about the use of animals in high school biology classes and science fairs. Many research scientists, as well as humane groups, have expressed concern over the unnecessary suffering caused by untrained and unskilled young people experimenting on live animals to illustrate principles that are already well established. In addition, Russell's observations about humane education are just as germane here as in the context of higher learning. In response to this situation, some scientists have been prompted to try to influence the direction taken by animal experiments at the preuniversity level. In the United States the work of F. Barbara Orlans, author of the highly readable and instructive volume *Animal Care from Protozoa to Small Mammals*, is exemplary, and in Canada the whole area of high school science fair experimentation in biology has been under nationwide regulation since 1975, owing to the combined efforts of the Canadian Council on Animal Care and the Youth Science Foundation. Meanwhile in the United States the 7,000-member National Association of Biology Teachers has been working hard in recent years to refine and strengthen its code for the use of animals in high school student projects.[20]

At one level of analysis, indifference to suffering on the part of those who are confronted by it or must deal with it in some way on a daily basis is understandable and even to a certain extent excusable. A natural reaction to being constantly bombarded by the distress of others is to deny or deflect it, to steel ourselves to it and direct at least a large part of our attention elsewhere. This reaction—perhaps in fact explainable by its obvious evolutionary significance as advantageous to survival—is in fact a psychological process of compartmentalization similar to that of the Nazi doctors described in chapter 5, except that it has a positive aspect and is normally self-limiting. A psychiatrist, for example, may be exposed to his patients' anguish, self-loathing, remorse, morbid thoughts, fears, and other wrenching emotional outpourings for several hours a day. If he allows himself to become too involved with them personally, he fails as a therapist and his own mental stability may be threatened. He must be able to hold his patients' woes at a suitable distance to treat them and lead his own life. If, however, he removes himself too far from his patients' subjective experience, he loses the ability to hear their pleas for help and to make the essential human response without which therapy likewise fails. He must, in short, strike a balance between these extremes of distance and empathetic closeness. The same is true in the practice of medicine generally and indeed in all professions in which human relations play a vital role.

It is most important to see, then, that the problem of indifference to suffering is a danger that is not unique to the practice of laboratory animal science. It may be easier for many people to slip into an attitude of indifference toward animal suffering because of the pressures of professional training in the sciences or because they regard the pain of animals as of lesser moral significance than that of humans. But just as a great many individuals trained in medicine have expressed concern over the problem of indifference to suffering in themselves and their colleagues, so have a great many animal experimenters agonized over the painful and stressful procedures they have found it necessary to administer and have invested considerable time, energy, and grant money in an effort to reduce unnecessary suffering. (To believe that animal suffering is of less moral significance than that of humans is not to believe that it is of little or no moral significance.)

There is no simple answer to the problem of indifference to suffering. It is highly misleading therefore to accuse scientists engaged in animal research of developing in themselves and their students a Nazilike mentality. As I have pointed out, the same psychological and ethical issues arise wherever individuals face the daily challenge of coming to terms with suffering. Perhaps all that can be said in general is that professionals who confront suffering routinely must exercise constant vigilance over their feelings and continually cultivate attitudes of compassion both in themselves and others through education, discussion, reflection, and the practice of self-discipline. The formation of humane attitudes is not automatic, nor subject to a ready-made formula. Clearly, the best chance professions dealing with human or animal care have to instill feelings and principles of humaneness in their members is to act early through the educative process. Failing this, those who are singled out by their peers or supervisors (or who single themselves out) as exhibiting callous attitudes or behavior should be given counseling or, in extreme cases, prevented from achieving or retaining professional certification.

It is important to remind ourselves too that humaneness and compassion in the best sense are not taught so much as they are the products of healthy personal development (see my earlier comments on the human psychological effects of cruelty to animals in chapter 3).

REPLACING ANIMALS IN RESEARCH

Among the community of scientists using animals in their laboratory work, there has been a growing realization of the need to reduce the number of animals in research. This trend is seldom acknowledged by critics of animal use in the laboratory, and especially by those who are bent on abolishing all animal experiments (or all except those that have obvious lifesaving medical benefits). Furthermore, few members of the concerned public seem to be aware of it. However this may be, many scientists have turned their attention over the past two decades to the problem of reducing animal use, and some encouraging developments have taken place, which I examine later.

It would be gratifying to those concerned with the infliction of suffering in animal experiments to learn that the motive for reducing animal use in research is purely ethical in nature, but this is not the case. There is, of course, an ethical dimension to many scientists' motivation to replace animals in their work, but other factors play perhaps an even greater part, such as the desire to refine statistical methods in the interests of greater precision of results; the desire to take advantage of simpler experimental models; and economic considerations prompted by the increasing shortage and correspondingly high cost of certain laboratory animals (a healthy chimpanzee, for example, now reportedly costs $10,000.)[21] I am not, however, suggesting that the existence of mixed motives casts doubt on the sincerity of scientists' ethical commitments, but only indicating that here, as in human behavior generally, the impetus to change springs from complex sources. But a more important point needs to be reiterated here: As an increasing number of scientists are becoming aware, ethical imperatives and the principles of good science—both of which obviously affect the nature of research and supply motives for the quest for alternatives to the use of live animals—furnish convergent rather than divergent objectives, that is, the concerns of ethics and of sound scientific inquiry overlap and their aims coincide at a certain point. As scientist Carol M. Newton has remarked,

> I think people of good faith are far in the majority in all aspects of this issue. I do feel that the biologists, not just for humane reasons, but

actually for reasons of good science, are getting the most out of hard work in the laboratory. They increasingly are motivated to use good statistical and biomathematical techniques in research.

I think that the people in humane work are quite right to press for more responsible scientific work as far as animals are concerned, but again I believe this all converges. I think that the good quality of scientific work will meet the same objectives as the request for responsible work with animals.[22]

A number of researchers have formulated principles to serve as guidelines for the replacement or reduction of animal use in experimentation. The best known of these are the "3 R" principle of reduction, replacement, and refinement first put forward in 1959 by Russell and Burch and referred to earlier; Newton's "3 S" principle of good science, good sense, and good sensibility; and Harry C. Rowsell's "3 R" tenet: "the right animal for the right reason."[23] These sets of principles are more or less self-explanatory and have to do not only with the replacment of animals but also with the cultivation and maintenance of humane attitudes, while acting as stimuli to the development of more sophisticated tools for research that can someday lessen the demand for live animals. Newton's principle of good sense calls in addition for knowledge (for example, of normal animal behavior) to replace ignorance (a common source of unintended suffering) in the selection, care, and handling of animals. Rowsell's tenet encapsulates the doctrine that researchers must justify their use of animals in general and the use of a specific species, but also give careful thought to the replacement of higher by lower species whenever possible.

Although prospects for reducing the use of animals in research are becoming ever more favorable, especially in the area of product development and testing, there is virtually unanimous agreement among working scientists that animals will never be replaced entirely in the laboratory. Scientific inquiry can and does make use of innovations in technique and method that replace animals or require fewer or lower-order organisms, and most of these novel approaches have been inspired by other than ethical considerations. But for certain basic physiological studies and for other kinds of studies deemed indispensable for the general progress of the biological and behavioral sciences, only live, fully functioning animals will suffice as experimental subjects or models. Because of this, a significant number of animals will, so far as we can see at present, continue to be used for knowledge-oriented research (as opposed to product development and testing).

The grounds for these judgments are furnished by, among others, D. H. Smyth, Emeritus Professor of Physiology at the University of Sheffield, whose 1978 book *Alternatives to Animal Experiments* is the most exhaustive and balanced presentation to date of the alternatives debate and of the pros and cons of available and conceivable alternatives. Smyth points out that "the rational practice of medicine, dentistry and veterinary science requires a detailed knowledge of how living tissues work." He then goes to explain carefully, and in plain language,

> The cells of the body are organised into tissues, which usually contain more than one kind of cell. . . . The organs of the body are formed by a number of tissues and cells. . . .
>
> In general, the organ functions because of the coordinated activity of all the different kinds of cells. This has one very important result which has great significance in relation to alternatives. The organ will have properties which would not be apparent from studying the individual cells which compose it, or even the separate tissues which compose it. . . .
>
> The various organs of the body do not function in isolation, but are mutually dependent on the activities of each other. . . . This kind of coordination can only be studied on whole animals, and could never even be guessed at from [, e.g.,] experiments on tissue culture.[24]

Smyth indicates, in addition, that the homeostatic (or self-regulatory) mechanisms of the body "would not be seen in experiments on separate organs." They are also "not present in tissue cultures, and [this] constitutes a very major difference between experiments on whole animals and on tissue cultures."[25] Thus the crucial physiological reason why animals are indispensable for research lies in the systematic interconnectedness of cells, tissues, and organs which constitute an integrated, living being. Many criticisms of research, it would appear, spring from a lack of understanding of this most basic characteristic of living systems, which a better acquaintance with the biological sciences would reveal. Further, it is curious to note that those who have championed the cause of alternatives to animals in research, on the grounds that animal experiments yield piecemeal information that may be unreliable when applied to humans, fail to appreciate that a holistic perspective can be assured only by the very sort of work with live organisms which they wish to reject.

Smyth observes that "different methods of research must be used according to the level of biological organisation we are investigating." [26] This basic truth is the key to the entire range of alternatives to animal experiments. The availability of an alternative is a function of the degree to which the biological or behavioral properties under investigation reveal complexities that are understandable only in relation to an integrated, functioning organism, similar in relevant respects to *Homo sapiens*. For example, tissue culture (the maintenance of living tissues outside the body) "can provide basic information about cell physiology and behaviour"; [27] it can also be used for toxicity testing, cancer research, and the production of vaccines (though experts in this field all agree that it can serve only as an adjunct to animal experiments, not as a replacement for them [28]). In contrast, whole animals are required for other forms of research that must be conducted, if at all, on the macro level. Thus chimpanzees— whose status as laboratory animals has been thrown into question by recent discoveries about their linguistic abilities—are often the experimental subjects of choice because of their extremely close genetic, physiological, and hematological relationship to humans (see chapter 2, second section). To illustrate, consider the following:

> A vaccine for hepatitis B, which afflicts 40,000 Americans annually and is carried by 200 million others worldwide, was recently developed through experiments on chimps. Chimpanzees, along with other apes, are the only species known to develop the virus-caused disease. In humans, hepatitis B is a fairly severe and sometimes fatal disease. Thanks to the new vaccine, untold numbers of cases can now be prevented. Chimps remain essential in the fight against hepatitis B, because each new batch of the vaccine that is made must be safety tested in a virus-free chimp. Chimpanzees are also being used in research to develop tests for another form of hepatitis called non-A, non-B.
> . . . Chimps have the same blood types as people and are used for studies of blood diseases, such as sickle-cell anemia. Experimental surgery on chimps has produced advances in organ transplantation and joint replacement. Behavioral experiments—the very research that has stimulated concern for the animals—have yielded important clues for the treatment of autistic and mentally retarded children. [29]

There are, then, clear limitations in the nature of things to what can be accomplished by introducing alternative procedures to replace animals in research, for the simple reason that living matter is incredibly complex and the whole is always greater than the sum of its parts.

Still, the number of animals needed in research can be reduced significantly by alternatives and by refinements to experimental design and methods of analysis, and the amount of suffering caused by experiments can be lessened by using the right animal for the right reason.

The field of research into alternatives is too vast to be surveyed adequately or conveniently here, and in any case this has been done very well elsewhere.[30] It may be useful, however, to note briefly the wide variety of possibilities now open to experimenters. Smyth canvasses the following (with special reference to medical research, but alternatives available to behavioral scientists may be found among them as well):[31] (a) dummies, such as mannequins, used for teaching purposes, automobile crash research, and the like; (b) mechanical models, which can be used to demonstrate the workings of different physiological systems; (c) computers, which, as we might surmise, have a broad range of applications—rapid data processing, information storage and retrieval, the refinement of experimental procedures, the simulation of events in certain living systems, the modeling of whole animals (for teaching purposes), the prediction of drugs' effects, the design of new drugs, and so on; (d) in vitro methods, or the analysis of tissues kept alive outside a donor organism, which have applications to the production of vaccines, antitoxins, and antisera; (e) tissue culture (a type of in vitro technique); (f) lower organisms and plants, including microorganisms (used for "studying the properties of living matter when organised as separate independent cells" and in the Ames test for carcinogens, and so on), invertebrates (used for basic physiological and biochemical studies), and eggs (used to culture viruses in embryological studies and for analyzing the effects of drugs on fetal development); (g) humans as subjects (epidemiological studies, experiments on human volunteers); (h) mass spectrometry and gas chromatography— refined forms of chemical analysis that allow for studies of human or animal blood in greatly amplified detail, sometimes effecting a reduction in the number of experiments performed; (i) audiovisual aids, which can in the schoolroom and laboratory sometimes replace demonstrations on live animals; (j) saturation analysis and radio-immunoassay, which are complex chemical techniques used chiefly for the detection of hormone concentrations in the blood and which promise to replace many older, standard forms of bioassay (defined as the "process of using living tissue to measure the presence or amount of some chemical substance"); and (k) miscellaneous cultures and laboratory tests, partly owing to which "the number of animals used for diagnostic purposes has been very greatly reduced in recent years.[32]

Several conclusions may be drawn at this point. First, there are many alternatives to animal experiments. Some may conceivably help to replace animals altogether in certain areas of research, whereas others may play a major or a minor role in reducing the number of animals needed. Although alternatives hold out the promise of diminishing sharply the amount of unnecessary animal suffering and death, it is evident that they will never come near to eliminating animal experiments.[33] Both the acquisition of basic scientific knowledge and the testing of vaccines, medications, surgical techniques, therapies, and so on will continue to require such research. If Smyth and others who have studied the prospects for alternatives are correct, it is easy to overestimate the likely impact of alternatives and to suppose, erroneously, that the complete replacement of animals in research is just a matter of time.

Second, the availability of present alternatives and also the likelihood of greater choice of alternatives in the future depend very much on the level or organization of living material under investigation. For less complex levels (cells, tissues) alternatives are more practicable than for more complex levels (whole organs, physiological systems, entire animals).

Third, as for the computer simulation of living systems, computers can only perform mathematical operations on data fed into them; therefore, as Smyth points out, "while the computer enables us to make more use of the data we get from animal experiments, and it may enable us to design and plan better experiments, it does nothing to replace experiments themselves." He stresses in addition that to model mathematically a whole animal or animal system in a completely adequate way, so that experiments with the model would yield exactly the same results as experiments with the living animal (and hence be able to replace it), we would need to know everything there is to know about the animal or animal system in question and would no longer need to do research on either animals or alternatives![34] In other words, as long as there is still important knowledge to be gained from the study of living systems, alternatives will serve as aids to research, steadily improving perhaps, but never becoming satisfactory surrogates for all categories of live animals.[35]

Fourth, according to Smyth at least, alternatives exist not primarily because of humane considerations but for purely scientific ones. For example:

> Tissue culture was first used for vaccine production in 1949, a long time before the present demand for alternatives. The driving force was the need to find a better protection against poliomyelitis. . . . Mass spectrometry and gas chromatography . . . are not new and do not require to be brought to the attention of biomedical research workers. Isotopes were first used in biochemical research by an American, Hevesy, in 1923, and the work was greatly stimulated by another American, Urey, in 1931. Since then there has been a continuous exploitation of their use by the best brains in biomedical science. . . . Radioimmunoassay was not developed as a way of reducing the number of animals used, but as a better method of estimating hormones.[36]

It would be prudent, then, to avoid jumping to the conclusion that but for a recalcitrant and unimaginative scientific establishment, laboratory animals could be spared their fate. It does not follow, of course, that concern for animal welfare is not also a spur to the development of alternatives. But those advocating greater reliance on and research into alternatives should realize that these cannot simply be willed into existence. A viable program of searching for alternatives would therefore recognize the principle, underscored earlier, that good science and good sensibility are converging interests.

Fifth, so far as animal experiments are believed by the scientists concerned to be indispensable for progress in biomedical and behavioral research, they are bound to continue. Indeed, a very strong impetus to animal experimentation was provided by the exposé at the Nuremberg trials of German medical atrocities during World War II; this and other subsequent revelations about abuses in peacetime medical research led to the development of strict ethical codes for experimentation on human subjects in many jurisdictions and research establishments, as well as to the World Medical Association's adoption of the Declaration of Helsinki in 1964. The latter reads, in part, "Clinical research must conform to the moral and scientific principles that justify medical research, and should be based on laboratory and animal experiments or other scientifically established facts."[37]

Sixth and last, the existence of alternatives, although having the effect of diminishing certain kinds of procedures using animals, may also act in the opposite direction to stimulate further animal experimentation which the newer techniques now render possible.[38]

The field of alternatives to animal research, then, may be seen as promising but also offering a mixed blessing rather than a panacea for resolving all laboratory animal problems. So far as *alternatives* is a useful buzz word, an effective rallying cry, it will continue to be heard on every conceivable occasion. The progress toward genuine alternatives to live animals in research will be slow and deliberate, not a stampede caused by pressures originating outside the scientific community. Scientists with a commitment to improving the lot of laboratory animals but who also want to pursue frontier research simply have to live with this situation, as do the critics of such investigations. As Sir P. B. Medawar has pointedly observed, "We must grapple with the paradox that nothing but research on animals will provide us with the knowledge that will make it possible for us, one day, to dispense with the use of them altogether."[39]

REPLACING ANIMALS IN PRODUCT TESTING

Many animals are routinely used in laboratories around the world for testing new commercial products, such as pharmaceuticals, food additives, cosmetics, and pesticides. These tests are required by regulatory legislation designed to protect the health and welfare of consumers, and they generally aim at establishing the degree to which new chemical compounds have potentially toxic or (in the case of cosmetics, for example) irritant effects. With an estimated "65,000 chemicals in common use already and another 1,000 being added every year,"[40] the magnitude of the task of testing is daunting, to say the least.

Although it may be argued reasonably that such testing is a form of scientific research since it is normally performed in a laboratory setting by individuals with scientific training and credentials, or at least under the supervision of such persons, I have not so far integrated this topic into my general discussion of the use of animals in experimentation for three reasons. First, product testing is a set of screening and safety evaluation procedures created in response to legislation requiring that certain manufactured articles be declared safe before marketing them. However, I wanted to keep the focus of the foregoing discussion on genuine scientific research, whose purpose is the discovery and advancement of knowledge. Animal testing is often confused by the media with research, leading to a negative impression of the latter, as when a bevy of immobilized rabbits awaiting the eye testing of some cosmetic product or the pyrogenicity (fever-causing property) testing of an injectable medication is represented as a typical research situation. Second, product testing raises ethical issues that are quite distinct from those generated by what I call true research. It would, of course, be naive to suppose that animal research and the testing of products on animals are totally unrelated endeavors, particularly as similar sorts of inferences to humans are drawn from both. Some might argue, however, that whereas research on animals can be justified and therefore should continue, animal testing—at least in its present form—is morally unacceptable. It is even conceivable that some would maintain the reverse, that testing can be justified in the interests of consumer protection, whereas experimentation (in whole or in part) cannot be. Third, although it is not likely that animal experiments will be replaced to a significant degree by alternatives in the near future (if ever), it appears probable that some of the standard product tests performed on animals, and which are among those most widely held to be morally objectionable, will be replaced before long by procedures that do not require animals. Indeed, it is arguable that the animal protectionists' drive for alternatives really amounts to a demand for change in the field of product testing more than anything else. (Their publications most often so direct their demands.)

There is little point in surveying here the legislative requirements for product testing and the procedures now in use, attempting to assess the pros and cons of each, since this has been done elsewhere by scientific writers familiar with this kind of laboratory work.[41] However, it may be useful to indicate a few areas where alternatives are making inroads into conventional ways of doing things.

The first of these is tissue culture, a technique that has been widely touted as the wave of the future. Tissue culture has been used successfully in the toxicology testing of various substances used in commercial products like those listed earlier. It has proved possible to observe microscopic structural alterations and to detect subtle biochemical changes in tissue cells preserved alive in vitro. Even though it is difficult to extrapolate from cellular reactions to reactions of entire organs and of entire organisms, toxicity can be identified at this simple level of organization. Furthermore, tissue culture offers the great advantage that human cells can be used, and thereby "the difficulty of species variation can be eliminated." [42] It goes without saying that if the objectives of toxicity testing could be met satisfactorily by employing tissue cultures alone, this method would be preferable from every point of view to live animal tests in which toxic reactions of substances fed by mouth, injected, or inhaled are indicated by a gamut of symptoms, from mild to extreme: "the animal looking quieter than usual, the coat losing condition, changes in breathing, changes in heart rate, loss of appetite, vomiting, diarrhoea, and in severer cases paralysis, convulsions or death." [43] The same would be true, obviously, in other areas where tissue culture either holds out some promise, such as in the testing of substances for carcinogenic properties (and of anticancer drugs), or is already well exploited, such as in the production of antiviral vaccines (for example, against poliomyelitis).

Another alternative that has attracted considerable attention is the Ames test for mutagenicity and carcinogenicity. This technique, which uses a mutated strain of the microorganism *Salmonella typhimurium*, has been demonstrated successfully in the analysis of 300 different chemicals. [44] A major improvement on the Ames test has recently been announced as well. This is the Hayes test, which uses genetically engineered *E. coli* bacteria to detect environmental carcinogens. [45]

A third area in which alternatives to conventional procedures are being vigorously pursued is cosmetics testing. The standard test for determining irritancy levels of cosmetics and toiletries generally is known as the Draize test. This test has gained a high degree of notoriety because it involves application of the chemical to be tested to the sensitive surface (epithelial cells) of rabbits' eyes. The animals are unable to escape or to engage in any kind of remedial behavior on their own behalf, and the effects on the eyes are carefully monitored over a period of hours or even days. The Draize test is perhaps the most clear example of a procedure that has aroused the central objection to using animals for product testing. As Smyth succinctly states, "Many people feel that large numbers of animals should not be killed to guarantee the safety of a product, particularly if it is one they themselves don't feel is necessary." [46] We often hear the argument that there is no need for yet another lipstick, shampoo, or deodorant and that if we want these things, we should buy only those that do not require animal tests to be marketed (and, if possible, those that contain no animal products either).

A further argument that has gained some currency among the opponents of current product testing procedures is that animals should not be sacrificed on account of human folly; if people wish to indulge their taste for inessentials like cosmetics, let them do so at their own risk. Products of this kind should be tested only on humans or released for sale with the warning that they are untested, in which case the caveat emptor principle strictly applies. The trouble with this position, however, is that even if we all agreed on which consumer items are inessential and which essential, we do as a matter of fact and common morality generally believe that society has an obligation to protect its members from self-harming behavior. It has a further obligation to prevent such behavior from taking place by, for instance, placing controls on potentially harmful substances: narcotic drugs, firearms, alcohol, and chemical compounds of unknown effect—cosmetics, pesticides, and so on; and, finally, to come to the assistance of those who have engaged, wittingly or unwittingly, in self-injurious behavior. Britain's Research Defence Society has stated the matter in this way:

> It may be argued that because cosmetics are used voluntarily, the user should not be protected from any harmful medical consequences of his or her act. This argument is not normally advanced, however, in respect of other voluntary self-damage (as in attempted suicide, alcoholism, traffic accidents, wounding and other general trauma requiring general surgery).[47]

A somewhat different approach is taken by F. L. Marcuse and J. J. Pear, who write,

> Antivivisectionists sometimes assert that animals should not be "made to pay" for human "sins." People have car accidents because of human "foolishness." People smoke too much and get lung cancer because they lack "willpower." But we live in a deterministic world, and the concept of "retribution" is not appropriate. Human life is more important to the culture than animal life is, regardless of the conditions that cause humans to engage in behavior that is dangerous to themselves.[48]

It would seem therefore that if these viewpoints are correct, we ought to acknowledge that cosmetics and their testing are here to stay and focus our attention instead on the alternatives to animal tests.

Recently—largely owing to pressures exerted by animal welfare lobbyists—Revlon and Avon, two giants of the cosmetics industry, have awarded very substantial grants to scientists at Rockefeller University for the express purpose of stimulating research into alternatives to the Draize test. Almost at the same time, the Cosmetics, Toiletry, and Fragrance Association awarded a grant to the Johns Hopkins Center for Alternatives to Animal Testing; Bristol-Myers also funded alternatives research by the British group Fund for the Replacement of Animals in Medical Experimentation (FRAME); the American Fund for Alternatives to Animal Research (with the support of other animal welfare groups and individuals) initiated a similar project at the Medical College of Pennsylvania; and the New England Antivivisection Society did likewise at Tufts University School of Medicine. To this date no breakthroughs have been announced, but encouraging signs of progress are evident.[49] Also, research into a number of other fruitful alternatives for product testing and for medical research generally has been funded since 1970 by the Dr. Hadwen Trust for Humane Research in Britain.[50]

Fourth and finally, some ideas have begun to emerge for easing animals' burden as test subjects in the measurement of lethal toxicity levels for different substances. The legislated standard procedure for ascertaining these at present in the United Kingdom, North America, Australia, parts of the Middle East, Asia, the Pacific, and Africa is the LD_{50} test. The name of this test is an abbreviation for "lethal dose 50 percent," or the amount of a substance resulting in death for half of a given group of experimental animals. Many reservations have been expressed about the LD_{50} test, ranging from the alleged inhumaneness of using it as an experimental tool (since test animals often have to be force fed the materials under investigation and cannot, in the nature of the case, be anesthetized, administered analgesics, or prematurely euthanized), the sheer crudity and apparent arbitrariness of the test as a method for obtaining a criterion of product safety, and its inability to determine the long-term effects of exposure to potentially inter-acting (synergistic) chemical substances to other, more scientific objections about, for example, the way of determining the time period over which a substance's (say, a drug's) potentially lethal effects are to be measured or the appropriateness of using "a test for lethal toxicity . . . as a test for non-lethal toxicity, or at least to give assurances about non-lethal toxicity."[51]

A *Report on the LD$_{50}$ Test*, prepared in England by the Advisory Committee on the Administration of the Cruelty to Animals Act 1876, indicates that when this test was first devised in 1927, its purpose was quite well defined:

> ... to overcome difficulties which arose in measuring the potency of highly toxic yet potentially beneficial medicines of natural origin such as diphtheria antitoxin, digitalis and insulin. Where the difference between a therapeutic and a toxic dose is narrow, it is clearly most important to know the strength of the preparation to be given as precisely and accurately as possible. In the absence of clear indices of biological action, ... lethality of such compounds was the only readily available property capable of precise and accurate determination.[52]

This original purpose, as noted earlier, has given way increasingly to the use of the LD$_{50}$ as an international standard for measuring antitoxicity levels. The committee established that roughly 5 percent of all experiments done in the United Kingdom during 1977—or 229,500—were of this sort. Having heard testimony from numerous experts representing diverse viewpoints, the committee came to the following conclusion: "The evidence given to us leaves no doubt whatever in our minds that at the present time for the proper safety evaluation of new substances some acute and chronic toxicity tests must be carried out on whole live animals." It also affirmed a statement of the British Medical Research Council that " 'the LD$_{50}$ test is the only reliable measure of acute toxicity and yields a result with the least possible expenditure of life.' "[53] However, the committee also recognized the fact that several factors could bring about a significant decline in the use of the LD$_{50}$ test: a tendency to turn to nonanimal testing once the type of toxicity a substance possesses has been established; the use of human volunteers as subjects; advances in the biochemical understanding of "the active principle in drugs"; the use of fewer animals per test; and the use of limit tests (dosing up to "some arbitrary level assumed to be safe")[54] whenever possible, as in the cosmetics industry. These trends would all represent positive steps in the direction indicated by Russell and Burch's "3 R" principle of replacement, reduction, and refinement. In addition, the adoption of uniform regulations for the laboratory testing of toxic materials and closer observation of animals undergoing tests could help reduce the quantity and duration of suffering experienced by them without affecting the statistical significance of the tests. It does not appear, however, that the LD_{50} test is likely to be phased out or entirely supplanted, as far as we can see into the future.

In sum, the search for alternatives to current methods of product testing is ongoing, stimulated by both humane and scientific considerations. But it is also a mixed bag: In some cases, progress and even breakthroughs can reasonably be anticipated, whereas in others, as long as animal experiments are generally believed vital for the protection of human health and welfare, it is difficult to see how certain painful procedures—or something very similar to them—can be eliminated. This conclusion is reinforced by the fact that alternatives have their own limitations, of which we are seldom made aware by those hastening to usher in a glorious new age of animal replacements. Consider the following observation by two authors working in the field of cancer research: "As yet, no single test or single battery of in vitro tests has emerged as the best suited for carcinogen testing or carcinogen screening. Nearly all of the tests produce both false negative and false positive results. (The Ames test, for example, was positive for Tris, the flame retardant, but negative for DES [diethylstilbestrol].)" [55]

I may point out too that clamoring for restrictions on the cosmetics industry to prevent the development (and hence the testing) of still more new compounds is naive behavior in a capitalist economy. It is mere utopian wish fulfillment to suppose that the drive to seek greater profits through the artificial creation of new needs can be checked without changing the system and society as a whole. In addition, in the present system such restrictions would act as restraints on trade, effectively penalizing small or new companies striving to capture part of a lucrative market. Whether or not we endorse our economic system, its basic dynamics can only be altered at the roots, not at the leaf tips. Much more realistic is the attitude taken by Bernard Rollin in a recent book generally critical of research and product testing: "The most currently viable hope for diminishing the total amount of suffering [in animal experimentation] is by refinement of existing procedures, by the introduction of anaesthetics and analgesics, by the mitigation of stress and anxiety, all of which attempt to deal with the current realities of research." [56]

Critics of cosmetics testing would be wise to avoid the inconsistencies that sometimes creep into their position. For instance, it appears that those who oppose the use of animals for product testing are also among the most vociferous supporters of consumer protection legislation. We cannot have it both ways, however: Either we endorse a policy of protectionism and accept its consequences, and hence animal tests, or we do not.

In addition, the foes of product testing on animals have often failed to notice that one of their favorite arguments against experimenting on nonhuman creatures—animals' similarity to us—is a double-edged sword. We cannot at the same time acknowledge that animals are so similar to humans that we must maintain high ethical standards in dealing with them and deny (as many do) the adequacy of animal models of human systems for the purposes of safety testing.[57]

REPLACING ANIMALS IN DRUG RESEARCH AND DEVELOPMENT

Smyth has pointed out (though without giving any figures) that "probably by far the largest use of animals in medical research is by the pharmaceutical industry."[58] The role of animals in drug research and development is manifold. Animals are involved throughout the preclinical stages of investigation. It has been estimated that "of the 7–10 years it takes for a new drug to reach the market, 4 on average are devoted to preclinical trials, in which animal experiments predominate."[59] To begin with, a new compound must be screened to determine what, if any, therapeutic effects it possesses. At the next stage, animal tests reveal the nature of the substance's activity within a living organism. Safety or toxicological tests are then initiated to discover what side effects the compound may have. These comprise the LD_{50} test (discussed previously), subacute safety tests, perinatal or teratological tests (which identify any effects the chemical exerts on fetal development), mutagen tests, carcinogen tests, and chronic use tests. Drug regulatory laws require that such tests be performed on a variety of species. Even during later clinical trials on humans, animal tests may continue to be used to arrive at a better understanding of the drug's metabolic behavior within a similar organism.[60] It is clear, then, that the pharmaceutical industry is committed to using a very large number of animals.

We must also bear in mind that most drug companies operate within a capitalistic, competitive economic system and that because of this, widespread or unnecessary replication of pharmaceutical research is virtually inevitable. G. J. V. Nossal comments pointedly on this feature of drug R and D in *Medical Science and Human Goals*:

> One of the worst features of research in the drug industry is the work which needs to be done to make and test products which are only marginally different from existing ones. As soon as a real therapeutic advance occurs, there is a great temptation for a competitor to come along with a drug differing slightly in chemical composition which can then be marketed without patent infringement. This kind of work is mentally stultifying and, with rare exceptions, of no benefit to mankind. . . . I fear . . . that to a degree this wastefulness is built into the system, and part of the price we have to pay for the free market framework.[61]

It may be unfortunate that given the profit-oriented economies of the West, there is no escape from this vicious circle. Excessive use of animals and unnecessary suffering appear to be assured by the prevailing method of doing business.

There are, however, some hopeful developments here too. As we saw earlier, drug design with the aid of computers promises to circumvent certain stages of R and D that normally require animals. The advantages to this technology are not only reduction or replacement of animals in particular procedures but also the increased accuracy of prediction of drugs' effects that is afforded by a detailed understanding of new compounds at the molecular level.[62] In addition, progress is being made in the development of novel in vitro techniques to replace animals. The latest and most startling of these is the use of enzymes extracted from mung bean roots to screen anticonvulsant drugs.[63]

This may be an appropriate place to comment briefly on another issue related to the replacement of animals in drug R and D. Antivivisectionist critics of the pharmaceutical industry frequently hold up the examples of thalidomide and DES as drugs that have had broad-ranging tragic effects on human lives and argue that such cases show the inadequacy of safety testing drugs on animals. The answer given by those who support animal testing is that although infallibility cannot be hoped for in such matters, the lesson learned from these drug disasters is that more rather than fewer animal tests are called for. As Smyth reports, for example, the United States was spared the epidemic of thalidomide deformities because the FDA prohibited its sale on the grounds of insufficient animal testing.[64] It may be that more refined and specialized knowledge of appropriate animal models acquired since this drug was first manufactured in 1957, plus the greater use of teratological tests and the information provided by the new science of drug design, can help avert similar tragedies in the future.

FUTURE PROSPECTS AND POLITICAL IMPLICATIONS

We have seen that the notion of alternatives to laboratory experimentation on live animals is ambiguous, having quite different meanings in different contexts and embracing a variety of approaches and innovations in methodology and technique. In addition, the future of alternatives, as I have indicated, is promising in certain areas but does not warrant so rosy a picture as some have painted nor support the call for a wholesale replacement of laboratory animals by surrogates.

In spite of these conclusions, however, the scientific community and its critics within the humane movement do not see eye to eye much of the time on the issue of alternatives, and continued confrontation and antagonism can be expected unless better communication and genuine dialogue between them comes about. Pressure for change, modernization, and accountability are, in general, desirable in most areas of life and work, at least so far as they lead to critical examination of routine assumptions and entrenched attitudes and values and to a greater sense of individual responsibility. This is no less the case in laboratory animal science than in other areas, and therefore public scrutiny of research using animals and sustained by tax dollars is a healthy sign—indeed, one that should be welcomed by the scientific community itself as a way of breaking out of its traditional insularity. That extramural criticism is not always greeted with enthusiasm by scientists will surprise no one. But just as in marital strife there are always two sides to the story, so are there here. The scientific community for its part has customarily been reluctant to avow its accountability to the public. It has been far too ready to assert, often condescendingly, that scientific matters are too complex to be understood by mere laypersons and consequently insufficiently willing to convey its methods and findings and their implications in terms accessible to nonspecialists. Animal welfarists, on the other hand, have too often been unwilling to exercise the patience and sophistication necessary to understand scientific objectives and procedures and the process out of which practical applications of laboratory studies emerge. They have been incautious about accepting half-truths, misrepresentations, and innuendos at face value and have frequently reacted emotionally rather than rationally; they have failed to seek full and adequate information even when it has been readily available.

Obviously, many opportunities have been lost in this adversarial opposition. Most important, the common interest that the two parties share, discussed earlier, has until recently been all but obscured from view. Since 1980 a steady flow of animal welfare legislation has been introduced into the U.S. Congress and various state legislatures, and enormous amounts of time and money have been spent deliberating over new bills and amendments to old ones. Both animal welfare and scientific organizations have given extended testimony before congressional committees, and the search continues for legislation that can command sufficient support to pass in both houses of Congress.[65] Most of the debate centers around NIH authorization bills and amendments to the federal Animal Welfare Act of 1966, revised previously in 1970 and 1976. Various versions of the legislation have proposed a diversion of up to 50 percent of federal animal research funds to the study of alternatives, as well as restrictions on the verification of results by duplicate experiments and other measures which the scientific community finds unacceptable.[66] (Similar legislation is under consideration in several Western European countries and is also pending before the Council of Europe, which is attempting to draft a Convention for the Protection of Vertebrate Animals used in experiments. A new laboratory animals protection bill, developed by Lord Halsbury and intended to replace the Cruelty to Animals Act 1876, is nearing parliamentary consideration in Britain.)

The scientific community can scarcely avoid perceiving the kind of impetus that lies behind these legislative reforms. The handwriting is on the wall, and if researchers want to preserve their independence and their proper role in society, they should seize the initiative to a greater degree than they have thus far. As one observer has commented,

> If we accept the thesis that highly restrictive legislation is socially undesirable, then the scientific community should be in the forefront of the effort to protect research animals, ameliorate their lot and strive toward eliminating their use. . . .

Those who are concerned with protecting the freedom of science must demonstrate leadership and take prompt action in regard to research animals, or else the absolutists will.[67]

Some initiatives that deserve special mention are the formulation of guidelines for pain research by the International Association for the Study of Pain and for neuroscience studies by the Society for Neuroscience; the adoption of a statement of humane animal use by the *American Journal of Physiology*, to which all research published by it is expected to conform; and the release for public discussion of the NIH's new draft policy on humane care and use of animals.[68]

It would be unfortunate if we neglected to take note as well of some efforts at dialogue and cooperation between the research community and its critics. In Canada the Canadian Council on Animal Care, "an autonomous advisory and supervisory body operating under the aegis of the Association of Universities and Colleges of Canada and supported financially by the Natural Sciences and Engineering Research Council and the Medical Research Council,"[69] has experienced a large measure of success in improving animal welfare. Since its founding in 1968, the CCAC has promoted voluntary guidelines for animal care and use in research facilities, both publicly supported and private. To a large extent it has set the standards of humaneness for these institutions, stimulating scientists to police themselves through a system of local animal care and ethics review committees. CCAC panels that conduct additional on-site inspections of research facilities always include laypersons representing the animal welfare movement. The council's *Guide to the Care and Use of Experimental Animals* is widely available and carefully followed.[70] (Its short statement of ethical principles is included as an appendix to this book.)

In the United States a growing number of conferences are bringing together experts in scientific research, animal behavior, philosophy, humane research, and other areas to discuss and debate issues of common concern in public forums. In addition, a few veterinary medical schools have introduced courses in veterinary medical ethics.[71]

In the United Kingdom a number of symposia have been conducted and their proceedings published.[72] These, together with related books, have also made a major contribution to increasing the prospects for further constructive examination of sensitive issues.

These indicators suggest that greater cooperation between scientists and welfarists and increased interest in humane animal experimentation are at least within the realm of possibility.

Whatever may result eventually on the legislative front, pressures will continue to mount outside and within the scientific community for a more widespread and enlightened attitude toward alternatives. Various symposia and publications cited and discussed in this chapter and noted in the bibliography will give the reader a sense of the activity going on currently in this area. One important aspect of the entire issue, to which the scientific community has not yet adequately addressed itself, is the degree to which the search for alternatives might correctly be seen as a function of imagination and hence could be encouraged by appropriately modified training in the basic experimental design at the postsecondary level. Two examples of such creative thinking are cited by Dallas Pratt in his 1980 book, *Alternatives to Pain in Experiments on Animals*.[73] One concerns the use of a low, reversible dose of amphetamine to produce the same behavioral deficit as that found in punishment-induced "learned helplessness" (see the section on "Behavioral Research with Notoriety" in chapter 4). The other experiment—the testing of behavioral responses under the effects of various drugs—introduces the deprivation of a small reward as punishment for failure to perform a required task, in place of electrical shock or some other aversive stimulus.[74]

There would seem, then, to be much room for improved communication and reeducation within the humane movement and the scientific community, as well as for meaningful contact between these two dedicated groups. Those advocating reforms in research using live animals will almost certainly help bring about some constructive changes in the way scientists are trained and their work done. But it is equally apparent that much energy and time and many resources will be wasted in further confrontation, rhetoric, and obstructionist tactics by both sides. The danger, as always, is that ignorance and irrationality will triumph. Perhaps it is the dialectic of progress in such controversial areas of human life that renders adversarial struggle inevitable. We must hope that better mutual understanding will carry the day; otherwise we will all be the losers.

In a very real sense there is no alternative to animal research. Abandoning animal research altogether, even though this might be favored by relatively few, is unrealistic and counterproductive because it would force society either to forgo certain obvious benefits in health and well-being or to turn to ethically unacceptable human research. Severe curtailment of animal research by legislation or other means would amount to a de facto decision that the pursuit of knowledge in certain crucial areas cannot be allowed to continue. To many this is also ethically unacceptable in a free society. Some but not all animal experiments will become unnecessary in time with the advent of genuine replacement techniques. Many of the experiments that remain will involve stress and pain in varying degrees. The inescapable dilemma is that although we can control some of this suffering, we cannot eliminate all of it, and we thus benefit from the deliberate harming of other sentient beings, which in the human sphere we pledge ourselves to avoid. There are individuals who state their own (theoretical) willingness to sacrifice severely defective humans—even their own children, if it came to that—for scientific research in place of healthy higher animals.[75] (Such generosity, however, is rarely extended to their own lives in the eventuality that they became gravely incapacitated and hence defective.) Fortunately, this is a tiny fringe minority. But a sizable and increasingly powerful minority of citizens, many of whom are thoughtful and legitimately concerned, is pressing for much tighter control over animal experimentation. We are at a crucial watershed at the present time, for these pressures are being felt by society as a political force issuing in a demand for legislative reform. It is therefore vital that everyone—scientists, legislators, animal protectionists, and other members of the public alike—realize that a choice has to be made about the future of research and seek a rational compromise in full awareness of the costs to us all (and to the animals) of restricted research.

7

Conclusion

AN ETHICAL AND HUMANE PERSPECTIVE
ON ANIMALS

I have attempted in this book to review a broad range of issues pertaining to the morality of using animals for experimental purposes. Questions concerning our attitudes toward animals, the evolutionary relationship between humans and animals, and how animals fit into our ethical scheme have been raised, and the positions arrived at, together with some considerations about the nature of scientific inquiry, have served as the foundation for discussing the ethics of experimentation using live animals and of the humane principles that should govern this widespread activity. Although my viewpoint throughout has been strongly proresearch, I have also made a case for the need to reduce or eliminate animal suffering wherever possible as well as to give greater and more thoughtful attention to these issues.

In concluding, I wish to address the question whether it is possible to condone the use of animals for human ends, specifically experimentation, and yet maintain a healthy and humane attitude toward them. Can we go on consuming laboratory animals at an astonishing rate and still value them enough to preserve and nurture our ethical sensibilities toward other species, indeed, toward nature as a whole? This is a large and complex question. But rather than just shrug and say, "It's anybody's guess," let us examine it briefly.

To speak of maintaining a healthy and humane attitude toward other creatures seems to me to mean this: to advocate a sane and reasonable policy about their coexistence with us within the same planetary ecosystem and to bear in mind at all times that many animals are sentient beings capable of suffering at our hands and on which it is therefore wrong to inflict pain unnecessarily. I see nothing in this understanding of humaneness that is in essence antithetical to animal experimentation. Therefore, to use animals as sparingly as we can, causing as little suffering as we can in the process, seems acceptable. It is not healthy, as I have defined the term, to use endangered species for experimental purposes—unless, of course, we did so under the most stringent conditions and to promote the species' survival chances. The process of trapping certain primates and transporting them to North America for experimentation has been reliably estimated to be responsible for a 70 percent mortality rate among the captive animals.[1] When it is added that many of the unfortunate survivors have been subjected to tests of the effects of nuclear, chemical, and biological weapons, it is not difficult for most of us to discern here an unhealthy—and inhumane—use of animals. Certainly, the governments of India and Bangladesh must have drawn a similar conclusion when they decided to ban the export of rhesus monkeys in 1978 and 1979 respectively, as must the government of Malaysia when it acted to prohibit trade in long-tailed macaques in early 1984.[2] Part of what makes cruelty to animals unhealthy is that it degrades us, and consequently such activities as these should be prevented in the interests of our own psychological and moral well-being, as well as in the interests of animals. Also, it is not humane to violate reasonable moral precepts relating to animals (see chapter 3) or those principles in terms of which "unnecessary suffering" is defined (see chapter 6).

Still, critics and opponents of animal experimentation may persist in asking questions like How do we show our respect for animals, our reverence for all life, by killing other creatures on a massive scale in the name of research? But, of course, we do not demonstrate our respect or reverence in this way; we demonstrate it rather by our attitudes toward what we do with animals and by the way in which we treat animals that we put to human uses. So I have chosen to interpret the foregoing question as Can we show respect toward animals and revere nature while still using millions of animals annually for research? To this I think the answer is yes.

The notion of respect is at best ambiguous in relation to animals. How can I show respect for a tortoise, an ostrich, a caterpillar, a maggot, a gnat, an amoeba—all of which are equally animals in the sense defined in the introduction? What should *respect* be taken to mean here? If it means "of a kind and to a degree appropriate to the given form of life," then this might at least make some sense, but it would then be questionable whether it is appropriate to cultivate the same attitude toward all animals. Respect is a concept that applies readily to persons. It is not at all clear how it is to be applied to animals, which are not, so far as anyone has been able to show, persons in the moral or in any other sense. Nor, I have argued (see chapter 1), can intrinsic value be ascribed to animals' lives. Therefore, I shall take the word *respect* to signify here dedication to a policy of caution, generosity, kindness, and minimal interference in our dealings with animals and their habitats, which in turn is derived from considerations about why cruelty to animals is wrong (see chapter 3).

Reverence, although essentially a religious concept, has its secular parallel in the sense of awe that the experience and study of nature inspire in us. As many scientists have realized themselves and shown to others, learning more through research about the living world of which we are a part increases our reverence for nature.[3] There are plentiful examples of areas of basic research from which such beneficial though intangible effects are derived. Many of these are exactly the kinds of research which antivivisectionists commonly label "trivial" and "merely curiosity oriented": the study of animal migration; of why fireflies flash; of bat navigation; of the mechanisms of sex in nonhuman species; of the symbiotic behavior of fish, like the cleaner wrasse, which feeds off the teeth of larger fish; of pleasure centers in the brain.[4]

Since the use of animals for human ends is morally permissible (can be justified), we are not required by any principles of obligation to demonstrate our respect for animals and our reverence for nature by refraining from using them for our own ends—even when this involves taking their lives. We maintain our respect and reverence for the biosphere by considering what we do with the utmost seriousness and by conducting ourselves—as in experimentation on living animals—with the greatest degree of critical self-awareness and responsibility. Only in this way can we retain our dignity and our sensitivity toward suffering wherever it occurs. Because we respect and revere those things to which we assign value in proportion to the desired experiences they give us, and because we are capable of sympathy with animals and of understanding our natural relationship to them, there need be no conflict between valuing animals, on the one hand, and experimenting on them, on the other, since using animals for experimentation also reflects our basic value commitments—namely, the priority or degree of worth we assign to human life and well-being and the relative use value we assign to other species as means to certain of our ends. There is no contradiction in this, though there may be (and probably always will be) conflicts of values which we must resolve, such as those that arise from experimentation on endangered species or from the infliction of suffering for relatively small but still significant gains in knowledge or for extended periods of time.

If, then, the guiding purposes behind animal experimentation are held to be (a) the alleviation of suffering (in the broadest sense) in both humans and animals and (b) the accumulation of knowledge to the extent that it may conceivably contribute to (a), research, humaneness, and respect for life are conceptually and emotionally compatible. To cite a recent study of the principles of humane education,

> Humaneness is a construct which describes an attitude on the part of an individual whereby he exhibits behavior patterns reflective of a balanced sensitivity to all things, i.e., a respect or reverence for all sentient creation. The goal is not only the survival of life forms but [their] survival in a world where cruelty and suffering are minimal.[5]

Although some readers will take issue with the position just set forth and no doubt think they find false sincerity in my view, I believe there is nothing here that is contrary to the spirit of Albert Schweitzer's ethics of reverence for life, or at least a secularized version of it. The gentle doctor grappled daily and profoundly with the moral burden of sacrificing life for the benefit of other life, remarking once with resignation that "reverence for life is an inexorable creditor!"[6] It has been noted of Schweitzer that "ironically, many of his efforts in Africa were devoted toward destroying life: the predators, the encroaching vegetation and the disease organisms among the native peoples."[7] Another commentator has observed in addition that Schweitzer "approved of animal experimentation carried out humanely."[8] It follows, I believe, that whatever contradictions may be thought to reside in the standpoint I have defended must be traced back to the irresolvable paradox with which we began—that of *Homo sapiens'* dual role as both an animal that is part of nature and a reflective, valuing being that stands outside nature.

RECOMMENDATIONS

In a work such as this, a section on recommendations may seem somewhat out of place. This book is after all not a report, nor was it commissioned by any interest group or agency. It is rather a product of personal interest and independent scholarship. Nevertheless, some readers who are responsible for resolving the problems of animal welfare at the practical, everyday level may find it valuable to have such a list, however brief, and others may derive some benefit from it as a guide to further thought and action. For these reasons I offer the following recommendations aimed at reducing animal suffering in scientific research.

1. Animal care and peer ethics review committees should be legally required at all facilities where animals are used for experimental purposes, whether publicly or privately financed.

2. Efforts should continue toward formulating a standardized code of ethics to govern all laboratory animal research that is both acceptable to scientists and capable of meeting reasonable animal welfare requirements.[9]

3. Efforts should continue toward formulating a standardized description of pain symptoms for each species of laboratory animal and toward formulating standardized criteria for assessing the degree of pain an animal of choice is experiencing, or is likely to experience, in a given experiment, to be used as guidelines for deciding on the acceptability of a given project or procedure.[10]

4. Laypersons should be represented on all ethics review committees. Veterinarians should be represented as well or at least be available for regular consultation.

5. Laboratory animal technicians should be required to achieve certification by the Canadian Association for Laboratory Animal Science (CALAS), the American Association for Laboratory Animal Science (AALAS), or the equivalent.

6. All individuals performing or assisting in research on live animals should have adequate training in animal care and handling, in experimental technique, and where appropriate in experimental design.[11]

7. University-level programs in the biological sciences and experimental psychology should require successful completion of training in experimental design and technique, and should include a course in which ethical issues of experimentation on animals are discussed fully and frankly.

8. Education in the humane treatment of animals should be featured at all levels of training in the biological sciences and in experimental psychology.

9. Animal care and experimental facilities, whether public or privately financed, should be subject to surprise inspections by government examiners empowered to require an improvement in conditions or the termination of research procedures on humane grounds. Sufficient funds should be allotted to this policing function to ensure that such visits actually take place. Government examiners charged with this responsibility should have relevant scientific and humane training.

10. Universal but nonrestrictive legislative standards should be enacted to guarantee that animal environments and care are conducive to maintaining natural patterns of behavior and the satisfaction of normal needs. The freedom to stand up, lie down, turn around, groom or preen, exercise, have social contact with other members of the species, and so on are basic conditions of this sort; cleanliness, adequate fresh air, water and food, light/dark cycles, general health, and similar factors should also be taken into account. The design of new facilities should incorporate features of the sort required to satisfy enlightened and reasonable humane standards. Accreditation, by the American Association for the Accreditation of Laboratory Animal Care (AAALAC) or the equivalent, of all research facilities in which animals are used and housed should be made legally mandatory.

11. "Scientists should be completely open with the general public concerning their procedures and the reasons for using them . . . [for] secrecy breeds suspicion and hostility which sooner or later must be allayed by openness." [12]

There may be additional areas which some may feel require such prescriptions. I have only touched on those matters that are of concern to the greatest cross section of individuals who have taken a constructive view of laboratory animal welfare. These recommendations represent not only the outcome of my own thinking on the subject of animal experimentation but also, I believe, a consensus of the views of individuals in the humane movement or practicing research with whom I have had discussions or whose work I have heard presented or consulted on my own. In my judgment, narrowing our attention to a relatively small number of matters, like those contained in the preceding list, offers the best promise of progress toward more humane standards for animal experimentation. Anyone with experience in the humane movement will, in any case, readily affirm that change comes about slowly and that setting our sights at a realistic level is enough of a challenge.

EDUCATION, LEGISLATION, AND CHANGING ATTITUDES AND BEHAVIOR

The foregoing recommendations mostly concern courses of action which the scientific community and its educational system are urged to follow. I have also, however, given certain indications of the role legislation might reasonably be expected to play in reforming animal research in the direction of greater humaneness. Before discussing this, however, let us look at education as a force for instilling humane attitudes.

It is generally assumed that education is the context that provides the most effective means of shaping children's values and attitudes. If we want people as adults to be humane toward animals, we should reach them with our message as early as possible, when they are still impressionable and therefore amenable to this kind of influence. We naturally tend to assume as well that if we want people's attitudes to change, education (in some form) is the route to follow. Unfortunately, the situation is not so simple. A distinction must be made, first of all, between attitude formation and attitude change. The influences that account for attitude formation appear to be better understood, and although the educational system is an important factor here, the consensus among psychologists is that many other competing sources also play a large role in this process—for example, family, peers, electronic communications and mass media, churches, and clubs.[13] Furthermore, education may itself be thought of as a package of experiences rather than just formal schooling. Nevertheless, since we have to begin somewhere and the problems of basic attitude formation must be tackled at various levels of society, education is one important place at which to try to exert an influence on developing minds. In this setting, for instance, adult examples of humane behavior and children's own early practical experiences with handling and caring for animals would be reinforced at a later developmental stage when the children's cognitive skills enable them to understand and see the force of, say, ethical arguments like the ones presented in this book.

Now what about people whose attitudes and values have already been formed? Here the common conviction is that ingrained beliefs, which have been reinforced by years of corresponding behavior and form part of a comprehensive and relatively inflexible worldview, are very difficult to change. A leading textbook on attitude research states,

> A person's attitude [toward an object] is determined by his salient beliefs about the object's attributes and by his evaluations of these attributes. At any point in time, a person holds a limited number of salient beliefs about any given object, action, or event, and those beliefs serve as the primary determinants of his attitude toward that object, action, or event.[14]

It would seem, then, that there is a significant role for education to play in attitude change as well as in attitude formation, for many people have a very limited knowledge and appreciation of animals' capacities or attributes.

But psychologists are far from agreement on the question of what factors are crucial in changing attitudes.[15] Also, the connection between attitude change and corresponding changes in behavior is much less straightforward than we might suppose. Martin Fishbein and Icek Ajzen, authors of the just-mentioned textbook, note that *"the effects of an influence attempt on change in beliefs, attitudes, intentions, and behaviors depend, in that order, on an increasing number of intervening processes* [i.e., variables]." Therefore, they continue, "the largest number of processes intervenes between an influence attempt and behavioral change."[16] Attitude research forces us to conclude, then, that it is very unclear what sorts of changes in belief lead to what sorts of changes in attitude and in turn to what sorts of behavioral changes toward the object in question. The consolation is that attitudes—even those that are firmly entrenched and emotion laden—can sometimes be changed by rational and other appeals. It therefore seems worth trying to do so, in the name of education in the broadest sense, even if the outcome is uncertain.

This brings us to the issue of the role of legislation in changing human attitudes, in this case, attitudes toward animals and more generally toward nature. It is a commonplace that "you can't legislate morality." What seems to be meant here is that merely changing laws cannot force people to reconsider and think differently about moral issues. If the emphasis is placed upon the "merely," then there is some truth in this assertion. But on the whole, it is false, as I think recent experience with civil rights legislation has shown especially vividly. Many people are fond of reiterating this piece of popular wisdom whenever radical social change is called for. "You can't legislate morality" has been the watchword of reactionaries and vested interests whenever the moral status quo is threatened by genuine, deep-cutting democratic reforms. Thus it was frequently heard during the 1960s when the civil rights movement in the United States had gathered its greatest momentum, and it has been heard again during the seventies and eighties as an explanation of why the feminist movement is supposedly following the wrong tactics (for example, pushing for adoption of the Equal Rights Amendment in the United States and—successfully—for equal rights clauses in the new Canadian Charter of Rights and Freedoms).

It is arguable, in my opinion, that although education and broader experience of the world do it better, legislation can help alter people's moral outlook to a significant extent. Indeed, it seems as if legislation sometimes acts as a catalyst for change in the area of intractable social problems, such as racial and sexual discrimination. Again taking the American civil rights movement as an example, it can be seen that compelling people to do what they ought to do anyway (in this case, treat blacks equally) gives them the exposure to new ways—an educational experience—that is necessary to produce more tolerant ways of thinking and acting; these ways in time become acceptable norms determining routine behavior in a manner that itself becomes second nature. Similar benefits to society have accrued in the area of women's equality and in the protection of the rights of the handicapped, the elderly, and other minorities. It may not be too much to say that legislative and judiciary bodies lead rather than follow public opinion in establishing norms of belief and behavior. Whether they should do so is debatable, but certainly evidence that they do is not lacking if we look at actual practice.

Could attitudes toward animals be changed by legislation? Evidently, many think so. Whether or not we support any particular new law, there would seem to be enough grounds for this belief that concerned individuals should be prepared to support fairly far-reaching animal welfare laws designed to control various abusive practices, just as they should support environmental protection legislation partly from the same motive.

Old ways die hard. We must exploit the possibilities for change that the educational system affords and recognize that some of the best hopes for eventual and lasting change rest there. But we must also remember that the majority of citizens—including all the decision makers and power wielders—are beyond the direct influence of educational institutions, and if their behavior is to be changed, legislation is probably necessary. Legislation is not a panacea for society's ills, but it does act to reinforce whatever moral stance society, for whatever reason, decides it ought to adopt.

Many would be prepared to acknowledge that the scientific community has, at least over the past few decades, begun to police itself a good deal more effectively in the area of animal experimentation. But a sizable body of opinion also holds that "self-regulation by the researchers themselves is not a rational way to insure [that] no abuse occurs: it is much too difficult to maintain an unbiased perspective."[17] We might reasonably accept that there is some truth in this observation and that consequently legislative vigilance of some kind is required in this area. Putting aside the fairly academic question of whether legislation can change morality, then, the real matter is that animals need protection from abuses perpetrated by humans. To the extent that laws proscribe certain practices and furnish the basis for enforcing such prohibitions, animals will benefit from legislation that is judiciously drafted, enforceable, and diligently enforced. If the point is to control certain forms of inhumane behavior, the law—whatever else may be said—is the most important vehicle toward which to direct our attention.

Whereas the greatest attention has been focused on the problem of drafting improved yet practically workable animal welfare legislation and on reforming and extending existing legislation, the idea of creating legal rights for animals has also begun to acquire some respectability in recent years. In chapter 3 I distinguished between moral and legal rights. Subsequent discussion supported the conclusion that animals do not have moral rights. We may now ask whether it makes sense to ascribe legal rights to them.

What does it mean for someone or something to have legal rights? Christopher Stone, in his excellent little book *Should Trees Have Standing?* (more illuminatingly subtitled *Toward Legal Rights for*

Natural Objects), offers the following analysis: "For a thing to be a holder of legal rights, nothing is more basic than that there be in the social structure some authoritative body prepared to review and call to question the actions of those who threaten it." In addition, however, Stone maintains that three other conditions must be met. These are as follows: "First, that the thing can institute legal actions at *its* behest—to have what the lawyer calls *standing*; second, that in determining whether to grant legal relief, the court must take *its* injuries into account; and third, that relief must run to *its* benefit."[18] By straightforward application, if animals are to be given legal rights, they must be considered to have legal standing in the sense just described, in which case a court-appointed guardian could press claims and seek redress on their behalf. This would mark a significant change in the law, since animals would acquire the status of "jural personhood," meaning that procedures concerning injury and redress would become applicable to them, just as if they were persons in the fullest sense instead of objects or mere property.

Stone argues strongly that all parts of the environment, whether inanimate or animate, should be given the same sort of legal standing or jural personhood. The chief gains from this maneuver would be two: (1) Injury to the interests of some other party (say, the animal's owner) would not have to be established first to gain access to the judicial process, since injury to the natural object (or animal) would qualify it to seek remedial legal action on its own behalf. (2) Redress would not be limited to compensation to other interested parties for damages suffered, but also would include reparations to the natural object (or animal) itself—which would now be the plaintiff—to restore it to its original state.

We should be very careful, however, that we understand exactly what assigning legal rights to animals would mean. Many defenders of animal rights go astray by confusing (a) the legal function of preserving and protecting basic moral rights with (b) the granting of legal standing or jural personhood in the sense under discussion. But it would seem obvious that a being which it is inappropriate to describe as having fundamental or inalienable moral rights cannot have these nonexistent rights enshrined in and defended by law. Hence only (b) furnishes a plausible context within which to discuss legal rights for animals.

So far as animals' legal standing is concerned, then, the rights they would acquire would presumably be limited to those that fall under the heading of due process rights—rights to make claims in a court of law, sue, appear and be heard in court, receive compensation, and generally to forestall decisions that would negatively affect the operation of their interests. This does not imply, however, that animals have (or should be seen as having) rights to life, liberty, happiness, and so on, which should be guaranteed by law. But many questions remain. How far should we extend the legal meaning of *animal*? What is in an animal's interest—being alive, or simply if alive, not being mistreated? What sort of legal standing should animals have—to do what and in what kinds of cases? Would animals' legal rights preclude their being used as means to humans ends, as in scientific research? or could such rights be understood simply as providing sanctions against inhumane experimental practices? What rights should animals have in disputes affecting the survival of an entire species, as opposed to those involving only the survival of an individual member of a species? Much careful thought must be put into these and other questions to define more precisely what animals' legal status should be before proceeding in this direction.

In thinking this matter through to its conclusion, we should beware of what Theodore S. Meth, a lawyer concerned with questions of ethics and animal use, terms "the dramatic satisfaction of outraged feelings" using the law as a means to this end. As Meth points out, restrictive legislation is "the preferred methodology of all absolutists, and therefore of the antivivisectionists," who often "have little respect for the pragmatic balancing of interests."[19] Suffice it to say that the alarm has been sounded again for those with a commitment to debate, compromise, and the preservation of progress through reasonably unfettered scientific inquiry.

OTHER APPLICATIONS

There are many other areas of animal use and abuse that have not been touched upon in this book, among them the following:

Agriculture (rearing animals for food; work animals)
Slaughtering
Transportation (animals as means of transportation; means of transporting animals)
Breeding and rearing (purebreds; fur-bearing animals; laboratory animals)

Marketing
Domestication (pets; wild animal taming)
Fishing (commercial and sport)
Hunting (including whaling and sealing)
Trapping, capturing, and storing
Live entertainments and spectacles (circuses, rodeos, races, cockfights,
     bullfights, and the like)
Zoos
Sex[20]
Motion pictures and television
Wildlife management and overexploitation of endangered species
Pest and predator control
Warfare and defense research

These obviously could form the subjects for many more chapters or
even books. Although I have elected to deal with only one central
topic (experimentation) and to treat it thoroughly, the arguments
and conclusions put forward here can be applied elsewhere. It is my
earnest hope and desire that individuals will take the initiative in
doing so, attempting to think these matters through carefully and
constructively.

Appendix

Canadian Council on Animal Care: Ethics of Animal Experimentation

These principles are formulated to provide guidance and assistance to all those utilizing vertebrates in the conduct of research, teaching, or testing.

In the establishment of ethical principles concerning animal experimentation, an effort has been made to incorporate the majority of the suggestions made by members of the Canadian Council on Animal Care, the Canadian Federation of Humane Societies, and scientists and other individuals concerned with the humane treatment of animals.

1. The use of any animal for experimental purposes should only be considered after all efforts to seek an alternative have been exhausted.

Those using animals should recognize the need to use the best methods on the smallest number of appropriate animals required to obtain valid information. Proposed experiments must be justifiable in terms of the declared objectives. The experimental design must offer every practicable safeguard to the animal.

2. In studies involving animals there must be reasonable expectation that such studies will contribute significantly to knowledge which may eventually lead to the protection and improvement of the health and welfare of either humans or animals.

3. Investigators have a moral obligation to abide by the humanitarian dictate that experimental animals are not to be subjected to unnecessary pain or distress.

4. If pain or distress are necessary concomitants of the experimental study, then these should be minimized both in intensity and duration.

5. An animal that is observed to be in a state of severe pain which cannot be alleviated should be humanely destroyed immediately. The method of euthanasia must, as an initial action, produce rapid unconsciousness.

6. Studies such as toxicological and biological testing, cancer research, and infectious disease investigation may require continuation until the death of the animal. This requirement, in the face of distinct and irreversible signs that toxicity, infectious processes, or tumour growth have been reached and are causing severe pain and distress, would clearly violate the principles outlined above. In such cases, alternative end points should be sought which would not only satisfy the objectives of the study but also give humane consideration to the animal.

7. In test procedures the investigator should be especially cautious with tests which may cause pain and distress. Acceptance should not be based on cheapness and ease of application.

8. Experiments involving the withholding of food and water should be short-term and have no detrimental effect on the health of the animal.

9. Prolonged physical restraint should only be used, if at all, after alternative procedures have been considered and found inadequate. The method of restraint must provide the animal with the opportunity to assume as many of its normal postural adjustments as possible, and to minimize mental and physical discomfort. Such an animal must receive exceptional care and attention. The same principles apply to the use of short-term physical restraint.

10. Painful experiments or multiple survival surgical procedures on an individual animal allowed to recover from the anaesthetic, solely for the instruction of students in the classroom or for the demonstration of established scientific knowledge in, e.g., exhibits, conferences, or seminars, cannot be justified. As a replacement, audio-visual techniques should be employed to convey such information.

11. It is accepted that where the animal is anesthetized and insensitive to pain during an entire experimental study and euthanized before regaining consciousness, there is no conflict of opinion concerning

the acceptability of experimental procedures as long as the studies abide by the principles enunciated in this document. This applies also to the conduct of an experiment which involves no pain or distress to the animal.

However, in the use of conscious animals an informed assessment of the degree of pain and its duration is required, in order to relate these to acceptable, or unacceptable, limits. Investigators must be especially prudent in their use of the following procedures:

a) experiments involving withholding pre- and post-operative pain-relieving medication;

b) paralyzing and immobilizing experiments where there is no reduction in the sensation of pain;

c) electric shock as negative reinforcement;

d) extreme environmental conditions such as low or high temperatures, high humidity, modified atmospheres, etc., or sudden changes therein.

It must be understood that the degree of pain involved should never exceed that determined by the humanitarian importance of the problem to be solved by the experimental study. The following experimental procedures must be restricted and used only when, on the basis of expert opinion, it is anticipated that their utilization will undoubtedly contribute knowledge or benefit to humans or animals:

i) prey killing and fighting;

ii) burns, freezing injuries, and fractures. These require anesthesia during procedures, followed by acceptable veterinary practices for the relief of pain.

12. Certain experimental procedures are known to inflict excessive pain and are thus unacceptable. These include:

a) utilization of muscle relaxants or paralytics (curare and curare-like) alone, without anesthetics, during surgical procedures;

b) traumatizing procedures involving crushing, striking, or beating in unanesthetized animals or in animals allowed to recover from the anesthesia.

The above principles should be applied in conjunction with those outlined in the "Guide to the Care and Use of Experimental Animals," as prepared and distributed by the Canadian Council on Animal Care.

NOTES

INTRODUCTION

1. See, for example, Jim Mason, "Guerrilla Tactics Among Animal Liberators," *Vegetarian Times* no. 44 (1981), 58–61; "Antivivisectionists Vandalize Canadian Universities," *Resource* (Canadian Council on Animal Care newsletter) 5, no. 1 (Winter 1980), 1; Arthur Lubow, "The Animals' Lib Case," *Montreal Star*, October 15, 1977, pp. F1–2.

2. "Editorial: "ALF Art Vandal Disgraces Animal Rights Movement," *One World* (Trans-Species Unlimited newsletter) 2 (April 1982).

3. "U.K. Research Centre Attacked," *Resource* 7, no. 1 (Fall/Winter 1982), 2.

4. Frank Jones, "Jeanne's Developed Animal Pragmatism," *Toronto Star*, February 20, 1984, p. A2.

5. "Group Saves Animals from Hospital Laboratory," *Kingston Whig-Standard* (Canadian Press Service), June 16, 1981, p. 1; "Hospital's Animal Testing Is Justified in the Name of Science, Council Says," *Kingston Whig-Standard* (Canadian Press Service), June 17, 1981, p. 56.

6. Interestingly, an article in *Animalia*, a publication of the World Federation for the Protection of Animals, although endorsing a "Universal Declaration of the Rights of Animals," speaks to this point with a degree of realism that is rare among animal rights enthusiasts:

> The protection of animals and the defence of their rights should not cause us to overlook the precarious state of the rights of most human beings.
> Those who struggle for animal rights must work just as hard for human rights, starting with the biological rights of the most disadvantaged groups—Senior Citizens, the Third World, the Fourth World, the handicapped, the sick and the dying. (July–September 1977 issue)

7. Brigid Brophy, "In Pursuit of a Fantasy," in Stanley and Roslind Godlovitch and John Harris, eds., *Animals, Men and Morals: An Enquiry into the Maltreatment of Non-Humans* (London: Victor Gollancz, 1971), 129.

8. See, for example, Tom Regan, *The Case for Animal Rights* (Berkeley, Los Angeles, London: University of California Press, 1983), 96–99.

9. Peter Singer, *Animal Liberation: A New Ethics for Our Treatment of Animals* (New York: New York Review/Random House, 1975), preface and chap. 1.

10. Based on figures supplied by the U.S. Congressional Office of Technology Assessment, in "The Ethics of Animal Testing," *The Economist*, April 7, 1984, p. 87.

11. Richard D. French, *Antivivisection and Medical Science in Victorian Society* (Princeton, N.J.: Princeton University Press, 1975), chaps. 9 and 10; James Turner, *Reckoning with the Beast: Animals, Pain, and Humanity in the Victorian Mind* (Baltimore, Md.: Johns Hopkins University Press, 1980).

1: FALLACIES IN OUR THINKING ABOUT HUMANS AND ANIMALS

1. "Baby Girl Mauled by Family's Puppy Loses Both Her Ears," *Toronto Globe and Mail*, October 10, 1979, p. 1.

2. "Puppy That Mauled Baby Won't Die Vows Official," *Toronto Star*, October 10, 1979, p. 1.

3. Hans Ruesch, *Slaughter of the Innocent* (New York: Bantam Books, 1978), 405–406.

4. Iris Nowell, *The Dog Crisis* (Toronto: McClelland and Stewart, 1978), 194.

5. Michael W. Fox, *Between Animal and Man* (New York: Coward, McCann and Geoghegan, 1976), 169.

6. Nowell, *The Dog Crisis*, 18.

7. Ibid., 20.

8. Ibid., 192.

9. "Got Problems, Pussycat? Blame Your Neurotic Owner," *Toronto Star*, February 23, 1980, p. B4.

10. Nowell, *The Dog Crisis*, 169.

11. Singer, *Animal Liberation*, 28.

12. For some interesting (though farfetched) thoughts on this subject, see Desmond Morris, *The Naked Ape* (New York: Bantam Books, 1969), 204–207.

13. See Robert S. Brumbaugh, "Of Man, Animals and Morals: A Brief History," in Richard Knowles Morris and Michael A. Fox, eds., *On the Fifth Day: Animal Rights and Human Ethics* (Washington, D.C.: Acropolis Books, 1978), 6–25; Singer, *Animal Liberation*, chap. 5.

14. John Stuart Mill, "On Nature," in vol. 10 of *Collected Works* (Toronto: University of Toronto Press, 1963–1977), 400.

15. For a careful recent discussion of the idea of living in accordance with nature, see Holmes Rolston, III, "Can and Ought We to Follow Nature?" *Environmental Ethics* 1 (1979), 7–30.

16. See, for example, Ian McHarg, "Man: Planetary Disease," B. Y. Morrison Memorial Lecture (Washington, D.C.: Agricultural Research Service, U.S. Department of Agriculture, 1971); Robert Ardrey, "Cain's Children," in *African Genesis* (New York: Atheneum, 1961), chap. 11.

An excellent and sensible critique of the writings on humans' supposedly innate aggressiveness by Ardrey and Konrad Lorenz may be found in M. F. Ashley Montagu, "The New Litany of 'Innate Depravity,' or Original Sin Revisited," in M. F. Ashley Montagu, ed., *Man and Aggression* (Oxford: Oxford University Press, 1968), 3–17. See also Abraham H. Maslow, *Motivation and Personality*, 2d ed. (New York: Harper and Row, 1970), chap. 9; and Floyd W. Matson, *The Idea of Man* (New York: Dell, 1976), chap. 3. John Passmore's reflections on certain environmentalists' "doomsday mood of paranoic melancholia" are germane as well. See his *Man's Responsibility for Nature: Ecological Problems and Western Traditions* (London: Duckworth, 1974), 194–195.

17. M. A. Edey, *The Emergence of Man: The Missing Link* (New York: Time-Life Books, 1972).

18. Carl Sagan, *The Dragons of Eden: Speculations on the Evolution of Human Intelligence* (New York: Random House, 1977), 87–90; Richard E. Leakey and Roger Lewin, *Origins: What New Discoveries Reveal about the Emergence of Our Species and Its Possible Future* (New York: E. P. Dutton, 1977), 158–59. Recent discoveries suggest that our early ancestors were not just carnivores but scavengers. See Sharon Begley with John Carey, "Man's Family Portrait," *Newsweek*, April 23, 1984, pp. 49–50.

According to John E. Pfeiffer, "Hominids have been meat eaters at least two million years ago and possibly much earlier" (*The Emergence of Man*, 2d ed. [New York: Harper and Row, 1972], 128). More recent archaeological evidence seems to bear this out. A 1977 dig, for example, unearthed 2.5 million-year-old tools and animal bone fragments buried together at a possible ancient campsite ("Discovery of Oldest Stone Tools Pushes Back Dawn of Human Culture ½ Million Years," *Kingston Whig-Standard* [Associated Press Service], February 2, 1981, p. 5).

19. Vitus B. Dröscher, *The Friendly Beast: Latest Discoveries in Animal Behavior*, trans. Richard and Clara Winston (New York: Harper and Row, 1972), 222.

20. Ruesch, *Slaughter of the Innocent*, 19.

21. S. Vokonyi et al., "Earliest Animal Domestication Dated," *Science* 179 (December 14, 1973), 1161; Leakey and Lewin, *Origins*, 176.

22. G. E. Moore, *Principia Ethica* (Cambridge: Cambridge University Press, 1903), 83–84. A similar extended thought experiment may be found in Donald Scherer, "Anthropocentrism, Atomism, and Environmental Ethics," *Environmental Ethics* 4 (1982), 115–123.

23. Nancy L. Zettler, "Revolution, Evolution or Extinction?: Which Type of Environmental Ethics Is Most Adequate?" (unpublished ms., 1983), 17.

24. A striking parallel between Moore's experiment and St. Anselm's famous ontological argument for the existence of God can be noted. In the latter too, as Kant showed, purely conceptual considerations are used illicitly to detach an idea from thought and give it life independent of the mind that entertains it.

25. See, for example, Holmes Rolston, III, "Values in Nature," *Environmental Ethics* 3 (1981), 113–128; E. J. Bond, *Reason and Value* (Cambridge: Cambridge

University Press, 1983), esp. chap. 5; J. Baird Callicott, "Intrinsic Value, Quantum Theory, and Environmental Ethics," *Environmental Ethics*, forthcoming; Ernest Partridge, "Values in Nature: Is Anybody There?" paper presented to Conference on Environmental Ethics: New Directions, University of Georgia, October 4–6, 1984.

26. Aldo Leopold, "The Land Ethic," in *A Sand County Almanac* (New York: Ballantine Books, 1970), 240.

27. Diversity alone, for example, does not ensure ecosystemic stability. See Eugene P. Odum, *Basic Ecology* (Philadelphia: Saunders College Publishing, 1983), 51–52, 416–418.

28. G. Tyler Miller, Jr., *Living in the Environment: Concepts, Problems, and Alternatives* (Belmont, Calif.: Wadsworth, 1975), 80.

29. See Mark Sagoff, "On Preserving the Natural Environment," *Yale Law Journal* 84 (1974), 245–267; Lawrence Haworth, *Decadence and Objectivity* (Toronto: University of Toronto Press, 1977), 25–27.

30. Thus an attempt by John B. Cobb, Jr., to save Moore's argument and to shore up the notion of intrinsic values in nature along these lines must fail. See Cobb's "Beyond Anthropocentrism in Ethics and Religion," in Morris and Fox, *On the Fifth Day*, 140.

31. Wayne Sumner, "Moral Concern and the Harp Seal Hunt," *Proceedings of Canadian Federation of Humane Societies Symposium on "The Canadian Seal Hunt: A Moral Issue,"* February 7, 1982, 39–40.

32. Singer, *Animal Liberation*, 266. Brigid Brophy goes even farther: "The proper question," she states in discussing the morality of killing a pig to eat pork chops, "is what value that individual pig's irreplaceable life holds for that individual pig" ("Crossing the Insuperable Line," *Times Literary Supplement*, January 16, 1981, p. 48).

33. For more discussion on the issue of whether animals can value their lives and the importance of this consideration for ethics, see Ruth Cigman, "Death, Misfortune, and Species Inequality," *Philosophy and Public Affairs* 10, no. 1 (Winter 1981), 47–64, and the critique of Cigman's article by Steve F. Sapontzis, "Must We Value Life to Have A Right to It?" *Ethics and Animals* 3, no. 1 (March 1982), 2–11.

34. Regan, *The Case for Animal Rights*; the summary that follows cites 81, 244, 245.

2: An Evolutionary Perspective on Humans and Animals

1. Simple and straightforward accounts of investigations of chimpanzee learning may be found in Eugene Linden, *Apes, Men, and Language* (Harmondsworth, Middlesex: Penguin Books, 1976) and Flora Davis, *Eloquent Animals: A Study in Animal Communications* (New York: Berkley, 1978). For a brief authoritative scientific survey, see E. Sue Savage-Rumbaugh et al., "Do Apes Use Language?" *American Scientist* 68 (1980), 49–61.

2. Cetacean behavior is explored in Joan McIntyre, ed., *Mind in the Waters* (Toronto: McClelland and Stewart, 1974); Karl-Erik Fichtelius and Sverre Sjölander, *Smarter Than Man?: Intelligence in Whales, Dolphins and Humans* (New York: Ballentine Books, 1974); Jacques-Yves Cousteau, *The Whale* (London: Cassell, 1972); and Robin Brown, *The Lure of the Dolphin* (New York: Avon Books, 1979); and whale communications in particular are described in Roger Payne, "Humpbacks: Their Mysterious Songs," *National Geographic* 155, no. 1 (January 1979), 18–25. A recording is included with this article.

3. Gordon G. Gallup, Jr., "Chimpanzees: Self Recognition," *Science* 167 (1970), 86–87. Gordon G. Gallup, Jr. et al., "A Mirror for the Mind of Man, or Will the Chimpanzee Create an Identity Crisis for *Homo Sapiens?*" *Journal of Human Evolution* 6 (1977), 311.

4. W. H. Thorpe, *Animal Nature and Human Nature* (New York: Anchor Press/Doubleday, 1974), 307.

5. Stephen Walker, *Animal Thought* (London: Routledge and Kegan Paul, 1983), 386.

6. For more on the distinction between difference in degree and difference in kind, see Mortimer J. Adler, *The Difference of Man and the Difference It Makes* (New York: Holt, Rinehart, and Winston, 1967), chap. 2.

7. The phylogenetically accurate name for modern man is *Homo sapiens sapiens*. This differentiates our species from *Homo sapiens neanderthalensis*, for example.

8. Adler, *The Difference of Man*, 67–68.

9. Charles Darwin, *The Descent of Man and Selection in Relation to Sex*, 2d ed. (New York: Appleton, 1898), 128.

10. Richard M. Tullar, *The Human Species: Its Nature, Evolution, and Ecology* (New York: McGraw-Hill, 1977), 45.

11. "Molecular Study Links Man, Apes," *Toronto Star*, January 24, 1982, p. C8.

12. Tullar, *The Human Species*, 46.

13. Leakey and Lewin, *Origins*, 56–57.

14. Tullar, *The Human Species*, 256.

15. The entire range of findings that point to the biochemical similarity of humans and other primates is exhaustively discussed in John Gribbin and Jeremy Cherfas, *The Monkey Puzzle: A Family Tree* (London: The Bodley Head, 1982).

16. Jane van Lawick-Goodall, *In the Shadow of Man* (Boston: Houghton Mifflin, 1971) and other works; Geza Teleki, "The Omnivorous Chimpanzee," *Scientific American* 228, no. 1 (January 1973), 33–42; Geza Teleki, "Chimpanzee Subsistence Technology: Materials and Skills," *Journal of Human Evolution* 3 (1974), 575–594.

17. Leakey and Lewin, *Origins*, 66, 67.

18. Bernard G. Campbell, *Human Evolution: An Introduction to Man's Adaptations* (Chicago: Aldine, 1966), 288.

19. David Premack, *Intelligence in Ape and Man* (Hillsdale, N.J.: Lawrence Erlbaum Associates, 1976); W. A. Mason, "Environmental Models and Mental Modes: Representational Processes in the Great Apes and Man," *American Psychologist* 31 (1976), 284–294. For evidence of concept formation in other species, see A. J. Riopelle, ed., *Animal Problem Solving* (Harmondsworth, Middlesex: Penguin Books, 1967); D. L. Medrin et al., eds., *Processes of Animal Memory* (New York: John Wiley, 1976); R. J. Herrnstein and D. H. Loveland, "Complex Visual Concept in the Pigeon," *Science* 146 (1964), 549–551; R. J. Herrnstein et al., "Natural Concepts in Pigeons," *Journal of Experimental Psychology: Animal Behavior Processes* 2 (1976), 285–302. Chimpanzees' goal-oriented behavior is described in Leakey and Lewin, *Origins*, 188. See note 3 above for a reference to chimpanzee self-awareness.

20. Francine Patterson has reported her work with Koko, a seven-year-old female gorilla, whom she estimates to have a 375-sign "working vocabulary" (i.e., signs used "regularly and appropriately"). See "Conversations with a Gorilla," *National Geographic* 154, no. 4 (October 1978), 438–465.

21. See J. F. Mustard and M. A. Packham, "The Unrealized Potential of Animal Diseases in the Study of Human Diseases," *Canadian Medical Association Journal* 98 (1968), 887–890; Leo K. Bustad, "Pigs in the Laboratory," *Scientific American* 214, no. 6 (June 1966), 94–100.

22. David H. Hubel, "The Brain," *Scientific American* 241, no. 3 (September 1979), 46. See also T. R. Shantha and S. L. Manoska, "The Brain of the Chimpanzee," in G. H. Bourne, ed., *The Chimpanzee*, vol. 1 (New York: Karger, 1969); G. H. Yeni-Konshian and D. A. Benson, "Anatomical Study of Cerebral Asymmetry in the Temporal Lobe of Humans, Chimpanzees, and Rhesus Monkeys," *Science* 192 (1976), 387–389; Donald R. Griffin, "Prospects for a Cognitive Ethology," *Behavioral and Brain Sciences* 4 (1978), 528.

23. Boyce Rensberger, *The Cult of the Wild* (Garden City, N.Y.: Anchor Press/Doubleday, 1977), 190.

24. Thorpe, *Animal Nature and Human Nature*, 128.

25. Leakey and Lewin, *Origins*, 76, 155–157.

26. Adrian J. Desmond, *The Ape's Reflexion* (New York: Dial Press/James Wade, 1979), chap. 10; Rensberger, *Cult of the Wild*, chap. 12; Geza Teleki, "Primate Subsistence Patterns: Collector-Predators and Gatherer-Hunters," *Journal of Human Evolution* 4 (1975), 125–184; Natalie Angier, "Mother Nature's Murderers," *Discover* (October 1983), 79–82; Barbara Burke, "Infanticide," *Science 84* 5, no. 4 (May 1984), 26–31.

27. "Chimp Could Make Chump of Most Other Farm Hands," *Kitchener-Waterloo Record* (Associated Press Service), September 13, 1980, p. 24.

28. Tullar, *The Human Species* 95–96, 98.

29. George Gaylord Simpson, *The Meaning of Evolution*, rev. ed. (New Haven, Conn.: Yale University Press, 1967), 285.

30. Stephen Jay Gould, *Ever Since Darwin: Reflections in Natural History* (New York: W. W. Norton, 1979), 180.

31. Sagan, *The Dragons of Eden*, 39; see also Weston La Barre, *The Human Animal* (Chicago: University of Chicago Press, 1954), 75.

32. Stephen Jay Gould, "Evolution and the Brain," *Natural History* 84, no. 1 (January 1975), 24.

33. Peter Morgane, "The Whale Brain: The Anatomical Basis of Intelligence," in McIntyre, *Mind in the Waters*, 86, 88.

34. Harry J. Jerison, *Evolution of the Brain and Intelligence* (New York: Academic Press, 1973), 62.

35. John Napier, "The Evolution of the Hand," in *Human Ancestors: Readings from Scientific American* (San Francisco: W. H. Freeman, 1979), 43–49.

36. Leakey and Lewin, *Origins*, 41.

37. Campbell, *Human Evolution*, 295. Cf. van Lawick-Goodall, *Shadow of Man*, 218. These limitations are sometimes overlooked even by researchers themselves. For example, see Gallup et al., "A Mirror for the Mind of Man," 304.

38. Chimpanzees do, however, make tools in some sense. See Nancy Makepeace Tanner, *On Becoming Human* (Cambridge: Cambridge University Press, 1981), 69–75.

39. Harold M. Schmeck, Jr., "Earliest Use of Fire by Hominids Pushed Back Nearly 1 Million Years," *Kingston Whig Standard* (New York Times Service), November 17, 1981, p. 14.

40. E. Sue Savage-Rumbaugh et al., "Symbolic Communication Between Two Chimpanzees (*Pan troglodytes*)," *Science* 201 (1978), 641–644; E. Sue Savage-Rumbaugh et al., "Linguistically Mediated Tool Use and Exchange by Chimpanzees," *Behavioral and Brain Sciences* 4 (1978), 539–554.

41. Savage-Rumbaugh et al., "Symbolic Communication," 644 n. 12.

42. Savage-Rumbaugh et al., "Do Apes Use Language?" 52, 59, 60.

43. Ibid., 61.

44. Ibid., 52, 59.

45. H. S. Terrace et al., "Can an Ape Create a Sentence?" *Science* 206 (1979), 900, 901. See also Herbert Terrace, *Nim* (New York: Alfred A. Knopf, 1979), 394. Some important theoretical reservations relating to chimpanzee language learning are raised in Erich H. Lenneberg, "Of Language Knowledge, Apes, and Brains," *Journal of Psycholinguistic Research* 1 (1971), 1–29; see also the extensive discussion section in *Behavioral and Brain Sciences* 4 (December 1978): special issue on "Cognition and Consciousness in Nonhuman Species."

46. Thomas A. Sebeok and Donna Jean Umiker-Sebeok, "Questioning Apes," in Thomas A. Sebeok and Donna Jean Umiker-Sebeok, eds., *Speaking of Apes* (New York: Plenum Press, 1980), 396.

47. Norman Geschwind, "Specializations of the Human Brain," *Scientific American* 241 no. 3 (September 1979), 180.

48. Tullar, *The Human Species*, 32, 49.

49. Leakey and Lewin, *Origins*, 200.

50. Theodosius Dobzhansky and Francisco J. Ayala, *Humankind: A Product of Evolution*, Special Raymond Dart Lecture (Johannesburg: Witwatersrand University Press/Institute for the Study of Man in Africa, 1977), 12–13; C. F. Hockett, *Man's Place in Nature* (New York: McGraw-Hill, 1973), 101–115.

51. Bernhard Rensch, *Homo Sapiens: From Man to Demigod*, trans. C. A. M. Sym (London: Methuen, 1972), 155.

52. Adler, *The Difference of Man*, 191–192.

53. Walker, *Animal Thought*, 387.

54. For a critical discussion of Walker's and similar views, see Donald R. Griffin, *Animal Thinking* (Cambridge, Mass.: Harvard University Press, 1984), 134–143.

55. Tullar, *The Human Species*, 128.

56. Leakey and Lewin, *Origins*, chap. 9; René Dubos, *Beast or Angel? Choices That Make Us Human* (New York: Charles Scribner's Sons, 1974); René Dubos, *So Human an Animal* (New York: Charles Scribner's Sons, 1968); Alexander Alland, Jr., *The Human Imperative* (New York: Columbia University Press, 1972); M. F. Ashley Montagu, *On Being Human*, new and rev. ed. (New York: Hawthorn Books, 1966); Montagu, *Man and Aggression*.

57. Leakey and Lewin, *Origins*, 212–213; Leon Eisenberg, "The Human Nature of Human Nature," *Science* 176 (1972), 123–128.

58. Hockett, *Man's Place in Nature*, 258.

59. Tullar, *The Human Species*, 127.

60. Leakey and Lewin, *Origins*, 245.

61. Dobzhansky and Ayala, *Humankind*, 12; Thorpe, *Animal Nature and Human Nature*, 282. Tullar (*The Human Species*, 303) asserts that "man's cultural heritage is the most effective force molding his total genotype."

3: ANIMALS AND THE MORAL COMMUNITY

1. Jeremy Bentham, *An Introduction to the Principles of Morals and Legislation* (1780), chap. 19, sec. 1. Although Bentham is widely regarded as a hero by the animal liberation movement because of this remark, in the same passage he denies that animals have a right to life and asserts that in the absence of suffering there is no reason why we ought not to kill animals for food: "We are the better for it, and they are never the worse."

2. Pain and suffering are not equivalent, though many writers use them interchangeably. *Pain* is generally somatic in origin, whereas *suffering* is a more inclusive term, subsuming varieties of psychological distress and disagreeable physical sensations. Clearly, some animals can suffer, but it seems most improbable that they all can, since a certain level of mental complexity is presupposed when we speak of suffering, as is implied in the meanings of such subsidiary notions as anxiety, stress, anguish, apprehensiveness, despair, sorrow, worry, grief, lamentation, upset, and the like.

It is reasonable to assume, however, that at least all animals with nervous systems can experience pain. Whether their pain is like our own in kind or degree is not at all easy to establish, even leaving aside the conceptual problems created by talk about having another creature's experiences. The more complex a being's psychological life, the more properly is its pain to be described as suffering, and suffering may in turn be either augmented or diminished mentally. (Thus, for example, those who dwell on minor injuries aggravate their suffering, whereas others who exert some form of "mind over matter" may carry on uncomplainingly despite genuinely severe afflictions.)

3. Arthur L. Caplan, "Rights Language and the Ethical Treatment of Animals," in Laurence B. McCullough and James Polk Morris, III, eds., *Implications of History and Ethics to Medicine—Veterinary and Human* (College Station, Texas: Centennial Academic Assembly, Texas A & M University, 1978), 129.

4. Cf. H. J. McCloskey, "The Right to Life," *Mind* 84 (1975), 413.

5. This strategy is followed by Bernard E. Rollin in *Animal Rights and Human Morality* (Buffalo, N.Y.: Prometheus Books, 1981), pt. 1; but it is also a central feature of Singer's *Animal Liberation* and of other works. Indeed, the archetype of the argument is Bentham's frequently cited remark which I too have quoted at the beginning of this chapter.

6. Christopher W. Morris, "Comments on 'Rights and Autonomy,' by David Richards, and 'Autonomy and Rights: A Case for Ethical Socialism,' by Michael McDonald," paper presented to Conference on Human Rights, University of Waterloo, Waterloo, Ontario, April 17–19, 1980, 2.

7. Richard Wasserstrom, "Rights, Human Rights, and Racial Discrimination," in A. I. Melden, ed., *Human Rights* (Belmont, Calif.: Wadsworth, 1970), 104, 105.

As Alan Goldman has written, rights "carve out a moral space in which persons can develop as distinct individuals free from the constant intrusion of demands from others" ("The Source and Extent of a Patient's Right to the Truth," *Queen's Quarterly* 91 [1984], 126).

8. It may be objected that agents' autonomy is protected by the traditional right to liberty and that therefore there is no reason why animals should not be seen as possessing other rights, such as the right not to suffer or the right to live. (I owe this objection to Christine Pierce.) But the argument offered here is that rights only arise and make sense within a framework in which mutual recognition and accountability are typical characteristics of relationships, and it is clear that animals have no place in such a conceptual environment.

9. Carl Sagan, *The Cosmic Connection: An Extraterrestrial Perspective* (New York: Dell, 1975); John W. Macvey, *Interstellar Travel: Past, Present, and Future* (New York: Stein and Day, 1977).

10. For more on this interesting subject, see Roland Puccetti, *Persons: A Study of Possible Moral Agents in the Universe* (London: Macmillan, 1968), chap. 4.

11. A largely psychogenetic account has been given here of the reasons why the possession of autonomy or personhood (and only this) confers moral rights on a

being or entitles it to respect and equal moral concern; that is, the ascription of rights to such beings has been explained in terms of the conditions under which autonomous beings are disposed to ascribe rights to themselves and to other like beings. It may be argued therefore that a clinching philosophical argument for such ascriptions has not been provided; that it has not been shown why the possession of autonomy is a peculiarly relevant consideration, whereas possession of other characteristics, such as the capacity to suffer, are not.

I am not sure this kind of argument can be supplied, though I think that further reflections on the nature of autonomy, like those that occupy much of the rest of this chapter, go a good distance toward satisfying this demand. The reason such an argument cannot be given is that here we are up against the same problem of the fact-value gap that plagues all moral theories. By the same token, for instance, utilitarians cannot defend their key claim that the capacity to suffer is the singularly relevant criterion for the assignment of rights or the entitlement to respect and equal moral concern.

12. Joel Feinberg, "Human Duties and Animal Rights," in Morris and Fox, *On the Fifth Day*, 50 (author's italics).

13. For reasons of this sort, some critics of animal liberation have denied that speciesism constitutes a form of immorality comparable to racism and sexism—indeed, that it is immoral at all. For good arguments against the claim that speciesism is immoral, see the following: Leslie Pickering Francis and Richard Norman, "Some Animals Are More Equal Than Others," *Philosophy* 53, no. 206 (October 1978), 507–527; Cigman, "Death, Misfortune, and Species Inequality"; Meredith Williams, "Rights, Interests, and Moral Equality," *Environmental Ethics* 2 (1980), 149–161; Richard A. Watson, "Self-Consciousness and the Rights of Nonhuman Animals and Nature," *Environmental Ethics* 1 (1979), 99–129; Michael Wreen, "In Defense of Speciesism," *Ethics and Animals* 5, no. 3 (September 1984), 47–60.

14. Any alternative moral theory will have to confront the same problem; for since no society's resources are unlimited, the interests of disadvantaged individuals must always be weighed against those of everyone else.

15. For example, Singer, *Animal Liberation*, 80 f.

16. For a closer look at the family-of-man argument and a perceptive discussion, from a different perspective, of its bearing on the ethical problem of according preferential treatment to defective humans over animals, see Vinit Haksar, *Equality, Liberty, and Perfectability* (Oxford: Oxford University Press, 1979), 38–45, 71–79. See also Wreen, "In Defense of Speciesism," 53; United States Congress, Office of Technology Assessment, *Alternatives to Animal Use in Testing, Research, and Education* (Washington, D.C.: U.S. Government Printing Office, 1985), chap. 4.

17. Passmore, *Man's Responsibility for Nature*, 88–89.

18. See Helen Kohl, "The Strange Ones," *Canadian Magazine*, April 7, 1979, pp. 10–12, 14; Laura Schreibman and Robert L. Koegel, "Autism: A Defeatable Horror," *Psychology Today* 8, no. 10 (March 1975), 61–67; O. Ivar Lovaas,

"Behavioral Treatment of Autistic Children," in Janet T. Spence et al., eds., *Behavioral Approaches to Therapy* (Morristown, N.J.: General Learning Press, 1976), 185–201. The techniques described by Kohl and others, it should be noted, are based largely on knowledge about the efficacy of rewards and punishments in learning acquired initially through animal experiments.

19. For example, it may not be society's obligation to provide the same educational opportunities to retarded youngsters as to those of normal intelligence, but it may be obliged to train them specially to their maximum capacity to help them earn their own livelihood and be productive members of society.

20. For example, Tom Regan, "The Moral Basis of Vegetarianism," *Canadian Journal of Philosophy* 5 (1975–1976), 187, 189, 200.

21. Feinberg, "Human Duties and Animal Rights," 58; cited by Regan, "Moral Basis of Vegetarianism," 187.

22. D. W. Baxter and J. Olszewski, "Congenital Universal Insensitivity to Pain," *Brain* 83 (1960), 381–393; Ronald Melzack and Patrick Wall, *The Challenge of Pain* (Harmondsworth, Middlesex: Penguin Books, 1982), 15–19.

23. Indeed, one pain specialist has commented, "It would seem, then, that despite rare exceptions, the absence of normal pain sensation has little effect on normal personality development" (Richard A. Sternbach, *Pain: A Psychophysiological Analysis* [New York: Academic Press, 1968], 109). It would be interesting to know the nature of the "rare exceptions" to assess their impact on the moral argument under discussion here, but unfortunately Sternbach gives no further details.

24. Singer, *Animal Liberation*, 23.

25. For a sympathetic discussion of the problem, see Jan Narveson, "Animal Rights Revisited," *Animal Regulation Studies* 2, no. 3 (August 1980), 229–233.

26. Robert Nozick, *Anarchy, State, and Utopia* (New York: Basic Books, 1974), 49. See also Robert Nozick, *Philosophical Explanations* (Cambridge, Mass.: Belknap Press/Harvard University Press, 1981), 577–578.

27. John Stuart Mill, *Utilitarianism* (1863), chap. 2.

28. Caplan, "Rights Language and the Ethical Treatment of Animals," 133.

29. See Thomas Nagel, "What Is It Like to Be a Bat?" *Philosophical Review* 83 (1974), 435–450; and Michael Levin, *Metaphysics and the Mind-Body Problem* (Oxford: Clarendon Press, 1979), chap. 6, sec. 9.

30. See Michael Levin, "All in a Stew About Animals: A Reply to Singer," *The Humanist* 37 (September 1977), 58.

31. The oldest humane society is the RSPCA, founded in 1824.

32. Emily Stewart Leavitt, *Animals and Their Legal Rights: A Survey of American Laws from 1641 to 1978*, 3d ed. (Washington, D.C.: Animal Welfare Institute, 1978), 11–12.

33. An analysis of the historical development of humane attitudes is too complex to attempt here. The reader is referred to Gerald Carson, *Men, Beasts, and Gods: A History of Cruelty and Kindness to Animals* (New York: Charles Scribner's Sons, 1972).

34. See, in this connection, the following: G. C. Grindley, *The Sense of Pain in Animals* (London: Universities Federation for Animal Welfare, n.d.; reprinted from *Animal Year Book*, 2 [1933]); John R. Baker, *The Scientific Basis of Kindness to Animals* (London: Universities Federation for Animal Welfare, 1948).

35. See, for example, Singer, *Animal Liberation*, 49; Charles R. Magel, *Humane Experimentation on Humans and Animals or . . . Muddling Through* (Chicago: National Anti-Vivisectionist Society, 1980), 21.

36. For example, J. E. Lovelock, *Gaia: A New Look at Life on Earth* (Oxford: Oxford University Press, 1979).

37. Immanuel Kant, "Duties Towards Animals and Spirits," in *Lectures on Ethics* (pub. posthumously, 1924), trans. Louis Infield (London: Methuen, 1930), 241.

38. Eileen S. Whitlock and Stuart R. Westerlund, *Humane Education: An Overview* (Tulsa, Okla.: National Association for the Advancement of Humane Education, 1975), 9–10.

39. Ibid., 10–11 (my emphasis).

40. Compare this example:

From (3) If I apply the brakes, then the car will stop
it does not follow that
    (4) If I fail to apply the brakes, then the car won't stop
For I may, omitting to do so, smash into a tree!

41. Donna Jacobs, "A Link: Child Abuse, Animal Abuse," syndicated "Creatures" column, *Kingston Whig-Standard Magazine*, November 7, 1981, p. 24.

42. Cited by Jacobs, "A Link."

43. Richard Taylor, "On the Basis of Morality," in Michael Allen Fox, ed., *Schopenhauer: His Philosophical Achievement* (Brighton, Sussex: Harvester Press; New York: Barnes and Noble, 1980), 104–105.

44. Iain Douglas-Hamilton, cited by Donna Barnett, "Wildlife: Devastations and Defence," *Kingston Whig-Standard Magazine*, September 27, 1980, p. 22.

45. I think the account of our proper ethical relationship to animals I have given is an adequate response to a dilemma posed by Stephen R. L. Clark in *The Moral Status of Animals* (Oxford: Clarendon Press, 1977). Clark argues the following concerning humane laws: "Either the evil they seek to prevent is the suffering of animals," in which case animals have rights—at least the negative right "to be spared wanton ill-treatment"—"or it is the moral corruption of human beings" (12–13). But we need not accept this choice, as the grounds for our obligations to animals are varied and considerably more complex than Clark allows.

46. The question of unnecessary suffering is treated in chap. 6.

47. Leavitt, *Animals and Their Legal Rights*, 28–32.

48. R. D. Guthrie, "The Ethical Relationship Between Humans and Other Organisms," *Perspectives in Biology and Medicine* 11, no. 1 (Autumn 1967), 54, 55.

49. See, for instance, the discussion of replacement in W. M. S. Russell and R. L. Burch, *The Principles of Humane Experimental Technique* (Springfield, Ill.: Charles C. Thomas, 1959), chap. 5.

50. Griffin, "Prospects for a Cognitive Ethology."

51. Andrew F. Fraser, "Sentient Behavior," *Applied Animal Ethology* 3 (1977), 1–3; M. W. Fox, "From Animal Science to Animal Rights," paper presented to the First World Congress on Ethology Applied to Zootechnics, Madrid, October 25–27, 1978.

52. Simpson, *The Meaning of Evolution*, 285–286.

53. Sagoff, "On Preserving the Natural Environment," 222. The same point has been made in the context of defending intensive livestock production:

> The confinement approach to animal production has brought many positive benefits. . . . This is especially so regarding the animals' major requirements. . . . Shelter from the climatic elements has been provided, so the pigs no longer need suffer from extremes of the thermal environment. Steady supplies of nutritious feed and sanitary water are available, and special care is taken to ensure that each animal gets its required share of both. Young pigs are protected against predators. Sanitary environments are much more easily achieved and maintained. Daily inspection of each animal is possible, and attention to disease and injury is prompt. (Stanley E. Curtis, "Welfare of Animals in Animal Science Research," paper presented to Animal Welfare Committee of the U.S. Animal Health Association, Louisville, November 4, 1980; reproduced and distributed by American Association of Swine Practitioners, 75.)

54. This objection is entertained by Philip E. Devine in "The Moral Basis of Vegetarianism," *Philosophy* 53 (1978), 500; Nozick, *Anarchy, State and Utopia*, 45–47; John Vyvyan, *The Dark Face of Science* (London: Michael Joseph, 1971), 197; Leonard Nelson, "Duties to Animals," in Godlovitch, Godlovitch, and Harris, *Animals, Men and Morals*, 152–153 (reprinted from *A System of Ethics*, trans. N. Gutermann [New Haven, Conn.: Yale University Press, 1956]); F. L. Marcuse and J. J. Pear, "Ethics and Animal Experimentation: Personal Views," in J. D. Keehn, ed., *Psychopathology in Animals: Research and Clinical Implications* (New York: Academic Press, 1979), 325–326.

55. As is argued, for example, by Kant in *Groundwork of the Metaphysics of Morals*, 2d ed. (1786) and by Bernard Gert in *The Moral Rules: A New Rational Foundation for Morality* (New York: Harper and Row, 1973).

56. See, for example, Singer, *Animal Liberation*, 267–268.

57. See Paul Edwards, "Life, Meaning and Value of," in Paul Edwards, ed., *The Encyclopedia of Philosophy*, vol. 4 (New York: Macmillan/Free Press, 1967), 473.

58. I owe this objection to Peter Sabor.

59. These and other absurdities may be found in Peter Tompkins and Christopher Bird, *The Secret Life of Plants* (New York: Harper and Row, 1973). See also "The Green Machine," transcript of NOVA program, January 11, 1978, published by WGBH Educational Foundation, Boston.

60. In any event, as Alan Herscovici points out, the Jains' unusual practices are based "not on compassion for the suffering of other creatures, but on the principle of non-activity," that is, of minimizing their "'attachments' to the physical world," (*Second Nature: The Animal Rights Controversy* [Toronto: CBC Enterprises, 1985], 38).

61. Singer, *Animal Liberation*, 263.

62. See note 13 above.

4: ANIMALS IN RESEARCH: UNDERSTANDING THE CONTEXT

1. Committee on Laboratory Animal Facilities and Resources, Institute of Laboratory Animal Resources, *National Survey of Laboratory Animal Facilities and Resources* (Washington, D.C.: National Institutes of Health, March 1980), 17, 20, 21. Estimates of total U.S. animal use for experimental purposes vary widely. Andrew Rowan gives an estimate of 90,000,000 for 1976–1977 in David Sperlinger, ed., *Animals in Research: New Perspectives in Animal Experimentation* (Chichester: John Wiley, 1981), 259, and of 70,000,000 for the current level of use in *Of Mice, Models, and Men: A Critical Evaluation of Animal Research* (Albany: State University of New York Press, 1984), 67. In "The Electronic Guinea Pig," *Discover* (September 1983), 77, Natalie Angier gives the figure of 60,000,000 for current annual U.S. use.

Some interesting tables and graphs correlating the number of animal experiments performed with medical discoveries over the past century, as well as epidemiological data relating the incidence of various diseases to the intensity of related animal research, may be found in Sir William Paton's *Man and Mouse: Animals in Medical Research* (Oxford: Oxford University Press, 1984).

2. Canadian Council on Animal Care, "Number of Vertebrates Used in Institutions" (Ottawa: CCAC, 1974), cited by Dallas Pratt, *Painful Experiments on Animals* (New York: Argus Archives, 1976), 12.

3. U.K. Home Office, "Statistics of Experiments on Living Animals, Great Britain, 1978" (London: H. M. Stationery Office, 1979).

4. Robert A. Brown, "History of the Humane Movement and Prospects for the 1980s," paper presented to Conference on Medicine, Animals, and Man, University of Illinois Medical Center, Chicago, May 21, 1980.

5. Ruesch, *Slaughter of the Innocent*, 85, 198.

6. Frank Stilley, *The $100,000 Rat and Other Animal Heroes for Human Health* (New York: G. P. Putnam's, 1975).

7. Marcuse and Pear, "Ethics and Animal Experimentation." See also "Vivisection—Vivistudy: The Facts and the Benefits to Animal and Human Health," a Symposium presented by the American Public Health Association and the Conference of Public Health Veterinarians, San Francisco, November 2, 1966, *American Journal of Public Health* 57 (1967), 1597–1626.

8. Robert W. Leader, "The Kinship of Animal and Human Diseases," *Scientific American* 210, no. 1 (January 1967), 210–216.

9. Fred C. Davison, "Historical Perspectives of Biomedical Experimentation," in Institute of Laboratory Animal Resources, *The Future of Animals, Cells, Models,*

and *Systems in Research, Development, Education, and Testing* (Washington, D.C.: National Academy of Sciences, 1977), 12. For more on the role animals have played in the development of cardiac surgery, see Walter C. Randall, "Is Medical Research in Jeopardy?" *The Physiologist* 26, no. 2 (1983), 73–77; reprinted from *Hospital Practice* 18, no. 2 (February 1983).

10. See Harry F. Dowling, *Fighting Infection: Conquests of the Twentieth Century* (Cambridge, Mass.: Harvard University Press, 1977), chaps. 1–4 and 12.

11. International Committee on Laboratory Animals, "The Need for Animal Experimentation," Resolution adopted by the ICLA Governing Board, Cairo, January 1979; cf. "Vivisection—Vivistudy."

12. Stilley, *The $100,000 Rat*, 123.

13. Patricia Hluchy, "Mighty Mice Hold Genetic Hope," *Toronto Star*, January 8, 1983, p. B7.

14. Jonathan B. Tucker, "An End to Pain," *Omni* 1, no. 5 (October 1979), 87–91, 107.

15. The dimensions of the pain problem and the frontiers of research are well described in Claudia Wallis et al., "Unlocking Pain's Secrets," *Time*, June 11, 1984, pp. 60–70. See also Michael Allen Fox, "Ethical Considerations in Painful Animal Research," in H. L. Fields, R. Dubner, and F. Cervero, eds., *Advances in Pain Research and Therapy*, vol. 9 (Proceedings of the IVth World Congress on Pain, Seattle, Aug. 31–Sept. 5, 1984) (New York: Raven Press, 1985).

16. J. Wolpe, *Psychotherapy by Reciprocal Inhibition* (Stanford, Calif.: Stanford University Press, 1958); H. J. Eysenck and Michael Eysenck, *Mindwatching* (London: Michael Joseph, 1981), chap. 6; R. Ulrich, T. Stachnik, and J. Mabry, eds., *Control of Human Behavior*, vols. 1 and 2 (Glenview, Ill.: Scott, Foresman, 1966); Schreibman and Koegel, "Autism."

17. D. S. Tuber, D. Hothersall, and V. L. Voith, "Animal Clinical Psychology: A Modest Proposal," in Keehn, *Origins of Madness*, 381–387.

18. J. Wolpe, "Parallels Between Animal and Human Neuroses," in Keehn, *Origins of Madness*, 31.

19. Gordon G. Gallup, Jr., and Susan D. Suarez, "On the Use of Animals in Psychological Research," *Psychological Record* 30 (1980), 212. See also chap. 3, footnote 18.

20. Neal Miller, contribution to "Understanding Psychological Man: A State-of-the-Science Report," *Psychology Today* 16 (May 1982), 52. See also Frederick A. King, "Animals in Research: The Case for Experimentation," *Psychology Today* 18 (September 1984), 57.

21. Dr. William G. Webster, Department of Psychology, Carleton University, personal communication, March 16, 1983).

22. The reader may wish to consult the following publications: Pratt, *Painful Experiments*; Jeff Diner, *Physical and Mental Suffering of Experimental Animals: A Review of Scientific Literature, 1975–1978* (Washington, D.C.: Animal Welfare Institute, 1979).

23. Thomas H. Maugh II, "Perfluorochemical Emulsions: Promising Blood Substitutes," *Science* 179 (February 16, 1973), 669–672.

24. Thomas H. Maugh II, "Blood Substitute Passes Its First Test," *Science* 206 (October 12, 1979), 205.

25. Maugh, "Perfluorochemical Emulsions," 669.

26. Richard Ryder, *Victims of Science* (London: Davis-Poynter, 1975), 69–70; Singer, *Animal Liberation*, 47; see also Nicholas Humphrey, "Seeing and Nothingness," *New Scientist* 53, no. 789 (March 30, 1972), 682–684.

27. H. C. M. Walton, "Vivsection and the Press," *Conquest* (journal of the Research Defence Society) 167 (April 1976), 15. Cf. Robert Jones, "The Ignorance and Confusion That Still Surrounds Animal Experiments," *The Times* (London), May 8, 1975, p. 14.

28. Martin E. P. Seligman, *Helplessness: On Depression, Development and Death* (San Francisco: W. H. Freeman, 1975); Lawrence S. Wrightsman, Carol K. Sigelman, and Fillmore H. Sanford, *Psychology: A Scientific Study of Human Behavior*, 5th ed. (Monterey, Calif.: Brooks/Cole, 1979), 542–545; Leland C. Swenson, *Theories of Learning: Traditional Perspectives/Contemporary Developments* (Belmont, Calif.: Wadsworth, 1980), 210–213; Martin E. P. Seligman, "Learned Helplessness in Animals and Men," in Janet T. Spence et al., eds., *Behavioral Approaches to Therapy* (Morristown, N.J.: General Learning Press, 1976), 111–126; William R. Miller et al., "Learned Helplessness and Depression," in Jack D. Maser and Martin E. P. Seligman, eds., *Psychopathology: Experimental Models* (San Francisco: W. H. Freeman, 1977), 104–130. The account that follows is based largely on the last two sources.

29. Miller and Seligman found that human subjects who had been exposed to inescapable loud noise performed worse on an anagram test than a control group and identically to a non-pretreated group rated in advance as depressed on two mood diagnostic tests (Martin E. P. Seligman, "For Helplessness: Can We Immunize the Weak?" *Psychology Today* 3 [June 1969], 42–44; see also William R. Miller and Martin E. P. Seligman, "Depression and Learned Helplessness in Man," *Journal of Abnormal Psychology* 84 [1975], 228–238). The voluminous literature on learned helplessness in humans is reviewed in Seligman, *Helplessness*, chap. 3.

30. Miller et al., "Learned Helplessness and Depression," 104.

31. Seligman, *Helplessness*, 57, 76. Seligman has also remarked that "learned helplessness seems general among species that learn, so it can be used with some confidence as an explanation of a variety of phenomena" (*Helplessness*, 28). Besides depression, the concept has been used to explain anxiety and sudden death phenomena (e.g., death upon hearing bad news, voodoo death).

32. There is an extensive literature on this subject, including: Harry and Margaret Harlow, "The Young Monkeys," *Psychology Today* 1 (September 1967), 40–47; Harry F. Harlow, "The Nature of Love," *American Psychologist* 13 (1958), 673–685; Harry F. Harlow, "The Heterosexual Affectional System in Monkeys," *American Psychologist* 7 (1962), 1–9; H. F. Harlow and S. J. Suomi, "Nature of

Love—Simplified," *American Psychologist* 25 (1970), 161–168; Harry F. Harlow et al., "Total Social Isolation in Monkeys," *Proceedings of the National Academy of Sciences* 54 (1965), 90–96; S. J. Suomi et al., "Reversal of Social Deficits Produced by Isolation-Rearing in Monkeys," *Journal of Human Evolution* 3 (1974), 527–534; S. J. Suomi and H. F. Harlow, "Effects of Differential Removal from Group on Social Development of Rhesus Monkeys," *Journal of Child Psychology and Psychiatry* 16 (1975), 149–158; S. J. Suomi and H. F. Harlow, "Social Rehabilitation of Isolate-Reared Monkeys," *Developmental Psychology* 6 (1972), 487–496; Harry F. Harlow, *Learning to Love*, 2d ed. (New York: Jason Aronson, 1974); Harry F. Harlow et al., "Maternal Behavior of Rhesus Monkeys Deprived of Mothering and Peer Associations in Infancy," *Proceedings of the American Philosophical Society* 110, no. 1 (1966), 58–66; Harry F. Harlow, "Love in Infant Monkeys," *Scientific American* 200 (1959), 68–74. The following account is based on these sources.

33. Harlow and Harlow, "The Young Monkeys," 45.

34. However, the following observations by Harlow (*Learning to Love*) may be germane here:

> Actually, during the infant monkey's first week of life maternal love is indiscriminate, and during this period a monkey mother will respond with equal intensity to her own or to a strange infant of similar age. Earlier research had indicated that mothers are very upset by separation from their infants, but that their distress is somewhat allayed when they can see the infants. However, a more recent experiment . . . demonstrates that they are relieved by the sight of any infant until their own offspring are a week to ten days old. After that point only the sight of their own infants will satisfy them. Evidently a monkey mother develops feelings specific to her own infant only after she has interacted with it for a period of time. (P. 12)

35. John F. Travers, *The Growing Child: Introduction to Child Development* (New York: John Wiley, 1977), 342.

36. E. Mavis Hetherington and Ross D. Parke, *Child Psychology: A Contemporary Viewpoint*, 2d ed. (New York: McGraw-Hill, 1979), 153.

37. Donald B. Helms and Jeffrey S. Turner, *Exploring Child Behavior* (Philadelphia: W. B. Saunders, 1976), 127.

38. Deborah Lott Holmes and Frederick J. Morrison, *The Child: An Introduction to Developmental Psychology* (Monterey, Calif.: Brooks/Cole, 1979), 141.

39. Jere E. Brophy, *Child Development and Socialization* (Chicago: Science Research Associates, 1977), 25.

40. S. J. Suomi et al., "Monkey Psychiatrists," *American Journal of Psychiatry* 128 (1972), 41–46.

41. M. A. Novak and H. F. Harlow, "Social Recovery of Monkeys Isolated for the First Year of Life: I," *Developmental Psychology* 11 (1975), 453–465.

42. Hetherington and Parke, *Child Psychology*, 2d ed., 159.

43. Brophy, *Child Develoment and Socialization*, 27.

44. Holmes and Morrison, *The Child*, 150, 248.

45. This research is described in the following publications: Lester R. Aronson and Madeleine L. Cooper, "Desensitization of the Glans Penis and Sexual Behavior in Cats," in Milton Diamond, ed., *Perspective in Reproduction and Sexual Behavior* (Bloomington: University of Indiana Press, 1968), 51–82; J. S. Rosenblatt and Lester R. Aronson, "The Decline of Sexual Behavior in Male Cats after Castration with Special Reference to the Role of Prior Sexual Experience," *Behavior* 12 (1958), 285–338; K. K. Cooper et al., "Physiological and Behavioral Observations of Erection Before and After Section of the Nerve Dorsalis Penis," *American Zoologist* 4 (1964), 301; L. R. Aronson and M. L. Cooper, "Seasonal Variation in Mating Behavior in Cats after Desensitization of Glans Penis," *Science* 152 (1966), 226–230; Lester R. Aronson and Madeleine L. Cooper, "Penile Spines of the Domestic Cat: The Endocrine-Behavior Relations," *Anatomical Record* 157 (1967), 71–78; Lester R. Aronson and Madeleine L. Cooper, "The Appearance of Seasonal Cycles in Sexual Behavior in Domestic Male Cats Following Desensitization of the Glans Penis," *Proceedings of the 18th International Congress of Psychology, Moscow* 1 (1966), 190–197; Lester R. Aronson and Madeleine L. Cooper, "Olfactory Deprivation and Mating Behavior in Sexually Experienced Male Cats," *Behavioral Biology* 11 (1974), 459–480; Lester R. Aronson and Madeleine L. Cooper, "Mating Behavior in Sexually Inexperienced Cats after Desensitization of the Glans Penis," *Animal Behavior* 17 (1969), 208–212.

46. Aronson and Cooper, "Desensitization of the Glans Penis and Sexual Behavior in Cats," 54, 57.

47. "U.S. Agency Will Review Tests on Cats at American Museum," *New York Times*, July 28, 1976, p. 27.

48. Nicholas Wade, "Animal Rights: NIH Cat Sex Study Brings Grief to New York Museum," *Science* 194 (October 8, 1976), 162.

49. "Animal Rights Groups Demonstrate Against Cat Research," *National Society for Medical Research Bulletin* 27, no. 9 (September 1976), 2.

50. "An Inquiry into an Inquiry Using Cats for Tests," *New York Times*, August 1, 1976, pt. 4, p. 7.

51. "Museum Ends Its Silence on Study of Cat Sex Lives," *New York Times*, August 17, 1976, p. 62.

52. Adverse criticism of Aronson's research from an animal welfare standpoint can be found in Pratt, *Painful Experiments on Animals*, 71–73, under the heading "Effects of Surgical Mutilation on Sexual Behavior of Cats"; see also Henry Spira, "Killing Cats Isn't the Way to Spend Our Tax $$$," *Health Street Journal* 1, no. 1 (October 1978).

53. "Animal Rights Groups Demonstrate," 2.

54. "Follow Up on the News: Sex Study of Cats," *New York Times*, September 19, 1976, p. 45.

55. Cited in "Animal Rights Groups Demonstrate," 2.

56. Ibid., 1,2. The reader is also referred back to the quotation from *Scientific American* on p. 35.

57. Wade, "Animal Rights," 164–165. Eugene Garfield gives a more positive assessment of the impact of Aronson's studies in "Citation Analysis and the Anti-Vivisection Controversy, Part I" and "An Assessment of Lester R. Aronson's Citation Record, Part II," *Essays of an Information Scientist*, vol. 3 (Philadelphia: ISI Press, 1980), 103–108, 316–325.

58. Brendy Zosky, "Beginnings: Hans Selye," *Today*, July 20, 1980, 3.

59. Ruesch, *Slaughter of the Innocent*, 110–114.

60. Hans Selye, *The Stress of Life*, rev. ed. (New York: McGraw-Hill, 1976), 90.

61. Ibid., 87–90, 289–290.

62. Hans Selye, *Stress Without Distress* (New York: New American Library, 1974), 14; Hans Selye, ed., *Selye's Guide to Stress Research*, vol. 1 (New York: Van Nostrand Reinhold, 1980), preface, p. vii.

63. These examples are taken from Hans Selye, *Stress in Health and Disease* (Boston: Butterworths, 1976). Selye also used electric shocks, blinding lights, and deafening noise as stressors (W. Gifford-Jones, "Doctor Game: Exercise Can Help Banish Depression," syndicated column, *Kitchener-Waterloo Record*, July 23, 1980, p. 34).

64. Selye, *The Stress of Life*, chap. 3; Selye, *Stress Without Distress*, chap. 1.

65. Selye, *The Stress of Life*, 56; Selye, *Stress in Health and Disease*, 1119–1120.

66. See, for example, Selye's experiments described in Selye, *Stress in Health and Disease*, 445–447, 644, 654, 805, 874.

67. Hans Selye, "Ischemic Necrosis: Prevention by Stress," *Science* 156 (1967), 1263.

68. See, for example, P. Blythe, *Stress Disease: The Growing Plague* (New York: St. Martin's Press, 1973); P. G. Bourne, *The Psychology and Physiology of Stress: With Reference to Special Studies of the Viet Nam War* (New York: Academic Press, 1969); B. S. and B. P. Dohrenwend, eds., *Stressful Life Events: Their Nature and Effects* (New York: John Wiley, 1974); D. C. Glass and J. E. Singer, *Urban Stress: Experiments on Noise and Social Stressors* (New York: Academic Press, 1972); H. Kraus, *Backache, Stress and Tension: Their Cause, Prevention and Treatment* (New York: Simon and Schuster, 1965); H. G. Wolff, *Stress and Disease*, ed. S. Wolf and H. Goodell, 2d ed. (Springfield, Ill.: Charles C. Thomas, 1968); L. Levi, ed., *Society, Stress and Disease, vol. 1: The Psychological Environment and Psychosomatic Diseases* (New York: Oxford University Press, 1971); R. S. Eliot, ed., *Stress and the Heart*, vol. 1 (New York: Fontana, 1974).

69. Some of these books are: Hans Selye, *The Chemical Prevention of Cardiac Necrosis* (New York: Ronald Press, 1958); Hans Selye, *Hormones and Resistance* (New York: Springer-Verlag, 1971); Selye, *Stress in Health and Disease*.

70. Wade, "Animal Rights," 166.

71. Harry F. Harlow, Editorial: "Fundamental Principles for Preparing Psychology Journal Articles," *Journal of Comparative and Physiological Psychology* 55 (1962), 893, 896.

72. Seligman, "Learned Helplessness and Depression in Animals and Men," 113; Miller et al., "Learned Helplessness and Depression," 107; Seligman, *Helplessness*, 28. See also note 31 above.

73. Thomas R. Dorworth and J. Bruce Overmier, "On 'Learned Helplessness': The Therapeutic Effects of Electroconvulsive Shocks," *Physiological Psychology* 5 (1977), 355–358.

74. Stephen J. Suomi et al., "Effects of Bilateral Frontal Lobectomy on Social Preferences of Rhesus Monkeys," *Journal of Comparative and Physiological Psychology* 70 (1970), 448–453.

75. Ibid., 452.

76. The following summary is based on an interview conducted on April 10, 1980.

77. This account is based on interviews and observations made on April 10 and May 2, 1980, and the publications cited below.

78. Since this was written the successful development of an advanced technique for producing cultured skin implants, using burn patients' own skin, has been announced. (See Anastasia Toufexis, "The Miracle of 'Test-Tube' Skin," *Time*, August 27, 1984, p. 44.) The technique was, incidentally, "a serendipitous finding . . . made . . . while studying cultures of a mouse tumor" by a Harvard University scientist.

79. Carl G. Grant et al., "Expansion of Lapine, Porcine and Human Skin *in Vitro* for Grafting onto Extensive Burns," *Burns* 7 (1980), 60n.

80. Ibid., 58, 68.

81. For a survey of the relevant literature, see G. Bredberg and I. M. Hunter-Duvar, "Behavioral Tests of Hearing and Inner Ear Damage," in H. Autrum et al., eds., *Handbook of Sensory Physiology*, vol. 5: Auditory System, pt. 2: "Physiology (CNS), Behavioral Studies, Psychoacoustics," ed. Wolf D. Keidel and William D. Neff (New York: Springer-Verlag, 1975), 261–306.

82. I. M. Hunter-Duvar and G. Bredberg, "Effects of Intense Auditory Stimulation: Hearing Losses and Inner Ear Changes in the Chinchilla," *Journal of the Acoustical Society of America* 55 (1974), 795–801.

83. Ivan M. Hunter-Duvar, "Morphology of the Normal and the Acoustically Damaged Cochlea," *Scanning Electron Microscopy* 2 (1977), 300, 421–428.

84. The following publications were also consulted. Flavio Coceani and Peter M. Olley, "Role of Prostaglandins, Prostacyclin and Thromboxanes in the Control of Prenatal Patency and Postnatal Closure of the Ductus Arteriosus," *Seminars in Perinatology* 4, no. 2 (April 1980), 109–113; Peter M. Olley and Flavio Coceani, "Use of Prostaglandins in Cardiopulmonary Diseases of the Newborn," *Seminars in Perinatology* 4, no. 2 (April 1980), 135–141; F. Coceani, P. M. Olley,

and J. E. Lock, "Prostaglandins, Ductus Arteriosus, Pulmonary Circulation: Current Concepts and Clinical Potential," *European Journal of Clinical Pharmacology* 18 (1980), 75–81.

85. F. J. Holland, W. G. Sherwood, D. DiBattista, and L. Luna, "The Ontogeny of Growth Hormone and Prolactin in the Rhesus Monkey Fetus," abstract of a paper presented to a meeting of the Endocrine Society, Los Angeles, June 1979.

86. Based on my observations at the animal care unit, Hospital for Sick Children and at the Primate Laboratory, University of Waterloo, in the spring of 1980.

87. See Nancy E. Simpson, "Prenatal Diagnosis of Genetic Diseases by Amniocentesis," in T. V. N. Persaud, ed., *Genetic Disorders, Syndromology and Prenatal Diagnosis*; *Advances in the Study of Birth Defects*, vol. 5 (New York: Alan R. Liss, 1982), 205–221.

88. For example, Dr. Geoffrey Sherwood of the Research Institute, Hospital for Sick Children, who has been conducting medical research on fetal and infant monkeys for some time.

89. See O. Sacks, *Awakenings* (New York: Vintage Books, 1973).

90. Richard J. Beninger, Stephen T. Mason, Anthony G. Phillips, and Hans C. Fibiger, "The Use of Conditioned Suppression to Evaluate the Nature of Neuroleptic-Induced Avoidance Deficits," *Journal of Pharmacology and Experimental Therapeutics* 213 (1980), 626. Other publications consulted in connection with this discussion include Richard J. Beninger and Anthony Phillips, "The Effect of Pimozide on the Establishment of Conditioned Reinforcement," *Psychopharmacology* 68 (1980), 147–153; Richard J. Beninger and Anthony G. Phillips, "The Effects of Pimozide During Pairing on the Transfer of Classical Conditioning to an Operant Discrimination," *Pharmocology Biochemistry & Behavior* 14 (1981), 101–105. For an overview of research in this area from a critical perspective, see Fritz A. Henn, "Dopamine: A Role in Psychosis or Schizophrenia," in Fritz A. Henn and Henry A. Nasrallah, eds., *Schizophrenia as a Brain Disease* (New York: Oxford University Press, 1982), 176–195.

91. So named because one of the earliest large-scale manifestations of the disorder occurred and was studied at Minimata Bay, Japan, where more than 120 residents of several fishing villages were afflicted and the link with mercury discharged in effluents from chemical plants was confirmed. The symptoms of Minimata disease are loss of sensation in the extremities (paresthesia); constriction of the visual field (astereognosis); decreased ability to understand rapid speech (dysphasia); hearing and speech impairment (dysarthria); loss of muscular coordination (ataxia); tremor; abnormal reflexes; general paralysis. Many of these symptoms indicate brain damage and are persistent, though not usually progressive. See Clarence T. Charlebois, "An Overview of the Canadian Mercury Problem," *Science Forum* 10, no. 5 (October 1977), 17–36.

92. See B. Wheatley, A. Barbeau, T. W. Clarkson, and L. W. Lapham, "Methylmercury Poisoning in Canadian Indians: The Elusive Diagnosis," *Canadian Journal of Neurological Sciences* 6 (1979), 417–422.

93. The following publications were consulted: M. von Grünau, "Luminance Dependence of Strabismic Amblyopia in Kittens," *Proceedings of the Physiological Society*, July 14–15, 1978, *Journal of Physiology* 284, 119–120; M. W. von Grünau, "The Role of Maturation and Visual Experience in the Development of Eye Alignment in Cats," *Experimental Brain Research* 37 (1979), 41–47; W. Singer, M. von Grünau, and J. Rauschecker, "Functional Amblyopia in Kittens with Unilateral Exotropia: I. Electrophysiological Assessment," *Experimental Brain Research* 40 (1980), 294–304; M. W. von Grünau and W. Singer, "Functional Amblyopia in Kittens with Unilateral Exotropia: II. Correspondence Between Behavioral and Electrophysiological Assessment," *Experimental Brain Research* 40 (1980), 305–310.

94. W. D. M. Paton, "R.D.S. Paper No. 1: Some Notes on Experiments Recently Criticized" (London: Research Defence Society, 1975), 8.

95. Barrie J. Frost, "Mechanisms for Discriminating Object Motion from Self-Induced Motion in the Pigeon," in D. Ingle, M. Goodale, and R. Mansfield, eds., *Analysis of Visual Behavior* (Cambridge, Mass.: MIT Press, 1982), 177.

96. B. J. Frost, "Moving Background Patterns Alter Directionally Specific Responses of Pigeon Tectal Neurons," *Brain Research* 151 (1978), 599.

97. B. J. Frost, P. L. Scilley, and S. C. P. Wong, "Moving Background Patterns Reveal Double-Opponency of Directionally Specific Pigeon Tectal Neurons," *Experimental Brain Research* 43 (1981), 174.

98. A recent example is the case of Dr. Edward Taub, whose laboratory at the Institute for Behavioral Research in Silver Spring, Maryland, was raided by police on September 11, 1981 because of a documented complaint by a volunteer about the condition of seventeen monkeys kept at this establishment. Taub's research, which involved the deafferentation of monkeys' limbs (severing of the sensory nerves), has made a major contribution to the development of methods for rehabilitating stroke victims and has applications to the treatment of neuromuscular diseases and to the understanding of biofeedback, especially its use in alleviating migraine and Raynaud's disease (a circulatory disorder). In November 1981 Taub was convicted on six counts of cruelty to animals by a U.S. District Court. The NIH's National Institute for Neurological and Communicative Disorders and Stroke suspended its support of Taub's research. An NIH spokesman affirmed that the case concerns the basic handling of animals and the cleanliness of research facilities, not the justification or value of the project in question. (See Constance Holden, "Police Seize Primates at NIH-Funded Lab," *Science* 214 [October 2, 1981], 32–33; Rowan, *Of Mice, Models, and Men*, 62–63, 175–176.)

On appeal Taub was cleared of all but one charge of cruelty. A second appeal led to the dismissal of this remaining charge on the technicality that federally funded research projects are not subject to state humane laws. At the time of writing, Taub's appeal of the suspension of his NIH grant was still under review by this agency.

5: SOME OBSERVATIONS ON SCIENTIFIC INQUIRY AND RELATED MATTERS

1. Julius H. Comroe, Jr., *Retrospectroscope: Insights into Medical Discovery* (Menlo Park, Calif.: Von Gehr Press, 1977).
2. Ibid., 12.
3. Ibid., 14, 15.
4. Ibid., 15.
5. Ibid., 68.
6. D. Caroline Coile and Neal E. Miller, "How Radical Animal Activists Try to Mislead Humane People," *American Psychologist* 39 (June 1984), 701.
7. Mahlon B. Hoagland, *The Roots of Life* (New York: Avon Books, 1979), 111, 118.
8. Comroe, *Retrospectroscope*, 4.
9. For some excellent examples of the blending of basic and applied research, see Frank Kendig and Lisa Buck, "Guinea Pigs," *Omni* 6, no. 5 (February 1984), 46-49, 92-94.
10. See Coile and Miller, "How Radical Animal Activists Mislead," which presents results of a survey of 608 articles published in leading experimental psychology journals from 1979 to 1983.
11. Hoagland, *The Roots of Life*, 134.
12. D. H. Smyth, *Alternatives to Animal Experiments* (London: Scolar Press/ Research Defence Society, 1978), 34.
13. Jaegwon Kim, "Explanation in Science," in Edwards, *Encyclopedia of Philosophy*, vol. 3, 160.
14. "Lab Rats Now Bred Diseased for Study," *Kingston Whig-Standard* (Canadian Press service), July 19, 1982, p. 3. See also Patrick Young, "Meet the Mighty Mice," *American Way*, November 1979, 32-38.
15. Interview with Dr. Derek Ilse, Director of Pharmaceutical Research, Ortho Pharmaceutical (Canada) Ltd., November 8, 1979.
16. For further discussion, see C. W. Hume, *Man and Beast*, rev. ed. (Potters Bar, Hertfordshire: Universities Federation for Animal Welfare, 1982), chap. 10.
17. Ruesch, *Slaughter of the Innocent*, 258-259.
18. Ibid., 29.
19. Singer, *Animal Liberation*, 70, 71.
20. Nicholas Wade, "Peer Review System: How to Hand Out Money Fairly," *Science* 179 (January 12, 1973), 158, 159, 161.
21. Ruesch, *Slaughter of the Innocent*, 349. Ruesch unfortunately does not document this claim. Despite hours of poring over the Nuremberg trial transcripts

and books on the trials, I have been unable to either confirm or refute his charge. Consultations with experts on the trials, some of whom were on the prosecuting staff, have also led nowhere. Inquiries directed to Ruesch himself have gone unanswered.

Compare the argument offered by Ryder in *Victims of Science*, 222 ff.

22. Tom Regan, "The Moral Basis of Vegetarianism," *Canadian Journal of Philosophy* 5 (1975–1976), 182.

23. Singer, *Animal Liberation*, x.

24. Richard Ryder, "Experiments on Animals," in Godlovitch, Godlovitch, and Harris, *Animals, Men and Morals*, 74.

25. William L. Shirer, *The Rise and Fall of the Third Reich: A History of Nazi Germany* (New York: Simon and Schuster, 1960), 979.

26. Elie A. Cohen, *Human Behavior in the Concentration Camp*, trans. M. H. Braaksma (New York: Grosset and Dunlap, 1953), 91; Shirer, *Rise and Fall*, 987; Robert E. Conot, *Justice at Nuremburg* (New York: Harper and Row, 1983), 295.

27. Victor H. Bernstein, *Final Judgment: The Story of Nuremberg* (London: Latimer House, 1947), 155–157.

28. Henry V. Dicks, *Licenced Mass Murder: A Socio-Psychological Study of Some SS Killers* (London: Sussex University Press/Chatto-Heinemann Educational, 1972), 154–155.

29. *Trials of War Criminals Before the Nuernberg Military Tribunals under Control Council Law #10*, vol. 6 (October 1946–April 1949), 58.

30. Ibid., 59, 60.

31. For an illuminating discussion of developments within the German medical profession from the Weimar Republic to 1945, including its long-term commitment to "racial purification," see Stephen L. Chorover, *From Genesis to Genocide: The Meaning of Human Nature and the Power of Behavior Control* (Cambridge, Mass.: MIT Press, 1979), chap. 5.

32. A contemporary history of this mentality and its impact on the world may be found in Leo Kuper, *Genocide: Its Political Use in the Twentieth Century* (New Haven, Conn.: Yale University Press, 1981).

33. See, for example, Shirer, *Rise and Fall*; Dicks, *Licenced Mass Murder*; Jewish Black Book Committee, *The Black Book: The Nazi Crime against the Jewish People* (New York: Duell, Sloan, and Pearce, 1946); Alexander Mitscherlich and Fred Mielke, *Doctors of Infamy* (New York: Henry Schurman, 1949); and *Trial of the Major War Criminals* (Nuremberg transcripts), vol. 20 (November 21, 1946–August 20, 1947), Case 1: "United States vs. Brandt et al." (commonly referred to as "The Doctors' Trial").

34. Bernstein, *Final Judgment*, 158; cf. Shirer, *Rise and Fall*, 979.

35. Statement by Dr. Andrew C. Ivy, Medical Scientific Consultant to the Prosecution in Military Tribunal No. 1, in Mitscherlich and Mielke, *Doctors of Infamy*, xii.

36. Statement by Gen. Telford Taylor, chief counsel for the Nuremberg war crimes trials, in Mitscherlich and Mielke, *Doctors of Infamy*, xx. (Taylor cites material from the trial transcripts.)

37. M. H. Pappworth, *Human Guinea Pigs: Experimentation on Man* (London: Routledge and Kegan Paul, 1967), 197–198. Pappworth is citing Dr. Andrew C. Ivy (see above, note 35). The statute in question was enacted November 24, 1933, according to Maurice B. Visscher (*Ethical Constraints and Imperatives in Medical Research* [Springfield, Ill.: Charles C. Thomas, 1975], 86). On the compartmentalization phenomenon, see also Eugen Kogon, *The Theory and Practice of Hell: The German Concentration Camps and the System Behind Them*, trans. Heinz Norden (New York: Octagon Books, 1976), chap. 22; and Richard L. Rubenstein, *The Cunning of History: Mass Death and the American Future* (New York: Harper and Row, 1975), chap. 4.

6: Unnecessary Suffering and Alternatives to Animal Experiments

1. Singer, *Animal Liberation*, 11–16.

2. Marian Stamp Dawkins, *Animal Suffering: The Science of Animal Welfare* (London and New York: Chapman and Hall, 1980), 2.

3. See Melzack and Wall, *The Challenge of Pain*; Tucker, "An End to Pain"; Roy A. Wise, "Pleasure and the Brain," *Queen's Quarterly* 90 (1983), 74–87.

4. Dawkins, *Animal Suffering*, 25, 35.

5. Ibid., 109, 111 (author's italics).

6. Ibid., 109 (author's italics).

7. Ibid., 66–67; Smyth, *Alternatives to Animal Experiments*, 34.

8. Dawkins, *Animal Suffering*, 49–50, 110.

9. Ibid., 110–111.

10. Ibid., 89.

11. Ibid., 111. Colin Tudge remarks ("Farmers in Loco Parentis," *New Scientist* 60 [October 18, 1973], 180), "We cannot assume that animals are unhappy simply because they are in situations that would make us unhappy; we cannot assume that they are unhappy simply because they look unhappy to the casual observer; but neither can we assume that they cannot feel unhappy—and indeed, there are more grounds for thinking that the brainier animals do suffer emotions comparable to our own, than that they do not."

12. Dawkins, *Animal Suffering*, 59, 88.

13. Ibid., 2, 102.

14. The following publications are good sources of information: Christine Stevens, "Laboratory Animal Welfare," in Leavitt, *Animals and Their Legal Rights*, 46–68; Province of Ontario, Bill 194, 1968–1969, "An Act Representing the Care and Provision of Animals for Research" (Toronto: Queen's Printer, 1969); Province of Ontario, Regulations 139/71, 140/71, 141/71, and 142/71, "Regulations Made Under the Animals for Research Act" (Toronto: Queen's Printer, 1971); Richard D.

Ryder, "British Legislation and Proposals for Reform," in Sperlinger, *Animals in Research*, 11–38; Richard W. J. Esling, "European Animal Experimentation Law," in Sperlinger, *Animals in Research*, 39–62; Margaret Morrison, "Legislation and Practice in the United States," in Sperlinger, *Animals in Research*, 63–78.

15. See chap. 4, note 98.

16. Committee on Care and Use of Laboratory Animals of the Institute of Laboratory Animal Resources, *Guide for the Care and Use of Laboratory Animals*, 4th rev. ed. (Washington, D.C.: National Research Council, 1978).

17. Committee on Care and Use, *Guide*, 3, 4, 7.

18. Ryder, *Victims of Science*, 17–18.

19. George K. Russell, *Laboratory Investigations in Human Physiology* (New York: Macmillan, 1978), vi. See also G. K. Russell, "Vivisection and the True Aims of Education in Biology," *American Biology Teacher* 34 (1972), 254–257.

20. F. Barbara Orlans, *Animal Care from Protozoa to Small Mammals* (Menlo Park, Calif.: Addison-Wesley, 1977); Harry C. Rowsell, "Canadian Regulations Governing Use of Animals at the Pre-University Level," in Orlans, *Animal Care*, 346–350; "Biology Teachers Adopt New Animal Rules," *Scientists' Center for Animal Welfare Newsletter* 2, no. 2 (April 1980), 1–2.

21. Linda Koebner, "Surrogate Human," *Science 82* 3, no. 6 (July/August 1982), 35.

22. Carol M. Newton, "Biostatistical and Biomathematical Methods in Efficient Animal Experimentation," in Institute of Laboratory Animal Resources, *The Future of Animals, Cells, Models, and Systems*, 167.

23. See chap. 3, note 49; Newton, "Biostatistical and Biomathematical Models"; Harry C. Rowsell, "The Right Animal for the Right Reason," *Proceedings of the Canadian Association for Laboratory Animal Science, 1978–79* (Calgary: CALAS/ACTAL, 1979), 211–220.

24. Smyth, *Alternatives to Animal Experiments*, 13, 26, 27.

25. Ibid., 28.

26. Ibid.

27. H. B. Fell, "Tissue Culture and Its Contribution to Biology and Medicine," *Journal of Experimental Biology* 57 (1972), 1–13; cited in Smyth, *Alternatives*, 118.

28. Smyth, *Alternatives*, 111–119.

29. Koebner, "Surrogate Human," 34, 35.

30. Smyth, *Alternatives*; Rowan, *Of Mice, Models, and Men*; Andrew N. Rowan, "Alternatives to Laboratory Animals: Definition and Discussion" (Washington, D.C.: Institute for the Study of Animal Problems, 1979); Andrew N. Rowan, "Alternatives and Laboratory Animals," in Sperlinger, *Animals in Research*, 257–283; Michael F. W. Festing, "The 'Defined' Animal and the Reduction of Animal Use," in Sperlinger, *Animals in Research*, 285–306; Dallas Pratt, *Alternatives to Pain in Experiments on Animals* (New York: Argus Archives, 1980); Fund for Replacement of Animals in Medical Experiments, *Alternatives to Laboratory Animals* (London: FRAME, 1974/75); Fund for Replacement of Animals in Medical

Experiments, *Alternatives to Laboratory Animals* (London: FRAME, 1977); National Anti-Vivisectionist Society, *Progress Without Pain* (Chicago: NAVS, 1973).

31. Smyth, *Alternatives*, chap. 7.

32. Ibid., 45, 120, 138.

33. This point of view was subscribed to by all the scientific participants in the symposium on *The Future of Animals, Cells, Models, and Systems* cited earlier—each of whom engaged in published debate with animal welfarists and antivivisectionists; it was also universally endorsed by the American Association of Pathologists' "Workshop on Needs for New Animal Models of Human Disease," *American Journal of Pathology* 101 (December 1980 Supplement). See also Randall, "Is Medical Research in Jeopardy?"

34. Smyth, *Alternatives*, 106, 160; see also Newton, "Biostatistical and Bio-mathematical Methods," 168.

35. F. M. Loew, "Animals in Biomedical Research: North American Practice," *Animal Regulation Studies* 2 (1979–1980), 144; Robin Marantz Henig, "Animal Experimentation: The Battle Lines Soften," *BioScience* 29, no. 3 (March 1979), 146–147.

36. Smyth, *Alternatives*, 116, 130, 133.

37. "Helsinki Convention," in *World Medical Journal* 11 (1964), 281; cited in Smyth, *Alternatives*, 125.

38. Smyth, *Alternatives*, 129, 133.

39. P. B. Medawar, *The Hope of Progress* (London: Methuen, 1972), 86.

40. Rowan, "Alternatives to Laboratory Animals," 15.

41. See, for example, Leavitt, *Animals and Their Legal Rights*; Sperlinger, *Animals in Research*, pt. 1; Smyth, *Alternatives*, append. 3 and 4 for a survey of legal requirements. For a survey of product testing procedures, see Smyth, *Alternatives*; Pratt, *Alternatives to Pain*; *The Future of Animals, Cells, Models, and Systems*; Samuel S. Epstein, *The Politics of Cancer*, rev. and exp. ed. (Garden City, N.Y.: Anchor Press/Doubleday, 1979), chap. 3.

42. Smyth, *Alternatives*, 111.

43. Ibid.

44. J. McCann, E. Choi, E. Yamasaki, and B. N. Ames, "Detection of Carcinogens as Mutogens in Salmonella/Microsome Test: Assay of 300 Chemicals," *Proceedings of the National Academy of Sciences* 72 (1975), 5135–5139; J. McCann and B. N. Ames, Discussion of "Detection of Carcinogens as Mutogens," *Proceedings of the National Academy of Sciences* 73 (1976), 950–954; Raymond Devoret, "Bacterial Tests for Potential Carcinogens," *Scientific American* 241, no. 2 (August 1979), 40–49.

45. "New Non-Animal Test for Environmental Carcinogens," *Resource* (Canadian Council on Animal Care bulletin) 7, no. 1 (Fall/Winter, 1982), 1–2.

46. Smyth, *Alternatives*, 59.

47. Research Defence Society, "R.D.S. Paper No. 3: Draft Answers to Common Questions" (London: RDS, 1975), 11.

48. Marcuse and Pear, "Ethics and Animal Experimentation," 316.

49. "The Draize Campaign—A Summary," *International Journal for the Study of Animal Problems* 3, no. 2 (April–June 1982), 94–97; "More Monies for Alternatives but No End in Sight for Animal Tests," *Society for Animal Rights Report* (February 1982), 5. FRAME publishes a journal of abstracts on alternatives (*ATLA Abstracts*) and the Johns Hopkins Center produces a newsletter. Ron Dagani, "Alternative Methods Could Cut Animal Use in Toxicity Tests," *Chemical & Engineering News* 61, no. 44 (October 31, 1983), 7–13.

In September 1984 the International Society for Animal Rights, Inc., one of the more visible and influential antivivisectionist organizations, issued a call for a renewed campaign against the animal testing of cosmetic products on the ground that the public's "moral outrage has not been silenced by the industry's grants to laboratories or by its talk of a search for 'alternatives'" (International Society for Animal Rights, "Victims of the Cosmetic Industry" [Clarks Summit, Penn.: ISAR, 1984]).

50. See, for example, Gill Langley, "Dr. Hadwen Trust Report," *Animal Welfare* (December 1979), 8–14.

51. Smyth, *Alternatives*, 61.

52. Advisory Committee on the Administrative of the Cruelty to Animals Act 1876, *Report on the LD$_{50}$ Test* (London: Home Office, 1979), 5.

53. Ibid., 5, 9, 13; Medical Research Council of the U.K., written evidence presented to the Advisory Committee on the Administration of the Cruelty to Animals Act 1876, cited by the Advisory Committee, *Report on the LD$_{50}$ Test*, 16.

54. Smyth, *Alternatives*, 66. The Research Defence Society of Britain has recommended that "any substance liable to be used on a considerable scale should be tested for safety, at a level which allows for the risk of misuse." It adds that "in making such tests, there is no general need, with substances of sufficiently low toxicity, to establish actually toxic levels, . . . it would be sufficient to establish a 'limit dose.' . . . What that level should be must depend on the substance, and the conditions and risk of high dosage" (Research Defence Society, "Notes on Safety-Testing: The Case of Cosmetics," January 14, 1976, 16).

A similar reform-minded recommendation has recently been put forward by the drug industry itself in a brief position paper entitled *The Role of the LD$_{50}$ Determination in Drug Safety Evaluation*, prepared by the Drug Safety Subsection of the Research and Development Section, Pharmaceutical Manufacturers Association (approved October 12, 1982).

55. Vincent T. Devita, Jr., and Harriet Page Kennedy, "Of Mice and Men: What Animal Tests of Carcinogens Mean to Us," *Connecticut Medicine* 44 (1980), 583; see also Epstein, *The Politics of Cancer*, 67–69.

56. Rollin, *Animal Rights and Human Morality*, 104–105.

57. Smyth points out, in addition, that those who criticize animal tests on the ground that species variability makes them unreliable are nonetheless "willing to rely on results from plants and bacteria, although the species variation in these cases is far greater" (*Alternatives*, 35).

58. Ibid., 40.

59. H. Bruhin and J. Gelzer, "Why Experiments on Animals Are Indispensable in Research, with Special Reference to Drug Development in Switzerland," *Animal Regulation Studies* 2 (1979–1980), 284.

60. This account is based in part on an interview with Dr. Derek Ilse, Director of Pharmaceutical Research, Ortho Pharmaceutical (Canada) Ltd., November 8, 1979.

61. G. J. V. Nossal, *Medical Science and Human Goals* (London: Edward Arnold, 1975), 46.

62. See Richard A. Lerner, "Synthetic Vaccines," *Scientific American* 248, no. 2 (February 1983), 66–74; and Angier, "The Electronic Guinea Pig."

63. "Moong Beans May Replace Animals for Drug Screening," *New Scientist* 94, no. 1309 (June 10, 1982), 702.

64. Smyth, *Alternatives*, 157–159. See also *Sunday Times* (London), *Suffer the Children: The Story of Thalidomide* (New York: Viking Press, 1979).

65. Jeffrey L. Fox, "Lab Animal Welfare Issue Gathers Momentum," *Science* 223 (February 3, 1984), 468–469.

66. William J. Broad, "Legislating an End to Animals in the Lab," *Science* 208 (1980), 575.

67. Theodore S. Meth, "The Limits of Legislation in Achieving Social Change," *International Journal for the Study of Animal Problems* 2, no. 3 (May–June 1981), 124.

68. Manfred Zimmermann, "Ethical Guidelines for Investigations of Experimental Pain in Conscious Animals," *Pain* 16 (1983), 109–110; Ad Hoc Committee on Animals in Research, Society for Neuroscience, "Guidelines for the Use of Animals in Neuroscience Research," May 9, 1984; American Physiological Society, "Guiding Principles in the Care and Use of Animals," pt. 2, *American Journal of Physiology* 246, no. 4 (April 1984); U.S. Department of Health and Human Services, "NIH Guide for Grants and Contracts" 13, no. 5 (April 5, 1984).

69. Canadian Council on Animal Care, *Guide to the Care and Use of Experimental Animals*, vol. 1 (Ottawa: CCAC, 1980), ii.

70. See Canadian Council on Animal Care, *Guide*, 2 vols. (available from Canadian Council on Animal Care, 151 Slater St., Suite 1105, Ottawa, Ontario, Canada K1H 5P3; $12.00; the set, postpaid).

71. For example, National Academy of Sciences, "Imperatives in Animal Use: Scientific Needs and Animal Welfare" (Washington, April 11–12, 1984); Rollin, *Animal Rights and Human Morality*, 112–117.

72. For example, Universities Federation for Animal Welfare, *The Rational Use of Living Systems in Bio-Medical Research*, Proceedings of a Symposium, October 7–8, 1971 (Potters Bar, Hertfordshire: UFAW, 1972); Universities Federation for Animal Welfare, *The Welfare of Laboratory Animals: Legal, Scientific and Humane Requirements*, Proceedings of a Symposium, September 30 and October 1, 1976 (Potters Bar, Hertfordshire: UFAW, 1977); David Paterson and Richard D. Ryder, eds., *Animals' Rights: A Symposium* (London: Centaur Press, 1979); Sperlinger, *Animals in Research*.

73. Pratt, *Alternatives to Pain*, 77–78.

74. S. Iversen and L. Iversen, *Behavioral Pharmacology* (New York: Oxford University Press, 1975); W. Pieper, "Acute Effects of Stimulants and Depressants on Sequential Learning in Great Apes," in G. H. Bourne, ed., *Progress in Ape Research* (New York: Academic Press, 1977).

75. Opinion: "Animal Rights Nonsense," *Nature* 305, no. 13 (October 1983), 562.

7: CONCLUSION

1. Lee Torrey, "The Agony of Primate Research," *Science Digest* (May 1984), 71.

2. Patricia Curtis, "New Debate over Experimenting with Animals," *New York Times Magazine*, December 31, 1978, p. 21; Peter Gwynne with Sharon Begley, "Animals in the Lab," *Newsweek*, March 27, 1978, 84; Torrey, "The Agony of Primate Research," 71; Rajan Moses, "Malaysia Bans Export of Research Monkeys," *Kingston Whig-Standard* (Reuter News Service), March 19, 1984, p. 1.

3. This point is made, for example, by W. Lane-Petter in "The Ethics of Animal Experimentation," *Journal of Medical Ethics* 2 (1976), 119; Jones; "The Ignorance and Confusion That Still Surrounds Animal Experiments"; and Guthrie, "Ethical Relationship Between Humans and Other Organisms," 59.

4. Sharon Begley with John Carey, "The Migration Enigma," *Newsweek*, October 15, 1979, pp. 111–116: E. W. Anderson, *Animals as Navigators* (London: The Bodley Head, 1983); Eugene J. Walter, Jr., "Why Do They Do What They Do?" *International Wildlife* 9, no. 5 (September–October 1979), 36; James A. Simmons, "The Sonar Sight of Bats," *Psychology Today* 2, no. 6 (November 1968), 50–57; "The Mechanics of Sex," in Philip Whitfield, ed., *The Animal Family* (New York: W. W. Norton, 1979), 8–31; "The Cleaner Wrasse," *Struggle Beneath the Sea* series, TV Ontario, March 23, 1983; Wise, "Pleasure Centers in the Brain."

5. Whitlock and Westerlund, *Humane Education*, 15.

6. Albert Schweitzer, *The Philosophy of Civilization, vol. 2: Civilization and Ethics*, 3d rev. ed., trans. C. T. Campion (London: A & C Black, 1946), 260.

7. David R. Klein, "The Ethics of Hunting and the Antihunting Movement," *Transactions of the Thirty-Eighth North American Wildlife and Natural Resources Conference* (1973), 259.

8. Maurice B. Visscher, "Animal Rights and Alternative Methods," *The Pharos* (Fall 1979), 13.

9. An ambitious attempt to accomplish just this objective is currently being undertaken by a Geneva-based group called the Council for International Organizations of Medical Sciences, established under the auspices of WHO and UNESCO. It plans to publish a set of Guiding Principles for the Use of Vertebrate Animals in Biomedical Research.

10. Some helpful steps in these directions have been taken by the Committee for Research and Ethical Issues of the International Association for the Study of Pain and in the Swedish codes of practice for animal experimentation. See Dana H.

Murphy, "The Problem of Pain: What Do Animals Really Feel?" *International Journal for the Study of Animal Problems* 3, no. 4 (October–December 1982), 275–82. See also Ralph L. Kitchell et al., eds., *Animal Pain: Perception and Alleviation* (Baltimore: Williams and Wilkins, 1983).

11. As of April 1, 1984, 468 U.S. institutions had achieved full accreditation by AAALAC, which was founded in 1965 (Franklin M. Loew, address to National Symposium on "Imperatives in Research Animal Use: Scientific Needs and Animal Welfare," National Academy of Sciences, Washington, D.C., April 11–12, 1984, session on "Utilizing and Caring for Research Animals: Varying Perspectives on Current Measures").

12. Marcuse and Pear, "Ethics and Animal Experimentation," 324–325. (A footnote indicates that the first coauthor demurred on this point.)

A similar view is expressed by Malone ("The Public Governance of Science and Research Animal Welfare"):

> If scientists demonstrate by their behavior their sure assumption of their responsibilities to their fellow humans as well as to their environment within as well as outside their institutions, then science has nothing to fear but much to gain from greater public interest and involvement in scientific endeavors. (P. 86)

13. Dr. John Berry, Department of Psychology, Queen's University, personal communication, March 16, 1983.

14. Martin Fishbein and Icek Ajzen, *Belief, Attitude, Intention and Behavior: An Introduction to Theory and Research* (Reading, Mass. and Menlo Park, Calif.: Addison-Wesley, 1975), 287.

15. See, for example, Peter Suedfeld, *Attitude Change: The Competing Views* (Chicago and New York: Aldine-Atherton, 1971); Jozef M. Nuttin, Jr., *The Illusion of Attitude Change: Towards a Response Contagion Theory of Persuasion* (London, New York, San Francisco: Academic Press; Louvain: Louvain University Press, 1975).

16. Fishbein and Ajzen, *Belief, Attitude, Intention and Behaviour*, 408 (authors' italics).

17. Lori A. Zurvalec, "Use of Animals—Medical Research: The Need For Government Regulation," *Wayne Law Review* 24 (1978), 1748.

18. Christopher D. Stone, *Should Trees Have Standing? Toward Legal Rights for Natural Objects* (New York: Avon, 1975), 29 (author's italics).

19. Meth, "The Limits of Legislation," 121.

20. See, for example, Gaston Dubois-Desaulle, *Beastiality: An Historical, Medical, Legal and Literary Study*, trans. A. F. Niemoeller (New York: Panurge Press, 1933); E. A. Rappaport, "Zoophily and Zooerasty," *Psychoanalytic Quarterly* 37 (1968), 565–587; and Nowell, *The Dog Crisis*, 29–33.

BIBLIOGRAPHY

Only references of general interest (mostly books) are included in this bibliography. Readers who wish to pursue individual topics will find numerous additional references in the notes to each chapter at the end of the text. An excellent, though already somewhat dated, source of bibliography on ethical issues in the treatment of animals is Magel's volume listed below. Those who are skeptical about the accomplishments of the biomedical and behavioral sciences and about the contributions of animals to their advancement are encouraged to consult works designated by *.

Adler, Mortimer. *The Difference of Man and the Difference It Makes.* New York: Holt, Rinehart, and Winston, 1967.

American Journal of Pathology. Special issue: "A Workshop on Needs for New Animal Models of Human Disease" 101, no. 35 (December 1980 Supplement).

Anderson, E. W. *Animals as Navigators.* London: The Bodley Head, 1983.

Animal Regulation Studies. Special issue: "Ethical Issues Concerning the Use of Animals in Agriculture and Scientific Research" 2, no. 3 (August 1980).

Arrington, Lewis R. *Introductory Laboratory Animal Science: The Breeding, Care, and Management of Experimental Animals.* Danville, Ill.: Interstate Printers and Publishers, 1978.

Attfield, Robin. *The Ethics of Environmental Concern.* Oxford: Basil Blackwell, 1983.

Baker, John R. *The Scientific Basis of Kindness to Animals.* London: Universities Federation for Animal Welfare, 1948.

Birx, H. James. *Human Evolution.* Springfield, Ill.: Charles C. Thomas, 1984.

Black, John. *The Dominion of Man.* Edinburgh: Edinburgh University Press, 1970.

Bleibtreu, John N. *The Parable of the Beast.* New York: Collier, 1969.

Boakes, Robert. *From Darwin to Behaviorism: Psychology and the Minds of Animals.* Cambridge: Cambridge University Press, 1984.

Bond, E. J. *Reason and Value.* Cambridge: Cambridge University Press, 1983.

Bond, Michael R. *Pain: Its Nature, Analysis and Treatment.* Edinburgh: Churchill Livingstone, 1979.

Bonner, John Tyler. *The Evolution of Culture in Animals.* Princeton, N.J.: Princeton University Press, 1980.

Borgese, Elizabeth Mann. *The Language Barrier: Beasts and Men.* New York: Holt, Rinehart, and Winston, 1968.

Bowman, John C. *Animals for Man.* London: Edward Arnold, 1977.

*Broadhurst, Peter. *The Science of Animal Behavior.* Harmondsworth, Middlesex: Penguin Books, 1963.

Brown, Anthony. *Who Cares for Animals? 150 Years of the RSPCA.* London: William Heinemann, 1974.

Brown, Robin. *The Lure of the Dolphin.* New York: Avon Books, 1979.

Calder, Nigel. *The Life Game: Evolution and the New Biology.* New York: Dell, 1975.

Campbell, Bernard. *Human Evolution: An Introduction to Man's Adaptations.* Chicago: Aldine, 1966.

Canadian Council on Animal Care. *Guide to the Care and Use of Experimental Animals.* 2 vols. Ottawa: Canadian Council on Animal Care, 1980, 1984.

Carpenter, Edward. *Animals and Ethics.* Report of the Working Party. London: Watkins, 1980.

Carson, Gerald. *Men, Beasts, and Gods: A History of Cruelty and Kindness to Animals.* New York: Charles Scribner's, 1972.

Clark, Kenneth. *Animals and Men.* New York: William Morrow, 1977.

Clark, Stephen R. L. *The Moral Status of Animals.* Oxford: Clarendon Press, 1977.

————. *The Nature of the Beast: Are Animals Moral?* Oxford: Oxford University Press, 1982.

Clark, Wilfred Le Gros. *Man-Apes or Ape-Men?* New York: Holt, Rinehart, and Winston, 1967.

Comroe, Julius H., Jr. *Retrospectroscope: Insights into Medical Discovery.* Menlo Park, Calif.: Von Gehr Press, 1977.

Conot, Robert E. *Justice at Nuremberg.* New York: Harper and Row, 1983.

Cousteau, Jacques-Yves. *The Whale.* London: Cassell, 1972.

*Cranach, Mario von, and Ian Vine, eds. *Social Communication and Movement: Studies of Interaction and Expression in Man and Chimpanzee.* New York: Academic Press, 1973.

Curtis, Patricia. *Animal Rights.* New York: Four Winds Press, 1980.

Cuschieri, A., and P. R. Baker. *Introduction to Research in Medical Sciences.* Edinburgh: Churchill Livingstone, 1977.

Darwin, Charles. *The Descent of Man, and Selection in Relation to Sex* (1871). 2d ed., rev. and aug. London: John Murray, 1896.

————. *The Expression of the Emotions in Man and Animals.* New York: Appleton, 1872.

Davis, Flora. *Eloquent Animals: A Study in Animal Communication.* New York: Berkley, 1979.

Dawkins, Marian Stamp. *Animal Suffering: The Science of Animal Welfare.* London and New York: Chapman and Hall, 1980.

DeBoer, J., J. Archibald, and H. G. Downie. *An Introduction to Experimental Surgery: A Guide to Experimenting with Laboratory Animals.* New York: American Elsevier, 1975.

Deely, John N., and Raymond J. Nogar, eds. *The Problem of Evolution: A Study of the Philosophical Repercussions of Evolutionary Science.* New York: Appleton-Century-Crofts, 1973.

de Luce, Judith, and Hugh T. Wilder, eds. *Language in Primates: Perspectives and Implications.* New York: Springer-Verlag, 1983.

Desmond, Adrian J. *The Ape's Reflexion.* New York: Dial Press/James Wade, 1979.

Dewar, James. *The Rape of Noah's Ark.* London: William Kimber, 1969.

Dewey, John. *The Ethics of Animal Experimentation.* Committee on Experimental Medicine of the Medical Society of the State of New York series. Rochester, Minn.: National Society for Medical Research, 1909.

Diner, Jeff. *Physical and Mental Suffering of Experimental Animals: A Review of Scientific Literature, 1975–1978.* Washington, D.C.: Animal Welfare Institute, 1979.

Diole, Philippe. *The Errant Ark: Man's Relationship with Animals.* Translated by J. F. Bernard. New York: G. P. Putnam's, 1974.

Dobzhansky, Theodosius. *Mankind Evolving: The Evolution of the Human Species.* New Haven, Conn.: Yale University Press, 1962.

Dobzhansky, Theodosius, and Francisco J. Ayala. *Humankind: A Product of Evolution.* Special Raymond Dart Lecture. Johannesburg: Witwatersrand University Press/Institute for the Study of Man in Africa, 1977.

Domalain, Yves-Jean. *The Animal Connection: Confessions of an Ex-Wild Animal Trafficker.* New York: William Morrow, 1977.

*Dowling, Harry F. *Fighting Infection: Conquests of the Twentieth Century.* Cambridge, Mass.: Harvard University Press, 1977.

Dröscher, Vitus B. *The Friendly Beast: Latest Discoveries in Animal Behavior.* Translated by Richard and Clara Winston. New York: Harper and Row, 1972.

Dubos, René. *So Human an Animal.* New York: Charles Scribner's, 1968.

————. *Beast or Angel? Choices That Make Us Human.* New York: Charles Scribner's, 1974.

Dworkin, Ronald. *Taking Rights Seriously.* Cambridge, Mass.: Harvard University Press, 1977.

Edey, M. A. *The Emergence of Man: The Missing Link.* New York: Time-Life Books, 1972.

Elliot, Robert, and Arran Gare, eds. *Environmental Philosophy: A Collection of Readings.* University Park: Pennsylvania State University Press, 1983.

*Epstein, Samuel S. *The Politics of Cancer.* Rev. and exp. ed. Garden City, N.Y.: Anchor Press/Doubleday, 1979.

Etyka. Special issue: "The Moral Status of Animals" 18 (1980).

*Eysenck, Hans, and Michael Eysenck. *Mindwatching.* London: Michael Joseph, 1981.

Farb, Peter. *Humankind.* New York: Bantam Books, 1980.

Ferry, Georgina, ed. *The Understanding of Animals.* Oxford: Martin Robertson, 1984.

Fichtelius, Karl-Erik, and Sverre Sjölander. *Smarter than Man? Intelligence in Whales, Dolphins and Humans.* Translated by Thomas Teal. New York: Ballantine Books, 1974.

*Foss, Brian, ed. *New Perspectives in Child Development*. Harmondsworth, Middlesex: Penguin Books, 1974.

Fox, Michael Allen. "The Use and Abuse of Animals." *Queen's Quarterly* 83 (1976): 178–187.

_____. "'Animal Liberation': A Critique." *Ethics* 88 (1977–1978): 106–118. (Reprinted in Shrader-Frechette, q.v.)

_____. "Animal Rights: Misconceived Humaneness." *Dalhousie Review* 58 (1978): 230–239.

_____. "Animal Suffering and Rights: A Reply to Singer and Regan." *Ethics* 88 (1977–1978): 134–138.

_____. "On Justifying the Use of Animals for Human Ends." *Animal Regulation Studies* 2 (1980): 191–203.

_____. "Animal Experimentation: Avoiding Unnecessary Suffering." *Federation Proceedings*, American Societies of Experimental Biology, in press.

_____. "Ethical Considerations in Painful Animal Research." In H. L. Fields, R. Dubner, and F. Cervero, eds. "Advances in Pain Research and Therapy. Vol. 9. (Proceedings of the IVth World Congress on Pain, Seattle, Aug. 31–Sept. 5, 1984.) New York: Raven Press, 1985.

_____. "Human Values, the Value of Nature, and Environmental Ethics." *Proceedings of the 17th World Congress of Philosophy*. New York: Peter Lang, in press.

Fox, Michael W. *Between Animal and Man*. New York: Coward, McCann, and Geoghegan, 1976.

_____. *Returning to Eden: Animal Rights and Human Responsibility*. New York: Viking Press, 1980.

Fox, Robin, and Lionel Tiger. *The Imperial Animal*. New York: Delta, 1972.

French, Richard D. *Antivivisection and Medical Science in Victorian Society*. Princeton, N.J.: Princeton University Press, 1975.

Frey, R. G. *Interests and Rights: The Case Against Animals*. Oxford: Clarendon Press, 1980.

_____. *Rights, Killing and Suffering: Moral Vegetarianism and Applied Ethics*. Oxford: Basil Blackwell, 1983.

Friends of the Earth. *The Whale Manual*. San Francisco: Friends of the Earth, 1978.

*Galton, Lawrence. *Medical Advances*. Harmondsworth, Middlesex: Penguin Books, 1979.

Gardner, Martin. *Science: Good, Bad and Bogus.* Buffalo, N.Y.: Prometheus, 1981.

Godlovitch, Stanley, Roslind Godlovitch, and John Harris, eds. *Animals, Men and Morals: An Enquiry into the Maltreatment of Non-Humans.* London: Victor Gollancz, 1971.

Gould, Stephen Jay. *Ever Since Darwin: Reflections in Natural History.* New York: W. W. Norton, 1979.

Gribbin, John, and Jeremy Cherfas. *The Monkey Puzzle: A Family Tree.* London: The Bodley Head, 1982.

Griffin, Donald R. *The Question of Animal Awareness: Evolutionary Continuity of Mental Experience.* New York: Rockefeller University Press, 1976.

————. *Animal Thinking.* Cambridge, Mass.: Harvard University Press, 1984.

Grindley, G. C. *The Sense of Pain in Animals.* London: Universities Federation for Animal Welfare, n.d.; reprinted from *Animal Year Book*, 2 (1933).

Hahn, Emily. *Look Who's Talking.* New York: T. Y. Crowell, 1978.

Haksar, Vinit. *Liberty, Equality and Perfectability.* Oxford: Oxford University Press, 1979.

Hall, Rebecca. *Animals Are Equal: An Exploration of Animal Consciousness.* London: Wildwood House, 1980.

Harlow, Harry F. *Learning to Love.* 2d ed. New York: Jason Aronson, 1974.

Harlow, Harry F., and Clara Mears. *The Human Model: Primate Perspectives.* Washington, D.C.: V. H. Winston, 1979.

Harrison, Ruth. *Animal Machines.* London: Vincent Stuart, 1964.

Hass, Hans. *The Human Animal.* London: Hodder and Stoughton, 1970.

Herschel, Abraham J. *Who Is Man?* The Raymond Fred West Memorial Lectures, 1963. Stanford, Calif.: Stanford University Press, 1965.

Herscovici, Alan. *Second Nature: The Animal Rights Controversy.* Toronto: CBC Enterprises, 1985.

Hinde, Robert A. *Ethology: Its Nature and Relations with Other Sciences.* London: Fontana, 1982.

Hoagland, Mahlon B. *The Roots of Life.* New York: Avon Books, 1979.

Hockett, C. F. *Man's Place in Nature.* New York: McGraw-Hill, 1973.

Hornstein, Harvey A. *Cruelty and Kindness: A New Look at Aggression and Altruism.* Englewood Cliffs, N.J.: Prentice-Hall, 1976.

Howard, Jonathan. *Darwin.* Oxford: Oxford University Press, 1982.

Hume, C. W. *Man and Beast.* Rev. ed. Potters Bar, Hertfordshire: Universities Federation for Animal Welfare, 1982.

Hutchings, Monica M., and Mavis Carver. *Man's Dominion: Our Violation of the Animal World.* London: Rupert Hart-Davis, 1970.

Ideas: Men and Animals: Building a New Relationship with Nature. Toronto: CBC Transcripts, 1984.

Inquiry. Special issue: "Animal Rights" 22, nos. 1–2 (Summer 1979).

Johanson, Donald, and Maitland Edey. *Lucy: The Beginnings of Humankind.* New York: Warner Books, 1982.

Jonas, Hans. *The Phenomenon of Life: Toward a Philosophical Biology.* New York: Harper and Row, 1966.

*Keehn, J. D., ed. *Psychopathology in Animals: Research and Clinical Implications.* New York: Academic Press, 1979.

Keele, C., and R. Smith. *The Assessment of Pain in Man and Animals.* London: Livingstone, 1962.

Kerr, Frederick W. L. *The Pain Book.* Englewood Cliffs, N.J.: Prentice-Hall, 1981.

Kitchell, Ralph L., Howard H. Erickson, E. Carstens, and Lloyd E. Davis, eds. *Animal Pain: Perception and Alleviation.* Baltimore: Williams and Wilkins, 1983.

La Barre, Weston. *The Human Animal.* Chicago: University of Chicago Press, 1954.

Lancaster, J. B. *Primate Behavior and the Emergence of Human Culture.* New York: Holt, Rinehart, and Winston, 1975.

Lane-Petter, W., and A. E. C. Pearson. *The Laboratory Animal: Principles and Practice.* New York: Academic Press, 1971.

*LaPage, Geoffrey. *Achievement: Some Contributions of Animal Experiments to the Conquest of Disease.* Cambridge: W. Heffer, 1960.

Leakey, Richard E., and Roger Lewin. *Origins.* New York: E. P. Dutton, 1977.

Leavitt, Emily Stewart. *Animals and Their Legal Rights: A Survey of American Laws from 1641 to 1978.* 3d ed. Washington, D.C.: Animal Welfare Institute, 1978.

*Lewin, Roger. *In Defence of the Body: An Introduction to the New Immunology.* Garden City, N.Y.: Anchor Press/Doubleday, 1974.

Linden, Eugene. *Apes, Men, and Language*. Harmondsworth, Middlesex: Penguin Books, 1976.

Linzey, Andrew. *Animal Rights*. London: SCM Press, 1976.

Livingston, John A. *One Cosmic Instant: Man's Fleeting Supremacy*. New York: Dell, 1973.

————. *The Fallacy of Wildlife Conservation*. Toronto: McClelland and Stewart, 1981.

Lovelock, J. E. *Gaia: A New Look at Life on Earth*. Oxford: Oxford University Press, 1979.

Lubow, Robert E. *The War Animals*. Garden City, N.Y.: Doubleday, 1977.

Lyons, David, ed. *Rights*. Belmont, Calif.: Wadsworth, 1979.

*Maas, James B., ed. *Readings in Psychology Today*. 4th ed. New York: Random House, 1979.

McAlester, A. Lee. *The History of Life*. Englewood Cliffs, N.J.: Prentice-Hall, 1968.

McCloskey, H. J. *Ecological Ethics and Politics*. Totowa, N.J.: Rowman and Littlefield, 1983.

McCoy, J. J. *The Defense of Animals*. New York: Seabury Press, 1978.

McCrea, Roswell C. *The Humane Movement: A Descriptive Survey*. New York: Columbia University Press, 1910; reprinted College Park, Md.: McGrath, 1969.

McCullough, Laurence B., and James Polk Morris, III, eds. *Implications of History and Ethics to Medicine—Veterinary and Human*. College Station, Texas: Centennial Academic Assembly, Texas A & M University, 1978.

McIntyre, Joan, ed. *Mind in the Waters*. Toronto: McClelland and Stewart, 1974.

Magel, Charles R. *A Bibliography on Animal Rights and Related Matters*. Washington, D.C.: University Press of America, 1981.

Manning, Aubrey. *An Introduction to Animal Behaviour*. 3d ed. London: Edward Arnold, 1979.

Mannison, Don, Michael McRobbie, and Richard Routley, eds. *Environmental Philosophy*. Monograph Series, no. 2. Canberra: Department of Philosophy, Australian National University, 1980.

Mason, Jim, and Peter Singer. *Animal Factories*. New York: Crown, 1980.

Matson, Floyd W. *The Idea of Man.* New York: Dell, 1976.

Mayer, William V., David H. Neil, F. Barbara Orlans, and George K. Russell. *Perspectives on the Educational Use of Animals.* Proceedings no. 36. New York: Myrin Institute, 1980.

Melden, A. I. ed. *Human Rights.* Belmont, Calif.: Wadsworth, 1970.

Melzack, Ronald, and Patrick Wall. *The Challenge of Pain.* Harmondsworth, Middlesex: Penguin Books, 1982.

Midgley, Mary. *Beast and Man: The Roots of Human Nature.* Ithaca, N.Y.: Cornell University Press, 1978.

————. *Animals and Why They Matter.* Harmondsworth, Middlesex: Penguin Books, 1983.

Miller, G. Tyler, Jr. *Living in the Environment: Concepts, Problems, and Alternatives.* 2d ed. Belmont, Calif.: Wadsworth, 1979.

Miller, Harlan B., and William H. Williams, eds. *Ethics and Animals.* Clifton, N.J.: Humana Press, 1983.

*Mitruka, B. M., H. M. Rawnsley, and D. V. Vadehra. *Animals for Medical Research: Models for the Study of Human Disease.* New York: John Wiley, 1976.

Mitscherlich, Alexander, and Fred Mielke. *Doctors of Infamy.* New York: Henry Schurman, 1949.

*Montagna, William. *Nonhuman Primates in Biomedical Research.* Wesley W. Spink Lectures on Comparative Medicine. Vol. 3. Minneapolis: University of Minnesota Press, 1976.

Montefiore, Hugh, ed. *Man and Nature.* London: William Collins, 1975.

Morris, Richard Knowles, and Michael W. Fox, eds. *On the Fifth Day: Animal Rights and Human Ethics.* Washington, D.C.: Acropolis Books, 1978.

Morse, Mel. *Ordeal of the Animals.* Englewood Cliffs, N.J.: Prentice-Hall, 1968.

Munson, Ronald, ed. *Man and Nature: Philosophical Issues in Biology.* New York: Dell, 1971.

Myers, Norman. *The Sinking Ark: A New Look at the Problem of Disappearing Species.* Oxford: Pergamon Press, 1979.

National Research Council. *The Future of Animals, Cells, Models, and Systems in Research, Development, Education, and Testing.* Proceedings of a Symposium. Washington, D.C.: National Academy of Sciences, 1977.

————. Committee on Care and Use of Laboratory Animals. *Guide for the Care and Use of Laboratory Animals.* 4th rev. ed. Washington, D.C.: U.S. Department of Health, Education, and Welfare, 1978.

Neblett, William. *The Role of Feelings in Morals.* Washington, D.C.: University Press of America, 1981.

Nossal, G. J. V. *Medical Science and Human Goals.* London: Edward Arnold, 1975.

Nowell, Iris. *The Dog Crisis.* Toronto: McClelland and Stewart, 1978.

Nozick, Robert. *Anarchy, State, and Utopia.* New York: Basic Books, 1974.

Odum, Eugene P. *Basic Ecology.* Philadelphia: Saunders College Publishing, 1983.

Orlans, F. Barbara. *Animal Care from Protozoa to Small Mammals.* Menlo Park, Calif.: Addison-Wesley, 1977.

Orlans, F. Barbara, and W. Jean Dodds, eds. *Scientific Perspectives on Animal Welfare.* New York: Academic Press, 1983.

Pappworth, M. H. *Human Guinea Pigs: Experimentation on Man.* London: Routledge and Kegan Paul, 1967.

Passmore, John. *Man's Responsibility for Nature.* London: Gerald Duckworth, 1974.

Paterson, David, and Richard D. Ryder, eds. *Animals' Rights: A Symposium.* Fontwell, Sussex, and London: Centaur Press, 1979.

*Paton, William. *Man and Mouse: Animals in Medical Research.* Oxford: Oxford University Press, 1984.

Patterson, Colin. *Evolution.* Ithaca, N.Y.: British Museum (Natural History)/Cornell University Press, 1978.

Philosophy. Special issue: "Ethics and Animals" 53, no. 206 (October 1978).

Pratt, Dallas. *Painful Experiments on Animals.* New York: Argus Archives, 1976.

————. *Alternatives to Pain in Experiments on Animals.* New York: Argus Archives, 1980.

Premack, David. *Intelligence in Ape and Man.* Hillsdale, N.J.: Lawrence Erlbaum Associates, 1976.

Public Interest Report. Special issue: "Animal Rights" 30, no. 8 (October 1977).

Racle, Fred A. *Introduction to Evolution.* Englewood Cliffs, N.J.: Prentice-Hall, 1979.

Regan, Tom. *All That Dwell Therein: Animal Rights and Environmental Ethics.* Berkeley, Los Angeles, London: University of California Press, 1982.

————. *The Case for Animal Rights.* Berkeley, Los Angeles, London: University of California Press, 1983.

————, ed. *Earthbound: New Introductory Essays in Environmental Ethics.* New York: Random House, 1984.

Regan, Tom, and Peter Singer, eds. *Animal Rights and Human Obligations.* Englewood Cliffs, N.J.: Prentice-Hall, 1976.

Rensberger, Boyce. *The Cult of the Wild.* Garden City, N.Y.: Anchor Press/Doubleday, 1977.

Rensch, Bernard. *Homo Sapiens: From Man to Demigod.* Translated by C. A. M. Sym. London: Methuen, 1972.

Report of the Departmental Committee on Experiments on Animals. Littlewood Committee Report. London: H. M. Stationery Office, 1965.

Rhodes, F. H. T. *The Evolution of Life.* 2d ed. Harmondsworth, Middlesex: Penguin Books, 1976.

Roberts, Catherine. *Science, Animals, and Evolution: Reflections on Some Unrealized Potentials of Biology and Medicine.* Westport, Conn.: Greenwood Press, 1980.

Rollin, Bernard E. *Animal Rights and Human Morality.* Buffalo, N.Y.: Prometheus Books, 1981.

Rosenfield, Leonora Cohen. *From Beast-Machine to Man-Machine: Animal Soul in French Letters from Descartes to La Mettrie.* New and enlarged ed. New York: Octagon, 1968.

Rowan, Andrew N. *Of Mice, Models, and Men: A Critical Evaluation of Animal Research.* Albany: State University of New York Press, 1984.

Rowan, Andrew N., and C. J. Stratmann, eds. *The Use of Alternatives in Drug Research.* Proceedings of a Symposium at the Royal Society, London, April 11–12, 1978. London: Macmillan, 1980.

Ruesch, Hans. *Slaughter of the Innocent.* New York: Bantam Books, 1978.

————. *Naked Empress, or The Great Medical Fraud.* Zurich: CIVIS, 1982.

Russell, George K. *Laboratory Investigations in Human Physiology.* New York: Macmillan, 1978.

Russell, W. M. S., and R. L. Burch. *The Principles of Humane Experimental Technique.* Springfield, Ill.: Charles Thomas, 1959.

Ryder, Richard. *Victims of Science: The Use of Animals in Research.* 2d ed. London: National Anti-Vivisection Society, 1983.

Sagan, Carl. *The Dragons of Eden: Speculations on the Evolution of Human Intelligence.* New York: Random House, 1977.

Salt, Henry S. *Animals' Rights Considered in Relation to Social Progress.* Rev. ed. London: G. Bell, 1922; reprinted Clarks Summit, Penn.: Society for Animal Rights, 1980.

Savage, Jay M. *Evolution.* 3d ed. New York: Holt, Rinehart, and Winston, 1977.

Scheffer, Victor B. *A Voice for Wildlife.* New York: Charles Scribner's, 1974.

Scherer, Donald, and Thomas Attig, eds. *Ethics and the Environment.* Englewood Cliffs, N.J.: Prentice-Hall, 1983.

*Schwabe, Calvin W. *Cattle, Priests and Progress in Medicine.* Wesley W. Spinck Lectures on Comparative Medicine. Vol. 4. Minneapolis: University of Minnesota Press, 1978.

Sebeok, Thomas A., and Donna Jean Umiker-Sebeok, eds. *Speaking of Apes: A Critical Anthology of Two-Way Communication with Man.* New York: Plenum Press, 1979.

Seligman, Martin E. P. *Helplessness: On Depression, Development and Death.* San Francisco: W. H. Freeman, 1975.

Selye, Hans. *Stress without Distress.* New York: New American Library, 1975.

———. *The Stress of Life.* Rev. ed. New York: McGraw-Hill, 1976.

Serban, George, and Arthur Kling. *Animal Models in Human Psychobiology.* New York: Plenum Press, 1976.

Serjeant, Richard, ed. *The Spectrum of Pain.* London: Rupert Hart-Davis, 1969.

Shirer, William. *The Rise and Fall of the Third Reich: A History of Nazi Germany.* New York: Simon and Schuster, 1960.

Shrader-Frechette, K. S., ed. *Environmental Ethics.* Pacific Grove, Calif.: Boxwood Press, 1981.

Simpson, George Gaylord. *The Meaning of Evolution.* Rev. ed. New Haven, Conn.: Yale University Press, 1967.

Singer, Peter. *Animal Liberation: A New Ethics for Our Treatment of Animals.* New York: New York Review/Random House, 1975.

Sluckin, W., ed. *Fear in Animals and Man.* New York: Van Nostrand Reinhold, 1979.

Smith, Robert Leo. *Elements of Ecology and Field Biology.* New York: Harper and Row, 1977.

Smyth, D. H. *Alternatives to Animal Experiments*. London: Scolar Press/Research Defence Society, 1978.

*Sperlinger, David, ed. *Animals in Research: New Perspectives in Animal Experimentation*. Chichester: John Wiley, 1981.

Stent, Gunther S., ed. *Morality as a Biological Phenomenon: The Presuppositions of Sociobiological Research*. Rev. ed. Berkeley, Los Angeles, London: University of California Press, 1980.

Sternbach, Richard. *Pain: A Psychophysiological Analysis*. New York: Academic Press, 1968.

*Stilley, Frank. *The $100,000 Rat and Other Animal Heroes for Human Health*. New York: G. P. Putnam's, 1975.

Stone, Christopher. *Should Trees Have Standing? Toward Legal Rights for Natural Objects*. New York: Avon Books, 1975.

Tanner, Nancy Makepeace. *On Becoming Human*. Cambridge: Cambridge University Press, 1981.

Terrace, Herbert. *Nim*. New York: Alfred A. Knopf, 1979.

Thorpe, W. H. *Animal Nature and Human Nature*. New York: Anchor Press/Doubleday, 1974.

Tributsch, Helmut. *How Life Learned to Live: Adaptation in Nature*. Cambridge, Mass.: MIT Press, 1983.

Tullar, Richard M. *The Human Species: Its Nature, Evolution, and Ecology*. New York: McGraw-Hill, 1977.

Turner, E. S. *All Heaven in a Rage*. London: Michael Joseph, 1964.

Turner, James. *Reckoning with the Beast: Animals, Pain, and Humanity in the Victorian Mind*. Baltimore: Johns Hopkins University Press, 1980.

Tuttle, Margaret Wheaton. *The Crimson Cage*. Martha's Vineyard, Mass.: Tashmoo Press, 1978.

Universities Federation for Animal Welfare. *The Rational Use of Living Systems in Bio-Medical Research*. Proceedings of a Symposium, October 7–8, 1971. Potters Bar, Hertfordshire: UFAW, 1972.

————. *The Welfare of Laboratory Animals: Legal, Scientific and Humane Requirements*. Proceedings of a Symposium, September 30 and October 1, 1976. Potters Bar, Hertfordshire: UFAW, 1977.

van Lawick-Goodall, Jane. *In the Shadow of Man*. Boston: Houghton-Mifflin, 1971.

Verney, Peter. *Homo Tyrannicus: A History of Man's War Against Animals*. London: Mills and Boon, 1980.

Veselovsky, Z. *Are Animals Different?* London: Methuen, 1973.

Visscher, Maurice B. *Ethical Constraints and Imperatives in Medical Research.* Springfield, Ill.: Charles C. Thomas, 1975.

Viaud, Gaston. *Intelligence: Its Evolution and Forms.* Translated by A. J. Pomerans. London: Hutchinson, 1968.

Vyvyan, John. *In Pity and in Anger.* London: Michael Joseph, 1965.

————. *The Dark Face of Science.* London: Michael Joseph, 1971.

Walker, Stephen. *Animal Thought.* London: Routledge and Kegan Paul, 1982.

West, G. P., ed. *Encyclopedia of Animal Care.* 12th ed. Baltimore: Williams and Wilkins, 1977.

Westacott, Evalyn A. *A Century of Vivisection and Anti-Vivisection.* London: C. W. Daniel, 1949.

Whitfield, Philip, ed. *The Animal Family.* New York: W. W. Norton, 1979.

Whitlock, Eileen S., and Stuart R. Westerlund. *Humane Education: An Overview.* Tulsa, Okla.: National Association for the Advancement of Humane Education, 1975.

Wilson, Peter J. *Man, the Promising Primate: The Conditions of Human Evolution.* New Haven, Conn.: Yale University Press, 1980.

Wood-Gush, D. G. M., M. Dawkins, and R. Ewbank, eds. *Self-Awareness in Domestic Animals.* Proceedings of a workshop held at Keble College, Oxford, July 7–8, 1980. Potters Bar, Hertfordshire: Universities Federation for Animal Welfare, 1981.

Index

Designer:	U. C. Press Staff
Jacket design:	Robin Fox
Compositor:	Eisenbrauns
Printer:	Vail-Ballou Press
Binder:	Vail-Ballou Press
Text:	11/13 Janson
Display:	Palatino